Writing, Directing, and Producing Documentary Films

Alan Rosenthal

Southern Illinois University Press
Carbondale and Edwardsville

Edited by Dan Gunter
Designed by Shannon M. McIntyre
Production supervised by Natalia Nadraga

93   4

Library of Congress Cataloging-in-Publication Data

Rosenthal, Alan, 1936–
    Writing, directing, and producing documentary films / Alan
Rosenthal.
        p. cm.
    1. Documentary films—Production and direction. 2. Documentary films—
Authorship. 3. Motion pictures—Production and direction. 4. Motion picture
authorship. I. Title.
    PN1995.9.D6R65   1990
    070.1'8—dc20   89-48102
                                                                    CIP
    ISBN 0-8093-1636-6
    ISBN 0-8093-1637-4 (pbk.)

The paper used in this publication meets the minimum requirements of American National Standard for Information Sciences—Permanence of Paper for
Printed Library Materials, ANSI Z39.48-1984.♾

For
Bobby Cramer
and
Susan Fanshel

who have helped me in so many ways
over the years

Contents

Preface

I have always distrusted how-to books, whether they are about sex or about making a million. The authors of such texts seem to me a bit presumptuous in trying to teach you things best learned by experience.

And as in love and business, so in film. Documentary is learned by doing, by trial and error. This is not a how-to book. It is meant to be a companion to you along the way, helping you see some of the pitfalls and problems and helping you find solutions to the difficult but fascinating task of filmmaking.

Except in the last chapter, I have said little about the aims and purposes of documentary. Yet this is probably the most important question, and at some point we all have to answer it. For me, working in documentary implies a commitment that one wants to change the world for the better. That says it all.

Acknowledgments

First, my thanks to all those people and organizations who let me look at their films and burrow through their scripts. In particular, I would like to thank Will Wyatt of the BBC and Leslie Woodhead of Granada; both gave me immense help and made this book possible. I would also like to thank Jeremy Isaacs, David Elstein, and Jerry Kuehl, who helped me tie up some loose ends.

Thanks are also due to the University of California Press, which allowed me to publish notes and interviews from some of my previous books—in particular, discussions with Arthur Barron, Ellen Hovde, Sue McConnachy, Jeremy Sandford, George Stoney, Peter Watkins, and Charlotte Zwerin.

P. J. O'Connell's manuscript "Robert Drew and the Development of Cinema Verite in America" was essential to me in understanding the real workings of cinema verite, and I am grateful to P. J. for letting me reprint discussions with Ricky Leacock and Don Pennebaker.

I am, of course, tremendously grateful to the following stations and authors who allowed me to reproduce script extracts: the BBC; Granada Television Limited; the National Film Board of Canada; Thames Television; WNET; James Burke; Kate Davis; Jon Else; Jill Godmilow; David Hodgson; Stuart Hood; Antony Jay; Robert Kee; and Morton Silverstein.

Many of my friends assisted with this book, but six people above all helped guide my steps. The first was John Katz, who drank a lot of coffee with me and pointed me in the right direction. Later Ken Dancyger and Brian Winston went over different sections of the book and gave me very constructive and detailed criticism. My debt to them is enormous, and I also have to thank Brian for letting me reproduce extracts from one of his scripts.

Another tremendous influence on me was Antony Jay. I met Tony many years ago while writing another book. After talking to me about one of his films, he showed me the teaching notes he used at the BBC and gave me an informal half hour when we discussed scriptwriting techniques. Tony was then acknowledged as possibly the finest scriptwriter at the BBC and is now world famous for his joint scripting of the series "Yes, Prime Minister." That half-hour discussion was worth its weight in gold, and I have been grateful to Tony ever since.

Unbounded thanks also to Dan Gunter, who did a superb job of copy editing and helped translate my native English idioms into understandable American speech.

My last guiding light was James Simmons, my editor at Southern Illinois University Press, who waited patiently through all my delays and provided excellent advice and tremendous enthusiasm along every inch of the way. To all six my thanks and gratitude.

Writing,
Directing,
and Producing
Documentary Films

1

Introduction

In the last twenty years tremendous changes have taken place in documentary and nonfiction filmmaking. These changes include subject matter, form, and the very way documentaries and industrial films are made. However, despite the rise in the number of university film and video courses, very few books explain how to consider, create, write, and direct the "new" film. One object of this book is to fill that gap: to provide you with a thorough, down-to-earth grasp of documentary filmmaking, from idea to finished work. But above all this is a book about ideas and concepts. Its goal is to help you to think about the film as a totality before the camera is switched on. This approach may seem obvious, but it is not always so obvious in practice. Many people jump into a film, shoot hours of material, and then wonder what it's all about. To me, that is putting the horse before the cart with a vengeance.

In essence, this book is about the daily problems that the filmmaker faces from concept to finished film; from financing to distribution; from censorship and political problems to breaking into the networks; from the complexities of location shooting to problems of ethics and morality; from difficulties with the crew to the problems of dealing with real people and the complexities of their lives. Finally, the book deals with research, problems of style, varieties of approach, and the challenge of the new technologies.

This book does not deal with equipment. This omission is deliberate because this subject at least is thoroughly covered in other books and is well taught in most film schools and universities. And therein lies one of the problems. Most film schools provide a technical training that would have been unbelievable only a few years ago. Students leave having handled more editing equipment than Eisenstein ever did; they know how to take apart and rebuild a Nagra in ten minutes and how to light a set using the best techniques of Nestor Almendros and Vilmos Szigmond. So the last thing they need is additional advice on bounce or direct lighting. But students do tend to be deficient in *what* to say and *how* to say it. Documentary writing, for example, is often the weakest subject in the curriculum. One of the aims of this book is to redress the balance.

A second topic deliberately left out of this book is that of documentary history. The subject is tremendously important, but I assume that most readers of this book are familiar with the history of documentary filmmaking. If not, then Erik Barnouw's *Documentary* is the best introduction around. If you know some history, you can proceed without reinventing the wheel. If you are familiar with the films of Flaherty, Riefenstahl, Jennings, the Maysles, Drew, Leacock, and Pennebaker, you already have a good sense of evolving styles and objectives. So, for the rest of this book, I will assume that you learned about cinema verite on your mother's knee, and that you know that *Nanook of the North* is a film rather than a Canadian hockey star.

Origins

This book arose out of a series of discussions and seminars I had with students, first at the Australian National Film School and later at Stanford University. The students knew everything about technology but undervalued ideas. Most of them had grown up in the tradition of cinema verite, which one student interpreted to me as "shoot before you think."

Cinema verite has an absolutely vital spot in any film curriculum, but if mishandled it can act detrimentally on other film disciplines, especially writing. This is exactly what I found: raised on a diet of cinema verite, the students knew nothing about planning a standard documentary or industrial film and were completely lost when it came to writing commentary. Further exploration showed that they had a highly romantic vision of what happened on location and a completely unrealistic view of how a documentary film director worked. When I gently suggested that a documentary director's main task was listening to people, they thought I was joking.

One thing was clear. Though the students knew everything concerning the realities of feature filmmaking, they had only the faintest idea of what documentary was all about. So we talked, and gradually the idea of this book was born.

At first I thought the essay would discuss only writing, as that seemed to be the biggest problem. However, that soon seemed too limiting, because where did writing end? Writing was not just idea and commentary; it was the overall concept of the film. And if you look at the problem more broadly, don't documentary directors write the film as they go along? They have to face the unexpected. They have to make choices on the spot. They can shape the film any one of a dozen ways while supervising the editing. So how could you have a book on writing that failed to deal with directing?

Writing and directing are inextricably linked in the making of documentary and industrial films. I know that many people just write, and others just direct. But the usual situation is to find both tasks combined in one person, and necessarily so, because it is hard to say where one ends and the other begins. So once I was committed to exploring writing problems, it was inevitable that directing had to be covered as well.

Observations

This book is laid out in what I see as the natural progression of the documentary film. It starts with a discussion of ideas, research, and script structure; proceeds through preproduction and production; and then deals in depth with editing and commentary writing. By the time you have finished part 4 you should be familiar with the preparation and production of the standard documentary or industrial film. Part 5 deals in depth with a few distinct types of film and some special techniques. Thus, there is one chapter on the historical film and another on cinema verite. The final chapter, the "wrap," offers a perspective on the entire process.

Within this framework I have made one or two policy decisions. The first concerns the subject of video and film. This book is intended to help both film and video makers. Whether you are making a documentary on film or video, for at least half the time your path and approach will be exactly the same. Only during editing will the paths separate. Reasons for choosing video over film, or vice versa, will be discussed in chapter 3. But in terms of approach, scriptwriting, and directing, what applies to one applies to the other.

The book is also addressed to both documentary filmmakers and makers of other forms of nonfiction film—for instance, industrial, travel, and educational films. Obviously the objectives of these different kinds of film vary enormously. The documentary often has a strong reform and social purpose, while an industrial may serve to improve a company's corporate image or to act as a fund raiser. However, though their purposes differ, both genres share a great number of methods and techniques. For example, if you are dealing with research or scriptwriting, your methods will be as valid for the industrial film as for the documentary. Finally, on a practical level, most makers of nonfiction films float between the sponsored world and the world of documentary. Today they will make an investigatory documentary; tomorrow they will make an industrial film. The more knowledge you have of the techniques of both, the better off you are.

My last observation concerns money. Only purists, angels, and millionaires make films without thinking about money. Films costs money, usually a hell of lot, and the sooner you start thinking about that fact the better. Neither writing nor directing is done in a vacuum; scriptwriter and director alike must be aware of the budget limitations. Once you start talking about money, you might as well discuss fund-raising and the role of the producer. Both subjects are in fact discussed at length, and I make no apologies. Someone once expressed it this way: "The successful filmmaker has his head full of dreams, his eyes on the mountains, but his feet on the ground." That's put bluntly, but it makes sense.

Method

Though I didn't climb any mountains to consult the sages, I did try to talk to the best professionals around before writing this book. The questions were always "How do you work?" and "Why do you do things this way?" Occasionally I would also ask, "What is the most important thing that you have learned over the years?" This book is a distillation of their advice and represents how experienced professionals tackle film and video problems. But the book also comes out of my own experiences as a filmmaker and is affected by my quirks, background, and experience. I have been making films for about twenty years and have developed various techniques and approaches that make sense to me. They represent an attempt to put logic into that very peculiar process we call filmmaking.

However, a warning is in order.

First, all filmmakers are different. My method of filmmaking may not work for you. Our temperaments and our approaches to film may be light-years apart. And that's fine.

Second, this book is not sacrosanct. There are no rules in filmmaking. What is accepted as gospel today is rejected tomorrow. I hope that you will read the book, accept what is useful, and then go out, break all the rules, and make the greatest film ever.

Part I

From Idea to First Draft

2

Clearing the Decks

From time to time I meet with my partner, Larry, and we toss documentary ideas at each other. Larry sits, taking notes furiously, and I wander around with a cup of coffee. "How about," I'll say, "a series on cities. How we lived yesterday, today, and tomorrow, and how the environment has changed, and what the changes do to the quality of our lives. Or we could do the divided cities—Beirut and Berlin, Jerusalem and Belfast. Or we could look at abandoned cities like Angkor Wat or Fattipur Sikhri. Then there are the rebuilt cities like Tokyo or Coventry. And we could use material from the film *Metropolis* as a motif. Well, what do you think?"

Then it's Larry's turn. "I'd like to do *Union Jack over Eden* about the British writers and actors in Hollywood in the 1930s. There were hundreds of them, from Cary Grant to Boris Karloff. They even had a cricket team with David Niven and Erroll Flynn. And here's another idea. We take famous generals to the scenes of their battles and relive their experiences with them."

Of course, these are not just ideas of the moment. Our general reading and observation of politics and current events establish a whole body of potential material in our minds. This material matures over time, so we bring to the programming sessions a series of ideas that have been developing and that we now want to try out on each other. Some of the ideas are old, some new. Often the old ideas suddenly became feasible because an external event makes them newsworthy. Thus, the Armenian earthquake disaster rekindled my interest in cities.

Larry and I hold these sessions about once a month, trying to generate ideas based on topics that really interest us. Once we get an idea that seems worth spending a few months of our lives on, we begin to ask questions. Is it practical? Would it be high- or low-budget? Does it have broad or narrow audience appeal? What approach could we take to the subject? We are clearing the decks, seeing whether the first idea looks promising enough to develop. You could say that if the idea is fine, we should just go ahead, but we first ask one important question: Can we sell this brilliant idea? And if so, how?

It's all very well to be a writer, but usually the serious writer-director must also get involved in fund-raising from the beginning, particularly when the writer is also the producer. So the writer's job often becomes twofold. First, he or she must write a proposal, a document that presents the basic idea in an attempt to persuade some funding agency — sponsor, foundation, or television station — to back the film. Second, the writer must write the script. A good part of this book is devoted to the problems and questions surrounding the writing of the proposal. If you have the film given to you on a golden plate and don't have to worry about raising money or having to define your ideas to anyone, then you may want to skip those pages. But you may also want to drop me a note and tell me how you did it so easily, because I am green with envy.

Is a Script Necessary?

If somebody asked you to name seven or eight outstanding documentaries or documentary series, it's highly possible that your list might include *Nanook of the North, Hospital, Best Boy, Harlan County,* "The Brain," "CBS Reports," *The War Game,* and *Diary for Timothy.* What strikes us about the list? First, the sheer variety of the films. They range from Flaherty's classic description of Inuit life through an institutional portrait to Jennings's gentle observation of life in England at the end of World War II. *Best Boy* tells us about the life of a mentally retarded man; *Harlan County* deals with striking miners; *The War Game* is a horrifying documentary drama of the effects of an atomic bomb on a small British town. All are, in their own ways, outstanding examples of really excellent documentary films.

But what was the writer's part in these projects and in the success of the films? Apart from "CBS Reports" (a catchall series), only three of the works — *The War Game,* "The Brain," and perhaps *Diary for Timothy* — had anything resembling a full preproduction script or outline. All the other films were largely unscripted. Notes were probably jotted down and long discussions held as to what sequences to shoot, but no long preproduction scripts with suggested visuals and tentative commentary were prepared. Instead, most of there films were built on the editing table. Clearly, then, you can have a successful film without a script, or without a conventional script that defines action and progression and carefully lays in all the narration or guidelines for the narration. All this, of course, is illustrated by the success of cinema verite in the 1960s and by the esteem granted to Drew, Pennybaker, Wiseman, the Maysles, Leacock, and other pioneers of the genre.

Granted, you can have a film without a prewritten script, but you can't have a film without a concept. By *concept* I mean a comprehensive idea that will drive the film in a distinct direction according to a clear plan. But more of that later.

The Purpose of the Script

If verite filmmakers can dispense with a script, perhaps filmmakers in other genres can also abandon it. Think of the savings in hours, coffee, cigarettes, and frayed nerves if we can just make do with a few rough notes. What a beautiful dream!

So why a script? Because using a script is usually the most logical and helpful way to make a film. I think of the script as something akin to the architect's plan. Buildings can be erected without master designs and working drawings, and in the same way all sorts of films can be made without scripts, but there are a myriad reasons in both cases for writing down and formalizing the creative ideas. To put it very simply, a decent script makes the task of filmmaking a hundred times easier.

Why is that? How *does* the script help us and what are its prime functions?

1. The script is an *organizing and structural tool*, a reference and a guide that helps everyone involved in the production.

2. The script communicates the idea of the film to everyone concerned with the production, and it tries to do this clearly, simply, and imaginatively. The script helps everyone understand what the film is about and where it is going. The script is particularly vital to the sponsor, telling them in detail what the film is about and whether what has been loosely discussed in conference has been translated into acceptable film ideas.

3. The script is also essential to both the cameraman and the director. It should convey to the cameraman a great deal about the mood, action, and problems of the camera work. It should also help the director define the approach and the progress of the film, its inherent logic and its continuity.

4. The script is also an essential item for the rest of the production team because, apart from conveying the story, it also helps the crew answer a series of questions:

- What is the appropriate budget for the film?
- How many locations are needed and how many days shooting?
- What lighting will be required?
- Will there be any special effects?
- Will archive material be needed?
- Are special cameras or lenses called for because of a particular scene?

5. The script will also guide the editor, showing the proposed structure of the film and the way the sequences will fit together. In practice, the editor may read the original script but will eventually work from a slightly different document, *the editing script*. (For reasons discussed later, the editing script may differ radically from the original script.)

Implicit in the above comments is the idea that the script is a *working document* and *not a literary document*. It is the basis from which plans can be made and action carried out. It might incidentally be a superb piece of prose (unusual!), but that is not the prime requisite. The first object of the script is to show what the film is about and suggest how its main idea can be carried out in the best possible way.

I have suggested the analogy of an architect's plan, but the comparison works only to a certain point. A script is a guide or first battle plan, the best device for getting the film under way on the basis of the information known at the time of writing. However, in reality it is only a best-guess guide to uncharted territory. It states where you want to go and suggests what seems initially the best route.

But the actual experience of the filming may cause you to change many ideas. For example, planned sequences may just not work out. The marvelous person who seemed so alive and forthcoming during the re-search interview turns out to be flat and useless on camera. The vaunted pageant, which sounded so good when described to you and which you thought would provide the climax to the film, turns out to be abysmally dull. Or new possibilities may be discovered while shooting. Strange characters may turn up and marvelous, unexpected events happen even in the best-planned film. In each case you may need to drastically revise your thinking about both the film and the script. You may find yourself reev-aluating sequences, throwing some away, adding others, and even reorder-ing some of the main acts.

Another frequent problem is that theory does not always match reality. The script that looked so appealing on paper refuses to work when the material is assembled. You find, for example, that the whole rhythm of the film is wrong or that it is overloaded with information. At that point the script will have to be adjusted, and again sequences may have to be lost, cut, or reordered in a new logic. In most cases this can be done relatively easily, and the script can be altered to accommodate the changes without damaging the essential structure and message of the film.

The Overall Film Stages

In order to understand the problems involved in the script, it helps to visualize the entire production process, which is outlined below. In a prescripted documentary the film will probably go through the following stages:

1. Script development
    The idea and its development
    Discussion with sponsors or funding agencies
    Preliminary research
    Writing the proposal
    Discussion of proposal
    Agreement on budget
    Research

Writing the shooting script

Acceptance and modification of script

(At this point the writer can relax slightly, but only slightly, as he or she will probably be highly involved throughout the production as well.)

2. Preproduction (based on script)

3. Filming

4. Editing

The visual edit based on a revised editing script

Editing sound and laying in narration from an approved narration script

5. Sound mix

6. Final lab work

What can sometimes be confusing is that the word *script* is used in half a dozen different ways and may mean something entirely different depending where you are in the production. You will also hear the words *treatment* and *outline* bandied about, adding to the confusion. In reality, it is all quite simple:

The idea. We know what that is.

The treatment or outline is usually just a few pages sketching in what the film is about. It will suggest an approach and tell the overall story of the film. Its usual aim is to clarify the purpose and progression of the film with the funding agency.

The shooting script is the approved master plan. It usually has a fairly full description of all the visual sequences and an accompanying outline of the ideas to be discussed in the sequence or the tentative narration. As its name indicates, this script also suggests to the director what to shoot and will be used to make a daily shooting plan and a proper budget. As mentioned earlier, it also helps the cameraman see what special camera and lighting provisions have to be made.

The editing script (visuals) may be the same as the shooting script or something radically different. Normally the director sits down with the editor after filming to review the material already shot (called "rushes" or "dailies"). If the director decides to drop, add, or modify a sequence, he or she will probably draw up a new script or set of notes to guide the editor. This is what we call the editing script. What has to be emphasized is that during editing the rushes, not theory, must guide the film, and this material may necessitate many departures from the original script. Hence the occasional necessity to formulate a special editing script.

The narration script is not really a script but rather the final narration text that has to be read over the visuals. In most current-event or biographical documentaries the shooting script contains only a rough guide to the main ideas of the film. The writing of the exact narration is usually left until almost the end of the process, when all the visual material has been locked into place. However, even in films where a full narration has been written at an early stage, it is not unusual to see major changes being made in editing, necessitating a new narration script when the editing is almost complete. Recording and laying in the narration track is one of the last stages in the editing.

3

Getting to Work

The writer's first work on a project can be broken down into two stages: (1) from birth of the idea to completion and acceptance of the proposal, and (2) from the research stage to acceptance of the shooting script. A great deal of writing will be done at both stages but to different ends. The final objective of the first stage is to sell potential backers on the idea of a film. The objective of the second stage is to prepare a working document that will guide the film from shooting through completion.

So is the writer a huckster, a common salesperson? In many cases, yes! Occasionally a writer is invited into a project that has already been set in motion, where the sole task is merely to write the script. More often than not, however, the writer will also be the producer or will work closely with the producer; in that case, his or her first job is to get out a piece of paper that will sell the idea of the film.

Of course, there are other objectives during the first stage, such as clearing the head of the writer, formulating the ideas in a lucid way, and agreeing on objectives with the sponsor. Nevertheless, in most cases the real aim of the first stage is to get somebody to accept the proposal and fund a film that might cost anything from $5,000 to $250,000. There are four milestones on the way:

1. Delivering the *basic suggestion*
2. Discussing the suggestion or idea with the sponsor, TV station or support organization
3. Writing and delivering the proposal
4. Discussing the proposal and signing the contract

All four stages are usually necessary when the idea originates from you personally. If the idea or request for a film comes from a television station or a sponsoring organization, then you will most likely go straight to the proposal. In this chapter I want to deal with stages 1 and 2.

The Basic Idea or Suggestion

The basic suggestion is the written definition of the idea that gets the film moving. It can be a note, a letter, or a memo to raise someone's interest so that he or she will back the film. The key words are *raise interest*. The note can be formal or informal, jocular or serious, but whatever format it takes its purpose is to intrigue the reader, to stimulate his or her interest and imagination. The response you are looking for is "What a great idea! Let's think more about this."

The note or letter can be long, but more often than not it is short and to the point. If the idea is good then its attractiveness can be seen immediately. The task of the suggestive note is to say briefly what the film is about, why the idea is attractive to you, and why it might be of interest to the sponsor. Here are a few examples.

> *Help Me*
> If hospitals scare adults, then what are the effects of the institution on children? We believe that the problems facing children going into the hospital have been neglected for too long.
>
> We therefore propose to make a ten-minute film for children between the ages of four and ten which will help dispel their fears. There is a dire need to make such a film and we believe that the Wellington Hospital, with its worldwide reputation for the care and welfare of children as well as its reputation for healing, is the ideal institution to make and back such a pioneering film.
>
> We estimate the production cost to be in the region of $12,000.

The suggestion is brief but easily grasped. Such an idea would probably be accompanied by a letter suggesting a meeting to discuss the idea in more detail if there is any initial interest. The letter would also amplify why it would benefit the hospital to make such a film.

Another idea might be put this way:

> Dear Dr. Courts:
> Is it just coincidence or is it the fashion of the times? In the last month I have read at least three articles in magazines ranging from *Newsweek* to *The New Yorker* discussing the prevalence of student stress and teenage suicide.
>
> This started me thinking about your department, which has received so much well-deserved publicity in regard to its research on student stress and your innovative methods for dealing with the same.
>
> I would like to suggest doing a film with you on the whole subject of stress, which would serve to publicize your methods and approach around the world. We could do this either as

a straightforward instructional film, or we could play around a little more imaginatively and focus on two or three student types. We could take a first-year student and a graduate student as typical cases and examine their problems and treatment.

I think—and I don't believe I'm wrong—that there is a tremendous demand for such a film (or videotape). I also think it would be fairly easy to get the university and the Science Research Council to fund us up to the tune of $20,000, which should be sufficient. What do you say? Can we get together to discuss the matter further?

In the above two examples the writer-producer is the originator of the suggestions. However, it sometimes happens that a sponsor or a television documentary series throws out a suggestion in a generalized area. It is then up to the writer to develop a specific approach. A recent handout from the British Home Office read as follows:

Request for Suggestions

We wish to make various short films showing the problems confronting new immigrants to England, and the successful integration of the immigrants. We welcome suggestions from Producers which should be less than three pages in length and turned in in triplicate. The films should be under twenty minutes in length and should be capable of being executed on a budget of $15,000. Proposals must be submitted to this office by July 31st.

An interested writer-producer might have responded as follows:

The Orchestra

This is a film about a unique orchestra in Manchester composed of thirty Indians from New Delhi and Madras who have been in England five years. Some are fluent in English, but not all. Many were professional musicians in India, but they now have to support themselves in Manchester by learning new trades and professions.

Three years ago, under the leadership and inspiration of Asoke Badra, they decided to form a specialized Indian folk orchestra.

The orchestra rehearses three times a week and in the last year has given major concerts in Manchester and in London's Festival Hall. Next year the orchestra has been invited to appear at New York's Lincoln Center.

> We believe that a look at the orchestra and its members will
> provide a different and fascinating way of approaching the
> problems of immigrant absorption.

Implicit in this suggestion is the idea that one will explore individual
backgrounds, problems, and attitudes to the new country and come out
with a story of hope. Quite clearly the orchestra motif is a neat frame for this
exploration.

Though I thought about the orchestra idea, I never submitted it. I was
therefore very interested when, a few years later, I saw that Jim Brown, a
New York filmmaker and university professor, had just finished a documentary on the experiences of a Russian émigré orchestra in the United States.

The Discussion and the Agenda

The response to your initial suggestion has been favorable. The doctor,
the sponsor, the station, or the agency is intrigued. They are willing to
explore further, though they have told you they are far from committed.
They want to meet and, depending on the discussion, will decide how far
they want to pursue the matter. The following topics are likely to be on the
agenda: the subject matter and purpose of the film; its intended audience;
its approach; and its limitations, such as budget and timing. Knowing that
these topics will come up, you have to go over them carefully in your mind
so that you will have the answers at hand when a problem is raised. You will
also know what issues to raise with the sponsor so that there are no
misunderstandings once you start to work seriously on the film.

Subject Matter and Purpose

No matter what the film, and no matter who is supporting it, it is essential
that the boundaries of the topic and the purpose of the film be clarified from
the start. Aim for a target definition or basic assertion that states clearly
what the film is about, what it is trying to say and to whom, and what it
hopes to achieve. You must have those things straight before going into any
discussion. And the target definition isn't just for the sponsor; it will also
keep your thinking on track as the film progresses.

You also have to be clear from the start what you want the film to do. It
may have a multiplicity of purposes, but you should know what they are.
Will it merely entertain? Will it help in fund-raising? Will it alarm the
population to a hidden danger and shake them from their complacency, like
The War Game? Will it instruct? Is it meant to change certain habits and
behaviors? You may want the film to do all these things or none of them, but
you must be sure of your central purpose from the beginning.

In these early discussions you also need to probe the sponsor's attitude to
the subject. Why are they interested? What do they want? Ideally their

interests and attitudes will coincide with your own, but not always. Therefore, it is best to flush out any reservations on the subject at the beginning rather than be surprised by them later, at some cost to the film.

Audience

The objective of a film cannot be discussed in isolation. It always goes together with a consideration of the audience for whom the film is intended. You must know from the beginning something about your audience; either the sponsor tells you or you find out for yourself. You need to know who makes up the audience, how it can best be reached, and whether it is broad or narrow. The answers to these questions will influence your whole approach to writing the film. Writing for television is generally quite difficult because the audience is so broad. When doing a general documentary for television, you have to assume that you are writing for all groups between the ages of fourteen and seventy-five, for all levels of education, and for people from all varieties of social and religious backgrounds. These difficulties are addressed in detail later in the book.

What are the things you need to know about your potential viewers and related matters?

First, you need to define *the general composition of the audience*. Who exactly are the people who are going to watch the film? What are their ages? What are their politics? What are their religious beliefs? Is it a city audience or a rural audience? Is it sophisticated or unsophisticated, educated or uneducated? Is it an audience of professionals or manual workers? Obviously, you won't be asking all these questions all the time, but you will definitely be asking some of them because the answers to the questions will help you talk directly to the audience instead of above it, below it, or around it.

Next, you need to know in what *context* the film will be shown. Will it be shown in a school, a church, or a university? Is it going to be shown on television in prime time, or at an obscure midnight hour? If it is going to be shown on prime-time television, you might have to tone down your treatment. If it's going to be shown in the early hours, then you may have a small audience but you might get away with a much more revolutionary and radical approach to your subject.

Is the film going to be used for fund-raising at a massive dinner, or is it going to be shown in a small village hall? Is it intended for a specific audience in one country, or will it be shown around the world? Is it going to be shown in a television series or in isolation?

You must be certain to define *audience feeling* about the subject. What attitudes do they hold on the topic? Is it completely unknown to them, or is it a subject with which they are very familiar? Do they have any fears or resistance to the subject? Do they hold any taboos about it? Are there any prejudices with which one has to cope, or is the subject outside the normal experience of the audience? Are they likely to approve of the line taken in the film or to resist it? The practical ramifications of these questions are very important. For example, if you are making a film about birth control it is vital to know whether your target audience is Protestant or Catholic, conservative or liberal. In short, you should understand the culture and beliefs of the audience you are trying to reach and influence. Unless you understand these elementary points, the film may be technically well made and yet fail to put across the message.

Approach

One of the inevitable questions that comes up in the first discussion is "What approach are you going to use? How are you going to do it?" At that point I try to say as little as possible, at least if it is a new subject for me as a writer or if I do not really know the sponsor. I want time to become familiar with the subject before I jump in. Usually, though, the sponsor wants some hint of how you would approach the subject. If you have been thinking about the topic for years, you should have no trouble with this question, as you have probably thought of a way to do the film. The trouble starts when the subject is new and you know nothing about it.

Sometimes I just play for time. On major documentaries I try to make a strong case that I need to research and absorb the subject before I can guess at an approach. Yet sometimes when they ask, "How would you do it?" you have no option but to plunge right in, even though you know you may junk the idea as soon as you exit the room.

One of the first times that question was sprung on me was when I was doing a news item, and the director of the museum where I was filming asked me out of the blue how I would do a general film on the museum. At that stage I knew nothing about the museum except for having walked around it once. My spontaneous answer was that I thought we could look at the museum through the eyes of two eight-year-old children. It seemed to me that at their age there was a curiosity that would add freshness to the way the museum was observed. This would break the standard intellectual catalogue approach to museum filming. In the end I didn't get the film. Would silence have been better? I don't think so.

Conversely, a friend of mine did get a film because he ventured a fresh approach at the right time to people with a receptive imagination. And here again it was a case of jumping in while knowing nothing about the subject. The Vermont State Bureau of Taxes wanted to encourage people to pay their local taxes. David knew nothing about taxes but suggested a scenario where his hero dreams of leading a revolt against tax payment. Everybody supports him. He becomes the local hero, but suddenly there are thieves everywhere as there is no money for the police; likewise, there are no hospital services and no schools. The hero wakes in shock and pays his taxes. It was a very funny idea and powerfully put across the essential idea that taxes are necessary to make the social order work smoothly.

One difficulty that frequently arises is trying to get the sponsors to abandon an approach which they have been nursing for months but which you feel is wrong. For example, they may want to star the managing director, who is also the chief shareholder, but who would, in your opinion, be a total disaster for the film. If the idea is no good then it has to be killed early, but tactfully.

Leaving all discussion of approach until the research has been done is great in theory, but difficult in practice. This is particularly true of television quasi-news documentaries, where the time between idea, research, and filming is often so negligible as to be nonexistent. In reality you start thinking about approach from the beginning with later research either reinforcing your original hunch or showing its deficiencies.

Limitations

One of the objects of the first discussion is to distinguish the possible from the impossible and to bring a sense of reality into the planning, considering budget costs, time, and technical matters. You might think that this kind of discussion should just be between the sponsor and the producer, but as it seriously affects the script I believe in the writer being involved as well.

Cost limitations. One has to know at an early stage all the cost limitations, because the size of the budget largely determines what can and cannot be done. The grandiose designs of the sponsor (or yourself) may require $100,000 and so be absolutely impractical if $20,000 is the maximum available. The script must be capable of being executed within the confines of the budget. This is golden rule number one.

Most people who work in television documentary have an excellent idea of realistic costs. This knowledge is rarely shared by companies or charitable organizations who want films about their enterprises or projects. Sponsors are always shocked by the cost of filmmaking, and my heart no longer dives when they say, "What! Thirty thousand dollars! We were sure it wouldn't be more than five thousand. Maybe we should think of doing a slide show instead."

You must have a good sense of film costs before entering any discussion with the sponsor. In assessing the feasibility of doing your script, even at the earliest stages you should be considering days of shooting, length of editing, stock costs, and so on, not to mention a living wage or small profit for the writer-director. So you must think about all the expenses in order to tell the sponsor what your beautiful idea will cost and in order to see whether the film can really be brought in on the budget suggested by the sponsor or backer. Hence golden rule number two: Do not accept a budget that will be inadequate for your film concept. If you are given a budget limitation, then your script (but not necessarily your imagination) must be limited by that fact. You ignore that rule at your financial peril.

One of the problems of dealing with costs at this point of the proceedings is that you may also be at the bid stage. If you are the only filmmaker being considered for the project, and if the sponsor came to you with their ideas, then you are in a relatively good position to argue for the best budget under the circumstances. What is the best budget? You soon get a rough sense of the organization—whether it is wealthy or desperate, whether it lives from profits or donations. Once you have this picture in mind you will have a good idea where to pitch your bid.

When there is competition for the film, things are trickier. When other people are bidding for the same film the question becomes how to make a reasonable bid that will keep you in competition with everybody else and yet will leave you enough to make a quality film and a profit.

Time constraints. It is also vital to discuss timing at an early stage. Are time considerations going to be of importance to any aspect of the film? If so, they should be discussed early. For example:

1. Does the film have to be finished and ready for screening on a certain date, such as the annual meeting of the sponsoring organization or a political anniversary within a country? If so, is there enough time to make the film while still maintaining quality?
2. How do the physical seasons affect the filming and the completion date? Have you taken into consideration that you will be filming at the time of the heaviest snows or that the rainy season will prevent your helicopter shots?
3. Are you dependent on one individual, group, or situation for any length of time, and will a change in the availability of someone or a change in the situation jeopardize the film?

If you are wary of these restraints, then think twice before you go ahead. If you still feel apprehensive, drop the idea. You'll feel better in the long run. Let me give you the Houseman example.

In summer 1985 I thought that I had hit on a great idea. It struck me that John Houseman, the professor hero of the series "The Paper Chase," had in his real life as writer, producer, and director seen almost every major change in film, theater, and television in the United States between the years 1940 and 1980. He had worked with Orson Welles on *Citizen Kane*, produced *Lust for Life* with Kirk Douglas, and seemed to have known everybody and done everything in the mass media. Knowing this, I suddenly thought we could do a fascinating film looking at forty years of change in the media and pin it all to Houseman's recollections and reminiscences. Houseman was agreeable and enthusiastic. What stopped me in the end was Houseman's age. In 1985 he was already eighty-three. I knew it would take about eighteen months to raise the money and get the project moving, then another eighteen months to film and complete. Could I rely on Houseman's health for three years? It seemed to me too big a risk, and I dropped the project. Houseman died in 1988.

Film or video. One major issue must be sorted out at the start: Does the sponsor want a film or a videotape as the final product? This will also be a question for yourself even if no sponsor is concerned. The answer really depends on purpose and use rather than on technical considerations. You might prefer video

1. if the program is intended mainly for home or office presentation;
2. if the audience will have to go back and forth in looking at the film or if they will want to stop on one point for discussion or need to rewind quickly;
3. if a tremendous amount of shooting has to be done and you are wary of cost—here the low cost of videotape is of tremendous help;
4. if you want to make many copies yet keep the cost down;
5. if you want very elaborate effects and think they can best be done electronically.

You might prefer film

1. if the sponsor wants a theatrical screening to impress people or if you are thinking primarily of a hall or theatrical presentation;
2. if the quality of the photography is an important final consideration;
3. if you are going to have a very lengthy editing process: at the moment film editing is much cheaper than video editing, but that might change.

In fact, all these arguments are open to question because of the swift pace of change in video technology.

Feasibility. Before starting a new project, I hold a discussion in my head, rather than with the sponsor, concerning the project's feasibility. Occasionally I get the most fantastic ideas, then realize they are not very practical. Often extremely careful thought is required before saying yes to an idea.

About a week before I wrote this section, a producer friend of mine told me he was considering doing a film on the intelligence services of the world and asked me to help him with it. It sounded like a splendid idea, and he had already made two films on international terrorism. If anyone could pull it off, it was Mike. But as we started to think through the project, a number of problems started surfacing. Yes, it was easy enough to talk about spies, about the blowing up of the Greenpeace ship by France, about the Israeli intelligence seizure of Vannunu, about John le Carré, about the KGB men who had defected and the problems of the CIA and so on—but was that enough? The film was about intelligence, not spies and not thriller writers, though these elements would appear.

The real question was whether or not we could penetrate in any meaningful way the intelligence systems of the world—the CIA, the British MI5 and MI6, the Israeli Mossad. I doubted it. We could perhaps get interviews with people such as Peter Wright, the former British agent and author of

Spy Catcher, and in 1987 a whole heap of public evidence had been revealed about the methods of the Israeli Mossad, but I still didn't think it was enough. For the program to have bite we needed real inside interviews. Instead, the most we could get would be old stories and tales of incidents based on hearsay, innuendo, and wild guessing. We could do an interesting film, but it wasn't the one I wanted to make.

However, I hate abandoning ideas. If the subject is intrinsically interesting, then sometimes an alternative approach or a slightly different slant will show you a way in. Again, what at first sight seems a doubtful or unpromising idea often gets realized through sheer determination or imagination. In 1975, Roger Graef, a noted cinema verite filmmaker, wanted to make a film about the decision-making processes of big business in England. This necessitated entry into the most intimate boardroom discussions of the largest corporations, such as those controlling steel and oil. "You'll never get the necessary permissions," everybody said. "All decisions of big business are made by fat rich men in elegant boardrooms in secret." Graef persisted, and against all odds got three of the largest corporations in England to give him permission to film their boardroom meetings over six months. The resulting series, "Decisions," was one of the most fascinating ever to appear on television.

Sometimes it merely looks impossible but can be done.

Order of Progress

I have suggested that the logical development of your film is through the initial idea, then into meetings and discussions that lead into the proposal. However, the order is often reversed, and you have to submit a detailed proposal before meeting with the sponsor. There are few rules, and each case is different. But for the purpose of this book I have assumed that the discussions came before the proposal. So on with the proposal.

4
Writing the Proposal

Your initial idea has had a warm reception. You have met with the potential sponsors or the television department head, who like your ideas but want to know more. Now you have to write a formal proposal that will define your thinking in much greater detail. A proposal is first and foremost a device to sell a film. It may serve many other functions, such as clarifying your own thinking or showing your friends what you want to do, and it will provide information useful to all sorts of people. But its central purpose is to convince someone or some organization that you have a great idea, that you know what you want to do, that you are efficient, professional, and imaginative, and that you should therefore be given the contract for the film against any competition or be financially supported in the endeavor.

Sometimes a proposal is called for after a film has been awarded to a producer. However, for the next few pages I want to discuss the general writing of the proposal when its prime purpose is to sell the film.

Style and Main Topics

The best rule is to aim for simplicity, clarity, and brevity. Brevity may not always be possible, but it is a worthy ideal. Proposals for the National Endowment for the Humanities or the National Endowment for the Arts are often hundreds of pages long, but they are special cases. Few sponsors have the patience to read long proposals in detail; a concise proposal is much more likely to get their attention.

What should the proposal discuss and how should it be organized? There are no absolute rules, but it helps to remember that a proposal is usually written with a specific person or organization in mind, and you write for that person or organization. I usually include the following items in my proposals:

1. Film statement
2. Background and need
3. Approach, structure, and style
4. Shooting schedule

5. Budget
6. Audience and distribution
7. Filmmaker's biography and support letters

Film statement. The statement formally declares that you are making a proposal and usually suggests a working title. It indicates the length of the film and briefly defines its subject matter and audience. It probably includes the basic assertion or target statement mentioned earlier. Only a few lines are necessary, as indicated by the following examples:

> *University Blues*
> This is a proposal for a thirty-minute 16mm film on the future of Oxford and Cambridge Universities for general BBC television audiences.
>
> *Because We Care*
> This is a proposal for a forty-minute 16mm film on St. Winston's Hospital for showing to potential donors for fund-raising.

Background and need. The section on background and need sets out briefly any information necessary to acquaint the reader with the subject. You try to let the reader see why the topic is interesting and why such a film is needed or would be of interest as entertainment or information to a general audience.

Some years ago I wanted to do a film about nineteenth-century American utopian movements and started writing the proposal with a friend, Brian Winston. We called the film *Roads to Eden* and included the following sketch with the proposal:

> The most sustained and widespread efforts to remake the world took place along the expanding frontier in North America, mainly in the nineteenth century. Literally hundreds of communities with thousands of members were established, and the vast majority of them sought salvation through rigorous and what they thought of as ancient Christian practice.
>
> The discovery of the New World and the birth of modern utopianism occurred during the same quarter of a century. The one deeply influenced the other, and the New World immediately became a place in which tradition and history could be restarted and remade.
>
> The potency of America as a ready-made site for social experiment survived undiminished by failures, lunacies, or frauds for the next three centuries.
>
> Inspired with a vision of early Christian life traceable back to the communes of the Essenes, enriched by the monastic tradition and the example of primitive (mainly German) Protestant sects, the

> American Christian radicals set about building their Jerusalem.
> Out of a flurry of activity major groups emerged: Mormons,
> Shakers, Amish, Oneidans, Amanites, Rappites, and Zoarites.

Brian and I took fairly long in setting out the background, but we were
making a proposal for an hour-long major network film, which we also
hoped would be the basis of a series. We assumed most people would like
the idea of a film about utopias but would know nothing of their histories,
hence the detail.

When we had finished sketching in the background we set out our
reasons for wanting to do the film.

> In this film or series we will look at the past in order to
> ascertain where we might possibly go in the future, for the
> dream of a better world is not dead, only diminished.
>
> Thus, a series of questions underlies the film. How can we
> make a better life for ourselves, our families, and our children?
> What can we learn from the past about sexual mores, family
> structures, and social organizations? What do the visions and
> struggles of the utopians tell us about our own future?

The background sketch can be short or long. You must ask yourself, does
the reader have sufficient information about the central situation and
premise of the film to make a reasonable judgment about it? And have you
provided enough information to intrigue the reader to go further? The
background information should be a lure to fascinate the reader, to make
him or her say, "What a marvelous possibility for a film."

Approach, form, and style. I have already mentioned that I am wary of
defining approach, form, or style before I have researched the subject, as
the research usually suggests the best way into the film. Yet in most cases at
least a tentative approach will be asked for at the proposal stage. If the
original suggestion came from you, an approach will definitely be required.
This is the part of the proposal that most interests the reader. Talking is one
thing, but how will you actually do the film? Your ideas sound fascinating
and appealing, but how will you carry them out in practice? This is where
you come down to earth. If your approach and structure is tentative, then
say so, or indicate two or three approaches you would like to investigate
further.

The question of form and structure is discussed in detail later, but a few
words might help now. In most television documentaries the chosen form is
usually that of the *general essay* or *illustrative story*, and the style ranges
from the objective to the anecdotal or the personal. In the early 1970s
Thames Television in England put out a marvelous twenty-six-part series
on World War II called "The World at War." What was refreshing about the
series is that it ran the whole gamut of styles and structures. One film would

be an academic essay, while the next would be highly personal, telling the story of the war almost solely through the voices of the soldiers.

A few paragraphs back I set out the background for the utopia film. That was the easy part. But what approach should we use? It could be done, say in essay style:

> The film is set up chronologically as we tell the story of the communities from the seventeenth to the late nineteenth century, from the Shakers to the Zoarites. The film will include all the main communities but will concentrate on the Shakers. It will be built around drawings, contemporary pictures, old photographs, and contemporary shooting and will be told through a strong central guiding commentary.

This may sound a bit dry. Perhaps we could try a story form and an alternative structure:

> We will look at the utopian movements through two central charismatic characters, the leaders of Harmony and New Harmony. These two colonies were situated in southern Indiana. The first was a religious colony founded by the grim authoritarian preacher Emmanuel Rapp, from southern Germany. Eventually the colony was sold to the Scottish idealist Robert Owen, who wanted to found a workers' utopia.
>
> We will film exclusively at New Harmony, which is today still faithfully preserved as in the days of Owen and Rapp. Besides filming on location we propose using old diary extracts and the writings of Rapp and Owen as the binding narrative. The film will look at these communities through the lives of their leaders, who could not have interpreted the meaning of "utopia" more differently. However, we will also try to recapture the feelings of the community members of the time. The style will be evocative and poetic rather than didactic.

In the early 1980s Canadian filmmaker Michael Rubbo made a film called *Daisy*, about plastic surgery. I never read his proposal, but from the experience of the film I could imagine Rubbo setting out the proposal something like this:

> Why do people go in for plastic surgery? What are their fears and expectations? We wish to show something of the history and practice of plastic surgery to the general public.
>
> We think the best approach to a film of this kind is to follow one individual for six months, covering the period before, during, and after the operation. And we have found exactly the right person.

Daisy is an employee of the Canadian Film Board, an open, cheerful, and extrovert woman in her early fifties. Though still extremely attractive, Daisy feels that plastic surgery will improve her looks and general social well-being. She also thinks it will help her find a husband.

Daisy's experience will provide us with the spine of the film. However, we will also branch out from time to time to show the history of plastic surgery, the way it is practiced in present-day Montreal, and how it exists as a thriving business.

Even without major research you can often take a pretty good stab at the approach you would like to take and the tentative structure of the film. Some years ago I was asked to consider doing a film on the British prison system, a subject I knew very little about. My initial feeling, before I had undertaken any research, was that this should be a people film rather than an essay film, a personal film from both sides of the bars. In my first outline proposal I suggested a film around the experience of five individuals. The first two would represent the administration in the person of a guard and the warden. The other three characters would be a prisoner about to serve his first six-month sentence, the second a lifer, and the last someone who had served five years and whom we would follow in his first three months of freedom. I was fairly sure that I could find these types and that the different experiences of the five over half a year would provide an illuminating and moving picture of the prison system.

I set all this out in the proposal and also indicated that there would be minimal narration; instead, the film would hang on the thoughts, feelings, and comments of the five "stars." I was a bit worried about the extended shooting time and its effect on the budget and therefore sounded out the sponsors before I wrote the proposal. They agreed to provide a decent budget, and I was free to explore the above approach. Had the budget been a small one I would have cut down on my characters and shooting time or would have opted for an essay film that could have been shot in two weeks.

Where possible, I like to indicate early on whether there will be formal narration, direct dialogue, or a great deal of voice-over. I also occasionally say something about visual style if I think that will be a major element of the film.

Shooting schedule. The shooting schedule is an optional item in the proposal. You include it when time is of the essence: for example, when you have to capture a particular event or shoot within a particular season of the year. You also put it in when you want to protect yourself, so that you can turn to the sponsor and say, "The proposal says very clearly we would need six months, so don't tell me now I have to do it in three. It just can't be done."

Budget. I usually include an approximate budget in the proposal. However, I try to put off committing myself on paper until I have had a word with the sponsors. I don't want to scare them off until we have talked about cost and have received some feedback. Obviously, if you are sending a proposal to a foundation such as the National Endowment for the Humanities or the Rockefeller Foundation, you will have to provide at least an outline budget proposal.

Audience and distribution. A discussion of audience and distribution is another optional item. If a sponsor has requested a film to train factory workers, or if a television station has requested a film for a certain documentary series, then you will not have to say anything about distribution in the proposal. However, when you are trying to sell a sponsor or a foundation on your idea and have said that there will be massive demand for your film, then you have to prove your claim, at least on paper. You also have to talk about getting the film to this massive public. This section of the proposal therefore sets out in detail the possible channels of distribution for the film. A section on distribution is invariably required for a major proposal to a foundation.

Below is the section on distribution from Jill Godmilow's proposal for *The Popovich Brothers*. The film, eventually made in the late 1970s, took as its subject a Serbian musical family in Chicago. The film explored their music but also looked at the sense of family, traditions, and close bonding of the whole of the immigrant community of which the Popovich brothers were just part.

> We believe that filmmaking and film marketing are two halves of a full circle. A film that never reaches its audience is little different from a film that never gets made. It just costs a lot more.
>
> We have two major goals in the distribution of *The Popovich Brothers*. The first is to make it available to the Serbian community on all levels: to the churches, to the local lodges of the Serb National Federation, to high school systems with large enrollment, of Serbs and other Slavic groups, and to universities which have community-developed ethnic studies. Our experience thus far indicates tremendous interest and support for this project in the Serbian community, on a local and national level.
>
> Besides the Serbian community, there are four general distribution markets for this documentary film:
>
> 1. *Television:* Television sales—commercial, educational, and foreign—constitute the independent documentary's widest means of exposure to a mass audience and its most immediate and least expensively obtained source of income.
>
>   a. The commercial networks can buy up to thirty minutes of footage at $1,000 per minute and recut and narrate it for use as one segment of their program.
>   b. PBS, the national educational network, is also in the market for quality independently produced documentaries.
>   c. Foreign television sales.

2. *Print Sales:* Museums, public libraries, and university libraries have begun to buy films for their permanent collections. They are used for public screenings as well as borrowed for home use.

3. *Rentals:* Every nondramatic film must find its particular rental market, its own special-interest groups. *The Popovich Brothers* has a good market potential in areas such as music, dance, American history, ethnic studies, social anthropology, Slavic languages, and ethnomusicology.

4. *Theatrical:* The fourth general area of distribution for *Popovich* is theatrical. It is a limited market but an important one. The success of a theatrical campaign for a film like this one depends to a great degree on being able to open in New York, with the accompanying critical response and public excitement which can create a name for a film.

I have set out Jill's proposal at length because it is one of the best examples I have seen of lucid proposal writing. *The Popovich Brothers* was eventually made, received wide acclaim, and has been followed by other films by Jill Godmilow such as *Far from Poland*.

Curriculum vitae and letters of support. It helps to finish off the proposal by giving a short biographical description of yourself and the other principal filmmakers involved in the project. You should also affirm your track record by adding letters of recommendation or praise for your previous work. You should also include any support letters from individuals or organizations for your idea and any letters from television stations showing an interest in screening your film.

Examples

Depending on the objectives of the film, the same subject might require two entirely different proposals. Let us imagine we have been asked to put in two proposals for a university film. One is to be a standard documentary for general television audiences, the second a film to raise funds for the campus; the working title for both films is *Tomorrow Begins Now*. Below I have sketched out the main differences between the two proposals.

FILM A	FILM B
Introduction	
A half-hour film to *explore* the changing University.	A half-hour film to *raise* money for the University.
Background	
The changing university over the last twenty years. Ideas	The changing community. Education today. Desperate need

change. Communities change.

for a new kind of university. The answer as provided by our university.

Objectives

A reevaluation in the eyes of the public of the role and purpose of a university. For general television audiences.

To raise money for the university. For showing to small interest groups, dinner groups, and friends of the university.

Focus

The film is about a group of students, and we set out to explore their world.

The complexity of a university and the need it fills in a community. Also the future requirements of the university.

Format and Style

We follow three students for six months as they become involved in different student, educational, and political activities. The style is personal and intimate.

We follow two students and two professors through a typical day. The film is an overview of university activities rather than an analysis of the pros and cons of the university. We intend to stress the building program and the intake of students from culturally deprived backgrounds.

Narration

As little as possible. Use the students' voices instead.

We will use a standard expository narrator with occasional voice-overs by students and faculty.

Technique

Cinema verite.

Basic directed documentary style.

Point of View

We view the students as basically idealistic and an admirable force for good.

We see the university as a vital element in our growing nation, an element that must be supported if we are to survive.

The proposal for film A follows in broad terms the film *The Berkeley Rebels*, made by Arthur Barron for "CBS Reports" in 1965. CBS had told Barron that there was a lot of trouble at the Berkeley campus of the University of California; they suggested that he explore the situation in terms of the students' goals and see what kind of film he wanted to make.

Barron spent a month at Berkeley, returned to CBS, and wrote out the following preparatory notes. These notes are not exactly a proposal but show clearly the kind of film Barron wanted to make.

Focus. This film is not about the University of California; it is not about the class of 1965; it is not about the demonstrations which have taken place at California. These are all elements in our story but the film is basically about something else. It is about a selected group of students. Call them "activists," the new radicals, or "green baggers." This picture is about *them*. It seeks to explore their world. It seeks to answer these questions: Who are they? What do they want? Why are they important? It seeks to reveal the mood, posture, and attitudes of a new and different generation of committed students.

Point of View. We do not state a point of view directly but we do have an attitude to these kids, and hopefully it comes through. It is this: despite their faults (intolerance, immaturity, a tendency to see things in black and white, rebellion for its own sake, a certain disrespect for law and order) these kids are a positive and admirable force in American society. They are idealistic, brilliant, vocal, and *alive*. They are willing to say, "The Emperor wears no clothes." They are generous, compassionate, and moral. They take America's promises seriously. They are, in short, our conscience.

Style. This is a highly personal film. It is intimate. It is emotional. Its style is human revelation rather than reportage. It is told subjectively rather than objectively. It is more a diary than an essay, more an autobiography than a report, more a drama than journalism. Its goal is to enter the world of these kids rather than observe and report on it.

Narration. The rule here is to use as little as possible. Ideally, the story will be told completely in the words and voices of our kids. First person all the way. We intend to use a CBS reporter merely to set the scene, to indicate that (distorted or not) this is the way these kids see the world, and to conclude.

Format. The film is in three acts. Each act corresponds to an underlying cause of agitation and disaffection among the students. Act 1 follows Kate Coleman, a senior who will graduate in June. On a personal level it is the story of her satisfactions and dissatisfaction with California. On a broader level it is the story of the achievement and failure of mass education. Act 2 follows Ron and Sally, two unmarried students who live together. In this act we reveal these kids' attitude to authority, responsibility, their parents, the older generation, and individual morality. The message of this act is this: our kids feel the adult world is corrupt and morally bankrupt; they believe they must decide what is *moral* for themselves. Act 3 is "Mike and the New Politics." Mike is a grad student who teaches math. As we follow him we gain insight into the political mood and stance of his generation. Mike's politics are different in important ways from my generation which preceded him. We show how and why this is so, and we reveal what it means to youth today and in America.

The notes conclude with a description of the film techniques that Barron intends to use. They include actual scenes; fantasy scenes to reveal "inner states in an unusually imaginative and dramatic way"; and staged scenes where the students are directed and told to do something.

George Stoney is another excellent filmmaker, noted for such films as *How the Myth Was Made*, about Flaherty's work on Aran, and *All My Babies*. Stoney is also well known as one of the producers of the highly acclaimed *Wasn't That a Time* about the musical group the Weavers. One of the most interesting of Stoney's films is the dramatic documentary *A Cry for Help*, made to assist police forces in coping with the problem of suicide. The following extract from Stoney's proposal illustrates his technique:

> What is the average policeman's attitude towards suicide? We have made some efforts to discover this. Fifteen police departments held roundtable discussions on the matter following a set of questions designed by Dr. Rowland. We have interviewed personally policemen in ten other departments. Our inquiries have gone far enough to suggest that attitudes on suicide *in the abstract* vary quite widely among policemen as among laymen generally being affected by such fundamental things as family background, religion, education, etc. However, the average policeman's attitude towards the individuals involved in such incidents has been made startlingly clear.
>
> In tape after tape one hears them talk about "sympathy bidders." In interview after interview they have made no effort to conceal their hilarity and disgust in telling us about the "repeaters" or the "nuts who call up."
>
> Happily, we have found a good many policemen who have a great deal more understanding than this. Much of the material contained in the script has been developed with their help. However, it is to the average policeman that our film is directed.
>
> *What is our aim?* The primary goal of the film is to save lives by emphasizing the importance of suicide threats and attempts.
>
> While the film will be prepared primarily as a training film for the police, it should have instructional value for clergymen, social service workers, physicians and in fact the public in general.
>
> Emphasis should be on specific situations and how to handle

them, but these should be generalized as far as possible and emphasis should be on attitudes.

The film should enhance the learning of the police officer so that he will handle suicide situations better. This can be done without making him a psychiatrist. Yet it is necessary that the policeman be a student of human nature. In fact, he gets very good at understanding people. With such qualifications, and with some training, he can be a very helpful person.

Structure sketch. Although the attached treatment will result in a film which we hope will be a single dramatic unit, it can be divided for purposes of subject matter analysis into four sections:

1. Ways of preventing suicide and suicide attempts in jail.
2. Emergency rescue procedures outside jails.
3. The role of the police in prevention.
4. The policeman's personal attitude towards people who attempt suicide; how this can hurt or help him in dealing with them.
5. Understanding "the cry for help."

The film's first section deals with suicides and suicide attempts made by people who are in police custody. This is a problem almost every policeman will accept as part of his responsibility, and here we can give him some fairly simple instructions.

The film's second section tackles a more difficult problem: suicides and suicide attempts made by people not in custody. The second section of the film undertakes these things:

1. To present suicide as a statistically important problem in the overall well-being of the community.
2. To stress the importance of responding to these cries for help as literally matters of life and death.

In part 3 the film begins to deal more directly with the policeman's role in preventing suicide. To help develop in our viewers an understanding of people who attempt suicide we sketch four case histories, moving from one to another as our analysis demands.

5

Research

The proposal has been accepted. You have talked it through with the sponsors. You clearly know what the film is about and what it is meant to do. You have thought about audience. The contract has been signed and you have got the go-ahead. The next stage is researching the subject in depth. As a researcher, you need to combine the penetrating brazenness of the good journalist with the painstaking attention to detail of the Ph.D. candidate. You must be observer, analyst, student, and note taker. Over a period that can be as short as a few days or as long as a few months you must become an expert on the subject of the film, a subject you may never even have known existed a few weeks before—not easy, but always fascinating.

Research can be broken down into four sections: (1) print research, (2) photograph and archive research, (3) direct interviews, (4) on-the-spot involvement with the subject or location research. In practice you are likely to be involved in all four forms of research at the same time.

Printed Material

Within the limits of time, budget, sanity, and common sense, you try to read as much as possible about the subject. Your aim is simple: within a very short time you want to become, if not an expert in the field, at least a person with a superior knowledge of the subject. Print research can involve scanning the major bibliographies and print sources and reading books, papers, magazines, trade journals, articles, diaries, letters, and even congressional records and court trials. If the material is highly technical, complex, or jargonized, you should get somebody to help you so that the material becomes comprehensible to you as a mere mortal. If you do not understand the material, you will never be able to say anything sensible about it in a film.

Of course, there are problems all along the way. You will often read too much and in too much depth, making it difficult to isolate the valuable or relevant material. After a while, however, you learn to scan and to distinguish the important fact from the obscuring detail. Another problem

35

is that much of the material may be out of date or presented from a biased or self-serving point of view. Take care to check the date of the material and the credentials and background of the writer. When I think that the material comes from a highly interested and partisan source (particularly in films of a political or controversial nature), I try to check the biases of the informant as well. I also double-check statistics, remembering the old adage "There are lies, more lies, and statistics."

There is one point that I think is terribly important, certainly in investigatory films. Go back to the original sources for your information. Do not be content with second- or third-hand reports. If you are doing a film on World War I, don't just read a few history books. Instead, start digging out documents, wills, diaries, and contemporary newspaper accounts. If you are doing a film on government policy, you have to start digging into official records, state papers, memoranda, and the like. This is not easy, but it is necessary.

Photographs and Stock Footage

Your sources for photographs and stock footage are fairly obvious. Depending on the film, your sources may be government archives (such as the British Imperial War Museum or the National Archives), local and press archives, or television archives. You may be searching through local libraries, private collections, family albums, and attics, or looking at old videos shot by the industry you are investigating. Bear in mind that you are looking at the old films and photographs both as sources of information and as possible visuals in the film. If your objective is the latter, then you should inquire fairly early about permission to use the materials. But more on that subject later.

Once you have a general source for your material, it is not always easy to locate what you want. Archives are often arranged haphazardly, and though you know there is gold somewhere around it may be terribly difficult to find. Most archives list their collections by film title, by subject, and occasionally by filmmaker. If the archive is good, a film's title card should list the subjects of the principal scenes; for example, "Hitler reviewing his guards in Nuremberg. Peasants in costume. Hitler's hotel at night. Torchlight parade." Obviously, the better the archives are indexed, the easier it is to find material. Until recently, hunting through archives was an abominably difficult job. Today, with computer indexing, the subject has vastly improved.

Often films were originally indexed improperly if the archivist did not recognize the importance of certain materials. Thus, the material you want may exist, but may not be indexed. For example, you may be looking for war criminal X in German archives indexed in 1947. But if Captain X came into prominence only through investigations in the 1960s, he may appear on much of the stock footage but be unidentified in the files.

In short, archive research often depends as much on intuition, on asking and probing, as it does on hunting through the files.

Interviews

Your objective in direct interviews is to talk to as many experts in the field as possible. Again, as in print research, you have to make some shrewd guesses. Because time is limited, you try to assess which people are the best, the most important, the most knowledgeable, the most open, and you allocate your time accordingly. You are looking for people seriously involved in the subject, but who are they? They can range from the technical experts and authorities to the ordinary people who have undergone the experience documented in the film. Thus, in a film on World War II you might find yourself talking to historians, generals, ordinary soldiers, and victims of bombing raids. Your perspective and the breadth of your subject will dictate to whom you talk, and your questions will obviously range from the general to the specific depending on the topic.

Approached correctly and sympathetically, most people will be willing to talk to you about your research. Occasionally, however, you will run into difficulties if the subject is personally painful or controversial. Do you then go ahead or do you back off? Everyone has to sort that dilemma out personally. Several years ago I interviewed Sue McConnachy, one of the principal researchers for the television series "The World at War." I was interested in her difficulties in talking to Germans for the film, because she was investigating not just memory and experiences but also possible participation in war crimes and atrocities. Her comments were very interesting:

> Initially it was quite difficult to get people to open up. However, once the Germans agreed to see you and talk it was all much fresher than the English people's reminiscences because it hadn't been told before. They'd never been asked or questioned about the war by the younger generation. There was a feeling that whereas it was acceptable for dad in England to talk to the kids about when he was in Africa, India, or wherever, it *wasn't* acceptable in Germany.
>
> The problem was getting to the shadow figures and the possible criminals. This was often done through a series of contacts. One was in the position of being given confidential information which one was not supposed to broadcast or pass on. You were only allowed to go and see these people on the understanding that you gave nothing away.
>
> Now once you'd got into a position of trust, once you'd got on to the "circuit," you were handed on from one to the next. And it was almost an impossible situation as a researcher (and as a human being) because I was dealing with people who, in the

period of their lives that we were talking about, had not oper-
ated with the same code of behavior, morals, whatever you call
it, that I by nature and upbringing operate on. (From Alan
Rosenthal, *The Documentary Conscience* [Berkeley and Los
Angeles: University of California Press, 1980])

About the time I met McConnachy I also spoke to Peter Watkins about
the making of his famous anti–nuclear war film *The War Game.* Among
other subjects the film discusses civil defense procedures in England and
the psychological aftereffects of the dropping of a nuclear bomb on a
civilian population. Watkins commented:

The more films I do, the more I research. It's a growing pattern.
I tend to put more and more emphasis on the solid basis of
research. With *The War Game* I had to do a great deal of original
research because nobody had collated all the information into an
easily accessible form. . . . There is an extreme dearth of literature about the third world war. What literature there is is
stacked up on the shelves of the American Institute for Strategic
Studies and is never read by the public. So it was an extremely
esoteric subject for a filmmaker to delve into and quite hard to
find basic facts.

As far as research went and talking to people, you have to
differentiate between people in general and government bodies. The experts, professors and so on, were extremely cooperative and very interested. A few were a little skeptical of an
amateur blundering into their domain but they freely supplied
what little information they had. The government bodies were
different. In general they said no. (From Alan Rosenthal, *The
New Documentary in Action* [Berkeley and Los Angeles: University of California Press, 1971])

The Home Office, responsible for internal affairs and security in England,
refused to help Watkins in the making of the film. In fact, not only did it
refuse information, but it also withdrew all official help and tried to hinder
the research by preventing the Fire Service and the police from giving
Watkins details of their plans in the event of a nuclear holocaust. He noted
that "the only group that helped me voluntarily at that time was the Fire
Service, which appeared to me to be the only group in England that had a
realistic approach to the effects of a nuclear attack. They were the only
(semi-official) group willing to talk to me. And they did it unofficially.
Officially there was a complete clamp-down."

Reliance on only a few interviewees on anything controversial has its
dangers. In such a case it is best to interview, or try to interview, a broad
range of people so that you can contrast opinions and estimate how much of

what you are being told is biased or partisan. Obviously, you have to rely on common sense. You are not aiming for balance, you are aiming for the truth, and it could be that the extreme, one-sided view just happens to be the truth. During interviews you will ask both the easy and the awkward questions. Naturally, your technique will differ from subject to subject; sometimes you may have to play the probing investigator, but more often you are asking commonsense questions that any interested person would bring up.

In a technical film you may want to accumulate facts, find out about problems, systems of work, difficulties, successes, side effects, results. In a human or portrait film you will probably want to find out about human experiences, memories, change, thoughts, and the consequences that certain actions have wrought on peoples' lives, and so on. Often the interviewing will be difficult or painful as you touch on emotions and sensitivities. You are not just collecting facts about a subject but trying to gain a perspective that goes beyond the facts. An adjunct to this is that you always have to keep in mind whether you want the emphasis to fall on facts or on emotions, because each may pull you in a different way.

It is also important to be open to stories and think how they can be used. Remember that the stories you have may be more powerful than any facts you dig up. Let us assume you are doing a film about refugees from a South Atlantic hurricane. You could say, after your research, that thirty thousand people were evacuated and five hundred homes smashed. But it is better if you can also use personal anecdotes: "I was at home. The wind smashed everything. First the upstairs roof collapsed, then the wall. Finally the wind lifted my bed and threw it, with me in it, into the garden."

As usual, a warning. There is a tremendous difference between interviewing someone about the current scene and the past. In both cases you have to be aware of bias, but in talking about the past you also have to be aware of the pitfalls of memory and romanticism. Sometimes, of course, the events of the past are etched more strongly on the mind than are the events of yesterday. But not always. Whether impelled by love or hate, or just age, the memory can be a strange, distorting mirror. So beware.

Location Research

Finally, you should experience the subject *in situ*, on location. You go to see the factory at work, spend two weeks getting the feel of the university, take the plane trip, ride with the police in their patrol cars, watch the daily life in a small Vermont village, accompany the theater director to rehearsal, visit the beaches of Normandy where the Allied invasion took place, and watch the new tourists stream through Saigon. All the time you are trying to soak up the subject and get as close to it as possible.

Research is vital to most good films, and yet it is a difficult subject psychologically. This is because you know that only a fraction of the material you are accumulating will ever be used in the final film. As a colleague of mine, Jim Beveridge, once put it: "Research is like an iceberg. Seven-eighths of it is below the surface and can't be seen."

Defining Limits

People often go astray in failing to define suitable limits to their films. If your goal is clear, then you should be all right, but you may have problems if you approach a very broad topic—drugs, juvenile delinquency, international terror—with no guidelines. What do you do when the subject is seemingly limitless? You do some preliminary research and then make some quick choices. Using your common sense you have to select boundaries, and within those boundaries you must select three or four promising areas for further research and development. The boundaries do not have to be arbitrary. You will be guided by what you yourself are interested in, by current public interests, and, as always, by what is feasible and practical. Thus, you don't decide simply to do a film on drugs; you decide to do it on drugs and the young, or drugs and their sources in the Far East, or drugs and big business. Once your subject is limited, you can go ahead.

The trouble is that even with the most rational head in the world you sometimes try to do too much in one film. In the end your ambition may let you down, whereas a more modest film would have worked well. This happened to me on a film I did about automobile accidents. It was clear that the subject involved three diverse elements: people, including drivers, pedestrians, and accident victims; vehicles; and roads and road engineering. I could have concentrated on any one of those topics, but I decided to look into all three. I saw all the films, read all the books, talked to experts, and wrote to dozens of people around the world. And all the time new topics of interest kept opening up. I found out about a correction course for dangerous drivers. I was told about a society for bereaved families. I obtained photographs of cars of the future. A psychologist told me of hypnotic experiments on aggressive personalities.

I accumulated a mass of fascinating materials, yet the film came out a mess. My cardinal mistake, which later stood out a mile, was trying to cover the three topics of driver, vehicle, and roads instead of limiting myself to just one. The research had been great fun, but I didn't know when to leave well enough alone; thus I seriously weakened the film.

6

Shaping the Film

After the research you have to answer a few questions before tackling the draft script. Your main concern is how to shape the film into a logical and emotional whole. Here you are concerned with four topics: Approach, style, form, and structure. The topics often overlap, and it is sometimes difficult to separate them. Form runs into structure, and can you really distinguish approach from style? Because of this overlap, the topics may be covered in any order, but I find it easiest to think about approach and style before form and structure.

Approach

When all the mists have cleared away, there are usually two main choices for the overall approach: the essay or the narrative. My feelings in this matter are simple. An essay is fine, but it is hard to maintain viewer interest in such a piece if it exceeds thirty minutes. You can talk generally and interestingly about Palestine nationalism for half an hour, but if you want an hour-long film you should be doing the story of Arafat or the PLO. I also believe people really enjoy a *story*, especially one that seems to move forward with an easy progression. Therefore, my first tendency in thinking about a film is to see whether a good narrative approach is possible. Obviously, some of the best films combine both approaches, with a good story illustrating an abstract, intellectual idea. Mike Rubbo's film *Daisy*, mentioned earlier, is an amusing essay on the history of plastic surgery and its practice today. The essay, however, backs up the personal story of Daisy and her hopes and fears as she faces major plastic surgery.

When I have to confront what is obviously a broad essay topic—say, crime in the 1990s—I prefer to look at the general through the particular, finding a few cases that highlight the key problems of the subject. Helen Whitney did just that in her 1978 film *Youth Terror*. Although ABC assigned her the broad topic of juvenile delinquency, her film concentrates on the experience of a small group of teenagers in the suburbs of Brooklyn, New York.

Yet there is a dilemma in all this, an unresolved tension between the story film and the investigative essay. Looking at problems through individual stories and attractive characters makes for an entertaining film, but it may do so by sacrificing deeper, more meaningful information. Sometimes you find that you have told a great story, but the film itself has become too narrow, with the major problems only superficially treated. Another difficulty in the case-study film is that viewers may perceive the individual story as typical, whereas a more balanced consideration of the subject might reveal it to be idiosyncratic.

Most films need a *key* or *handle*, an angle from which to tell the story in the most interesting, riveting, and entertaining fashion. The key may be a character you have come across in research. It may be the oldest member of a factory now being shut down; it may be one of the soldiers who led an abortive raid. One example of a key or handle comes from my film *Part of Them Is Me*. The task of the film was to tell how various youth villages in Israel provide homes for immigrant children without parents and prepare them for life in a new country. A good subject, but ten films had been made on youth villages in the past five years, so it was difficult to find a new approach. During the research, though, I found that the villages were the recipients of a new arts program. Once a month a musician-teacher came to the villages and taught the children various aspects of music. One day I saw David, the music teacher, at work. He was about thirty-five and very charismatic. When I discovered that David had grown up in one of these villages himself twenty years before, I immediately saw him as the natural key. If we told the film through his eyes we could cover the history of the villages through his childhood memories and his travels as a teacher.

As a rule I like to see whether a character will give me a slant on the film. A character can provide warmth, empathy, and identification. Most of us are naturally inquisitive; we like to delve into people's lives, into their ways of thinking and modes of work, their problems and triumphs. Characters can also observe things, do things, have things happen to them. That's why people are the ideal film key. A character may also function as the key in a sponsored or industrial film. Such characters are often fictional, sometimes comic creations who help focus the situation through their problems and inadequacies or through their superhuman capabilities.

Besides being the key or handle to the film a chosen character can also give shape to what would otherwise be a formless current-events film. For instance, most of Pam Yates and Tom Siegel's *When the Mountains Tremble*, a film about the civil war in Guatamala, recounts rebel life, village encounters, pursuits, and sudden death. To bind the film together the directors use a Guatemalan Indian, Rigoberta Manchu, who tells the story of her family. Rigoberta is filmed in limbo in a studio and appears four or five times throughout the film describing the tragic fortunes of her family. Her vital presence gives the film its spine.

The trouble with this approach is that the character may strike viewers as a gimmick or a cliché. We have seen so many films based on the memories of the old professor, the fortunes of the new nurse, or the difficulties of the Vietnam veteran that it is hard not to groan when the film starts. But if the film is well done, we forget about the possible gimmickry, held by the authenticity of the situation.

Find the right key and half your troubles are over. Consider *Wasn't That a Time*, Jim Brown's film about the Weavers, a folk group extremely popular in the 1950s and early 1960s. Brown could have told the story very coolly from the outside, but he chose instead to portray the Weavers through the eyes of Lee Hays, the oldest member of the group. Irascible, irreverent, a man of tremendous charm and humor, Hays was cast as a storyteller, thus transforming a fine film into a superb one.

When the main focus of a film is people, there is usually no difficulty finding a key or handle, but you may run into trouble in films dealing with, say, abstract ideas, architecture, specific historic periods or geographical locations. The danger is that you may string together a series of film ideas without any imaginative force. Sometimes the sheer power of the material will make the films work; more often than not, however, what we see in the end is a series of facts tacked together in some logical but unexciting order. Unfortunately, there are no simple solutions, no magic formulas. Instead, you have to struggle with each film until you find the key, and then if it is good, it often seems inevitable.

When Meredith Monk was asked to make a commemorative film about Ellis Island, the old landing and investigation point for immigrants to the United States, the solution must have seemed simple to the sponsors. Give us a historical documentary based on old photographs and records and throw in a little bit of filming today. And give us plenty of facts as well. Monk's solution was much more imaginative and far more elegant. She abandoned the records and instead recreated the atmosphere of historic Ellis Island in dance and short vignettes. She frames the film by following a modern tour group as they are shown around Ellis Island; this portion is filmed in color. Into the tour she inserts black-and-white "postcards" that suddenly metamorphose into an animated group of nineteenth-century arrivals, a scene of Greek immigrants dancing, or a sketch of 1920s women painfully learning English while the teacher writes the word "microwave" on the blackboard. Viewers could have been threatened with a dry historical record, but they were granted instead a marvelous documentary that vividly captured the spirit of the place. A potential failure was transformed into a success because the filmmaker had bothered to find an original and stimulating road into the film.

Some while ago I was asked to do a film about the area around the Sea of Galilee in northern Israel—an extremely beautiful spot, interesting because of its historic and biblical sites and its contemporary development. The film had vast potential, but I wasn't sure how to bind everything together. Then I remembered that an annual marathon circles the lake. That seemed the obvious key. The marathon would give a certain tension to the film, and as we followed the runners I could dart off into history or whatever I wanted.

Finding a key is a lot of work and doesn't come easily. Is the search worth it? Absolutely.

Structure

The question of structure has been tremendously neglected in discussions of documentary films. One sees too many films that are structureless, that amble along showing an occasionally interesting interview or compelling incident but without any spine. There may have been an interesting key to the film, but somewhere along the way it was lost. One is left with a film without development, a film without a sense of form or shape. Just as every good book and play needs a structure, so too does the documentary film. It should present an interesting, well-shaped story, with pacing and rhythm that lead to a satisfying resolution.

It helps to think of structure as being either *natural* or *invented*. From the beginning one looks for a natural or one might say obvious and commonsense structure, one dictated by the material itself. By this I mean a form that is absolutely impelled on you by the nature of the material and is so strong and obvious that this seems to be the only way the story could go. Finding such a structure often seems like a gift from God. The classic examples of this kind of documentary are the films of Drew Associates made at the start of the cinema verite movement: *The Chair, Jane*, and *On the Pole*. These films concentrate on an individual at a crux in his or her life, tracing the crises they face and ending after the problems have been resolved.

The Chair, shot by Don Pennebaker and Ricky Leacock, covers five days in the life of Paul Crump, a black man sentenced to death. At the time of the filming Paul had apparently been rehabilitated, yet he faced execution in only a few days. The film follows his lawyer's last attempts and appeal to have the sentence commuted. We see Crump in his cell and discover that he has written a book; we watch Crump's layers in public and private action; we find that the church supports leniency; and we watch the warden as he tests the electric chair. What gives the film its tension is our knowledge that a final decision must come in just a few hours. The suspense attains its highest pitch on the day of the decision: Crump's sentence is commuted, and he is transferred to another prison.

Jane, made in 1962 by Don Pennebaker, follows Jane Fonda as she rehearses a Broadway play that seems destined for disaster. We watch the public and private difficulties, the stress of the weeks of preparation, the tensions of opening night. The newspaper reviews come in the early morning, and are murder. The play is quickly abandoned and the characters separate. This film, like *The Chair*, seems to follow an inevitable progression from the statement of the conflict to the inexorable climax.

Most of the Drew Associates films depend on what has been called "the crisis structure," a common literary and theatrical device. We are also familiar with this device from feature films, but despite its familiarity it still works amazingly well. Another common structural device is based on the principle of great change over a relatively short time; such change is both interesting and filmic.

Ira Wohl's *Best Boy*, a good example of this type of film, covers two years in the life of Philly, Ira's cousin. Philly is a fifty-two-year-old man with a mental age of six. Philly's parents have always taken care of him, but they are now in their late seventies. Concerned about Philly's future after their parents' death, Ira wants to enroll Philly in a school for the retarded where he can learn how to take care of himself a little better. The film becomes a riveting study in Philly's growing independence and self-assurance. The theme of change is underscored by contrasting shots at the beginning and end of the film: at the start of the film Philly is shown being shaved by his father; the last scene shows him shaving himself.

This ability to portray change is one of the gifts of documentary. The process fascinates most viewers, and when filmed in a natural and interesting framework the results can be superb. In 1980 I wrote a television proposal about young Israeli women, who must serve two years in the armed forces. In the proposal I suggested following three women through basic training: one daughter of a rich city family, one from a rural family, and the third a recent immigrant. I intended to talk to them about their hopes and fears for the future before they went into the army, then follow them for five or six weeks as they joined the same unit. I wanted to see what happened to them, away from home for the first time, transplanted in the hothouse environment of the army. I thought the army background would be fascinating, and we would probably see interesting changes in the women as they adapted to their new circumstances.

What pleased me enormously was that the film seemed to have an obvious structure. The first part would focus on the period before the army: the waiting, the hopes, the fears and the preparation. The second part would concentrate on the induction and the shock period of the first two weeks. In part three the women would go on a brief leave, and in part four they would complete basic training and disperse to their units. The subject was exciting; the proposal was exciting. But a glitch developed: television workers went on strike, and when work resumed the proposal was lost in budget cutbacks.

One of the more difficult problems for documentary filmmakers is finding structure where there is no obvious approach. Even if you have found a good handle to the film you can be faced with this problem. The previous chapter discussed a proposal for a film about a university whose object was simply to portray the university to a general audience. A film of this sort has no natural structure; depending on the writer, it could go in almost any direction.

In such a case we have to plunge in and make some arbitrary decisions. For starters we decide the film will concentrate on two students, two professors, and an administrator, giving us a human approach and contrasting perspectives on the university. While these characters lead us into the film and offer themselves as constant and easily identified figures, the film itself could yet go different ways: it could be built around a day at the university, or it could follow key university events, lectures, sports rivalries, examinations, and graduation ceremonies. Another approach, one well suited to a fundraising film, might use the homecoming celebration to contrast the university's past and present. In this case the film might begin with the preparations for homecoming; identify typical new students, graduating students, and alumni; head off into their stories; and conclude with the homecoming dance at which all the characters are present.

Given the right scriptwriter and director, any of these approaches could work, but one structural device, that of "a day in the life," does present problems. When this technique first appeared in the symphonic films of the 1920s, such as *Rien que les heures* and *Berlin*, it was comparatively fresh, but since then there have been perhaps too many days in too many lives. Now the technique must be used with caution. Occasionally, though, it can still be potent, as it is in *Royal Family*, which Richard Cawston made for the BBC. *Royal Family* is both a narrative about the British royal family and an essay on the function of the monarchy within the British constitution. Its form is quite simple: the first part presents an imaginary typical day in the life of the queen, while the rest of the film takes her through a typical year. The structure is not a masterpiece of intellectual invention, but it works extremely well—and that's the whole point. Given the intense curiosity about the life of the queen, particularly the private side, it was a case of the simplest, most obvious structure being the best.

Another example of a well-structured film built from very loose and amorphous material is *City of Gold*, made for the National Film Board of Canada by Colin Low, Wolf Koenig, and Roman Kroitor, with commentary by Pierre Berton. In 1956, while doing research in the Dominion archives, Low discovered a collection of glass-plate photographs of Dawson City, center of the Klondike gold rush of 1898, taken by E. A. Haig. Together with Kroitor and Koenig, Low planned a film about Dawson City based on these photographs, which covered all aspects of life in the boomtown. But what was to be the framework?

The solution provided by the directors and writer is beautiful. The film moves from the present to the past then back to the present, inscribing a circle that gradually completes itself. Beginning in Dawson City of today, we see a small restaurant, old-timers lounging around, and small boys playing baseball in the park. From there the camera directs us toward relics of the past—an old engine, a landlocked riverboat, a boarded window—and the commentary recalls the days when they were new.

Almost imperceptibly the film moves from location photography of the present into the past, as seen in Haig's photographs. The transitional shot is that of the foreboding, icebound Chilkoot Pass, which the goldminers had to conquer before heading to Dawson City. At first we think we are looking at location photography; only when the camera moves into the figures of the miners do we realize that we are looking at a photograph. Using the photographs, the film then recounts the journey downstream to Dawson City and the crazy life that awaited the gold-hungry miners. We see how gold was panned and follow the fortunes of the lucky and the disappointed. We look at Mounties, prostitutes, bartenders, and Dawson City on carnival day.

Then, almost unnoticed, the film moves from past to present, and with a shock we realize we are back in Dawson City today. The film closes with what almost looks like a repetition of the opening shots. The boys are still playing baseball, and the old men are still talking on the porches—but it's not quite the same. We have awakened from a dream, but now our perceptions are haunted by the memories of the past. It is a very satisfactory ending and more. The return to the present completes the circle, and we sense that perfect form has been achieved.

There is usually no one perfect approach to a film; all sorts of ideas can get you to the same goal. Often I like to play around with two or three ideas, debating the pros and cons of each, before making up my mind which to use. Thinking about alternatives is not just an intellectual exercise; it also helps you to check the flaws in each strategy.

Some time ago I was asked to do more or less the same film for two organizations in two successive years. Each organization supported a hospital and wanted me to make a film that could be used for fund-raising. I found the handle to the first film after about a week of research. The hospital I was dealing with was rather grim and old. Though most of the staff were locals, there were also about fifteen foreign doctors working there. Maybe that was the clue. I debated a couple of ideas and eventually decided the best approach was to build the film around three expatriate doctors from North America. One was a top surgeon who had been working at Mount Sinai Hospital in New York, where he had probably earned about $200,000 a year. The second was a middle-aged doctor from Phoenix who specialized in geriatric care, while the third was a young doctor from Toronto who cycled to work and wanted to specialize in family medicine.

My meetings with the doctors in the few weeks of research raised a number of questions in my mind. Why had these doctors given up prosperous careers to move to England and work in a shabby hospital? Answer: because they believed in the work. They thought the hospital was vital to the community and believed that the overall challenge more than compensated for the lousy pay and the poor conditions. From there on matters went smoothly. I would tell the doctors' stories in their own words: why they came, what impelled them, why they were enthusiastic about the hospital. The doctors were very warm and likable, and I hoped that their example and dedication would inspire the potential donors to give.

Having found the handle, it was then easy enough to find a structure for the film, which we eventually called *Because We Care*. The first part shows the doctors arriving at the hospital and going about their duties. During this part we are introduced to the doctors and get a feel for the hospital and the patients. The middle part of the film, intended as a breather, shows what the doctors do with their private time. We filmed them at home with their families, shopping, or camping. The third section, which shows the doctors at work in serious situations, digs a little deeper into the doctor-patient relationship. The film concludes with a quick look at building operations and the planning of a new hospital. The director of the hospital appears at this stage, talking directly to the camera. His function is to make explicit what had only been implied up to then: that the hospital really cares about its patients (a point vouchsafed to me over and over during research). The scene could have been propagandistic, but the preceding scenes had provided a strong basis for the director's sentiments.

Because We Care had no narrator, relying entirely on voice-overs. My second hospital film, *For the Good of All*, depended heavily on narration, but it seemed to work just as well. It was filmed only a year later and also had a fund-raising goal, but it took a totally different approach. My sponsors wanted a film that dealt with research, teaching, and care. I felt that was too wide and suggested instead that we narrow the film, concentrating on the care and healing aspects of the hospital. After a few discussions the sponsors agreed that we should focus on four areas: oncology, neonatal care, eye surgery, and cardiology. That still left the questions of approach and form, so I suggested to the sponsors that we look at the hospital through the eyes of the patients. We could use their voices to reveal how they felt about their illnesses and the hospital treatment. However, feeling that this material alone would not suffice, I also wrote in a few general scenes with standard narration.

After some work I thought that the approach was right but that we still needed something else to give a boost to the film. The answer was a framing device in the form of an outdoor symphonic concert featuring Isaac Stern and Rampal. Shots of the orchestra serve as interludes between the separate stories. At the end of the film the featured patients appear in the mass outdoor audience as the orchestra plays the *1812* Overture, with cannons roaring and fireworks exploding. It was all a little hokey and contrived, but it provided a splendid, upbeat spirit to the ending that the sponsors loved.

Style and Imagination

Four men see a beautiful woman on a hill and instantly fall in love. All want to court and marry her. One writes her a letter, plods up the hill, and lays it at her feet. The second rushes toward her and garlands her with flowers. The third stands on his head, then dances for her, while the fourth hires a plane that trails the message "I'll love you forever!" Each is exhibiting his own particular style in accomplishing his objective. One is thorough, plodding, another dynamic. The third tries comic relief, and the fourth adds a little imagination to the whole business.

Style is as important in documentary as in love, and it may be straightforward, comic, elaborate, fantastic—whatever you want. In brief, think of where you want to go, what you want to do, and then find the most appropriate style to reach the objective. But watch out for baffling boredom, the dull discourse, the esoteric essay, and long-winded piffle. For many people the documentary is synonymous with everything that is tedious. What hurts is the amount of truth in that comment. In the 1980s the form seems to have settled into familiar patterns, with too many documentaries being excruciatingly dry. This is unfortunate because there is no need at all for documentaries to be like that.

Many filmmakers seem to think there is a standard pattern for making documentaries. Nonsense. What should dominate your thinking about style (and many other things) is the knowledge that there is no prescribed, hallowed way of making documentaries. Grierson's group understood that in the 1930s when their experiments in editing and sound revolutionized documentary. And Drew, Leacock, Wiseman, Rouch, and others understood it thirty years later when they turned the documentary movement on its head with their ideas about cinema verite.

For starters, give your style a bit of freedom. Remember, the only boundaries are those of your imagination. The style used in most documentaries is straightforward, realistic, prosaic. But think for a minute. You could opt instead for fantasy, humor, farce, parody. But if these latter elements are so good, why aren't they more widely used outside the realm of industrial and educational films? One answer is that too many television stations demand news-style documentaries and frown on imaginative gimmicks and humor. I think they are misguided, and the limits they impose are to be regretted because imagination can invigorate even the dullest subject.

As a writer it is useful to remember that you can choose from a tremendous number of tools. Some people argue that a documentary should consist only of sequences filmed from real life, archival material, or stills. This stricture has always struck me as nonsense. If you want to use dramatic or fantasy sequences, then go ahead. A few years ago Carl Sagan's noted series "Cosmos" used every filmic trick the producers could think of. First, they designed a control cabin for a futuristic spaceship and used it as the main setting of the series. It was from this cabin that Sagan looked out onto different worlds. The films then played between the cabin, real locations, computer graphics, models, dramatic reenactments, and archival film. Purists may have quaked, but the series, done with verve and panache, became one of the most popular series on American television. Above all it showed what a documentary series could do with imagination and a decent budget.

The United States commercial networks, whose forte has been the news documentary, have unfortunately tended to restrict their documentary writers and producers to a very plain, realistic style. Sometimes the writers have rebelled at the constraints and have tried to burst out of the confines of the network method. One such writer was Arthur Barron, who talked to me at length about problems of style and imagination in *The Berkeley Rebels*, which he made for CBS Reports.

> I didn't want analyses or objective reporting. I wanted to invoke the world of the students with as much dynamism and strength as I could. After a big of discussion CBS agreed to go along with this approach.
>
> The film was a mixture of things. On the one hand there was the simple, diarylike following of people. But then I tried deliberately shaping scenes to evoke a particular mood. For example, I tried a sequence which I called "Facts, Facts, Facts!" One of the criticisms of the university was that the kids were being fed information and facts but were not being taught wisdom or how to think. So "Facts" was to illustrate this point.
>
> We had a bathtub filled with soap bubbles and suddenly out of this bathtub emerged a huge, bearded student with water dripping off him. He looks at the camera and says, "The square root of the hypotenuse is so and so," and then he sinks back into the water.
>
> In another shot I had a guy racing down a hill on a skateboard and as he goes past the camera he screams, "The Athenian wars began in. . . ." For another evocation sequence I took a dog and gave him molasses candy to eat. As he chewed it looked as if he was talking, and we put a voice under the dog with a German accent. (From Alan Rosenthal, *The New Documentary in Action* [Berkeley and Los Angeles: University of California Press, 1971])

The small touches that Barron wanted to add were very funny, but in his own words, they "drove CBS completely up the wall." In the end the network deleted both the "Facts" sequence and the dog sequence. Humor and imagination were elements they felt very uneasy about.

This inability to see where humor might work in a documentary seems to be a problem for many television executives and sponsors. Maybe that's the reason so many documentaries lack spark. In effect, the executives are saying that serious and important subjects can be treated only in a heavy, dull way. That's sheer nonsense, whether one is talking about documentary or features.

Stanley Kubrick's *Dr. Strangelove* was a brilliant farce, but at the same time it offered a devastating critique of nuclear strategy. Putting it simply, humor can enliven even the most serious documentary, perhaps saving it from drowning in its own profundity.

One of the best examples of humor enlightening a subject can be seen in the series "Connections," written by James Burke for the BBC. The series was really a history of technology, and the binding theme of all the stories was the strange and unexpected ways in which change has been brought about. Burke's sense of humor was exhibited both in his offbeat, throwaway commentary and in the visual jokes he inserted in his scripts. In *Distant Voices*, one of the films in that series, he discusses early experiments with electricity: "A flamboyant French friar called Nollet, who gave private courses in electricity to beautiful women, decided to run a charge through multiple monks to see if the effect would produce an uplifting experience. It did!" The visuals accompanying the narration show six monks joining hands and then receiving a communal shock from an electrical jar. Thus shocked, the monks jump up and down very solemnly in slow motion; in fact, they appear to be skipping to music, and the effect is quite hilarious.

Many feature films use the device of the running gag, and it also works quite well in documentary. In 1982 I had to do a low-budget film on sports for television. The film, essentially a sports survey, was informative and full of action, but it needed something to bind the separate sequences together. As an answer I wrote in four or five short scenes that utilized the services of a slightly plump friend of mind. In the first scene he plays an enthusiastic football fan who is content to watch everything on television. Later, in a sequence dealing with automobile racing, we see him in a close-up in his car, battling with the wheel. When the zoom opens we see that the car is being towed by a pickup truck. Another sequence features marathon walkers and concludes with an exhausted Dave in baggy, short pants thumbing a lift. I realize that these weren't the world's most marvelous gags, but they worked well in the context of the film. They also did something else: they told us silently that we shouldn't take sports too seriously.

Imagination and humor are tremendously useful elements for helping odd sections of films, and they can do wonders when they inform the picture as a whole. When this happens, as in *The Road to Wigan Pier*, the basic film can be turned into a small work of art. Made for Thames Television by Frank Cvitanovich, *The Road to Wigan Pier* deals with labor and mining conditions in England in the 1930s; it is based on George Orwell's book of the same name. What one expected from the title, and from a knowledge of Orwell, was a serious historical documentary using Orwell's text over stock footage of miners, coal pits, crowded factories, and slums. And that almost exactly describes the first half of the film.

I say "almost" because Cvitanovich does two other things that alter the feel of the film. The first departure from the expected approach is the insertion of six or seven industrial ballads between portions of the stock footage. The songs, sung in different mining locations by an English folksinger, comment humorously on Orwell's text, turning the film into a documentary musical rather than just a historical study.

The second suprise comes close to the end of the film. We have been following a history of the 1930s and expect the film to conclude with war breaking out in Europe, marking the end of an era. This expectation is shattered when the narrator suddenly asks, "But what of *your* dream of socialism, Mr. Orwell?" The scene abruptly shifts to a modern but empty television studio. The folk singer then appears, seats himself at the television control board, and studies the monitors. They flicker, and various British prime ministers appear on the scenes, ranging from Baldwin and Chamberlain to Churchill and Wilson. One after another, in sequences lifted from electioneering speeches, they promise Britain prosperity and a glorious future. However, the footage is edited in devastating fashion. When one politician states, "Britain never had it so good," he is answered by a politician on another screen exclaiming, "Rubbish!" When a Labor prime minister says the workers are going from strength to strength, a Conservative prime minister answers, "Utter poppycock and nonsense." Finally, when Harold Wilson talks about Britain's New Jerusalem, an edit cut makes Edward Heath respond, "Shut up, belt up, and go home." It's a wickedly funny satirical sequence, and we occasionally cut back to the folksinger in his cloth cap, watching the screen and grinning at all this political balderdash.

The film then abruptly takes another turn as the folksinger dashes down endless corridors of computers and revolving disks. As he pauses computer reels spin, cards spill out of machines, and various anonymous voices proclaim the appalling state of industry and labor conditions in the 1970s, implying that little has changed since Orwell's day. The conception of this last sequence is brilliant, changing a good documentary of mild interest to the general public into a very strong comment about present-day England.

Stuart Hood's *Crisis on Wheels*, a discussion of the automobile and its function in the scheme of things, is another very funny and imaginative documentary. Given the subject, Hood must have been tempted to fall into all the standard traps and make the expected film about mass production, automobile economics, car design, accident prevention, and sales. Hood neatly sidesteps the obvious, building the film around five or six slightly offbeat essays concerning cars. The first section deals with the car as the idol of worship, and I have set out an extract below:

Visual	*Audio*
A car radio in close-up.	The object of veneration in suburban avenues on Sunday morning.

A car is being washed.	[*Music:* Holy! Holy! Holy!]
A man kneels down and wipes the wheels.	An indispensable utility for all but the poorest. An object of affection—a member of the family. The good car—cherished and loved by all.
An automobile show with beautiful women seated on the tops of cars.	This religion has its priestesses and handmaidens. It also has its golden idols who require a daily offering of human sacrifices.
An advertisement of a car being put on top of a mountain.	The objects of veneration are set up for adoration and worship on pinnacles and high places.

One of the most amusing scenes in the film is called "The Car as a Home from Home." The section targets the massive traffic jams seen with increasing frequency around London's suburbs. To make his point about our growing inability to deal with traffic congestion, Hood imagines a scenario in which the traffic jam becomes absolute, and people grow accustomed to living in their cars for weeks on end. The scene was staged in Slough, a medium-sized town near Windsor Castle, and the text is given below. The visual side is only suggested in outline, but it is not very difficult to imagine.

Visual	*Audio*
A staged traffic jam of immense porportions	Over a Clifton Street, Harpendon, just outside London, it's still saturation point. No use offering anyone here a tow home.
	This jam started three weeks ago and it still hasn't moved an inch. Now that abandoned cars are liable to instant destruction, these drivers have decided to stay put. And most of them actually prefer their home on wheels. The women volunteers cope magnificently with morale, and early morn-

People serve tea between cars.

ing tea is the brightest spot of the day.

Paperboy

Postman delivers mail.

The jam may not suit anyone, but the paperboy is delighted. With everyone so close he can get through his rounds in a fraction of the time. The postman had a hard job at first coping with the number plates instead of name plates, but now the traffic-jam community is easing his task.

Mrs. Stacey's car

It's been a long weekend holiday for Mrs. Stacey. Now her fifteen-horsepower home is the smartest in the street. The kitchen is in the back; there's a telephone, and the television works off the car battery. At teatime Mrs. Stacey links up to the exhaust, lights the fumes, and pops on the kettle for a quick cup of tea.

It's marvelous stuff, and once again it shows what wit and imagination can do for a subject.

7

Beginning the First Draft

You are a few weeks into the film, and things are beginning to clarify in your mind. You have decided to do the film as story plus essay. You think that you have found the right approach and structure, and you are beginning to see a possible opening, middle, and end. Great! Now all you have to do is sit down and write your first draft. This may take the form of either a draft shooting script with ideas only, or a draft shooting script with commentary. In the first case you will merely set out the ideas you want to accompany the visuals. In the second case you will actually write a preliminary commentary, even though this may well change as the film progresses.

A draft shooting script with the ideas sketched out might look like this:

Visual	*Idea Line*
Jerusalem seen from the air.	The concept of Jerusalem as the highest ideal. Perfection. St. John's vision. Mention Jerusalem as religious center.
Crowded Jerusalem streets. People struggle against cars.	Jerusalem of the here and now. Discuss reality. A city of 25,000. The everyday problems.
Stand-up comments.	Commentator expresses the dilemma of modern Jerusalem. The tensions of the present. Balancing the spiritual and the practical. Where is the film going.

A draft shooting script with commentary might look like this:

Visual	*Audio*
Jerusalem seen from the air.	When he left Palestine in 1920 the British governor of the

capital said, "After Jerusalem there can be no higher promotion."

For him, as for millions of others, there was no counterpart to Jerusalem in the history of the West.

Jerusalem was the center of two faiths and holy to a third. It was the light. The guardian of ideals. The eternal city. The symbol of perfection.

Jerusalem seen on the ground. Crowded streets. People push against cars. Chaos.

But as well as the Jerusalem of the mind, there is also the Jerusalem of reality. There is the modern city developed in the last century, and the ancient city where 25,000 people still live and work within medieval fortress walls.

Which of the two forms should you choose? The answer is usually forced on you by the circumstances and by the nature of the film. Most sponsors, in a fairly simple situation, like to receive a full commentary script even though they know it will most likely change at a later date. Often the visuals or a list of ideas means little to them. By contrast, it is very easy to understand the film through the commentary. Even a television documentary department, familiar with all sorts of presentations, may require a full commentary script before letting you do a history or personality film. And the same may be true of foundations to whom you have applied for a grant. For many films, however, it is quite clear that you will only be able to write the commentary at the end. These may be political films, news documentaries, or any films that are constantly evolving or that are essentially built in the editing phase. In such cases the best you can do is set out the ideas you want to use to guide you through the film and write the commentary when the editing is finished.

When I have both options, I prefer to write a first draft (for my eyes only) using the idea form, then rewrite the script with commentary for presentation. This double work is not strictly necessary, but I find that it helps me concentrate my ideas.

Script Formats

By now you probably have a good idea of what the standard script format looks like because of all the examples so far. The usual practice is to divide your page into two sections, with the visuals described on the left side of the page and the audio portion (commentary or ideas) on the right, as below.

Visual	Audio
Ascot race track.	Once this was known as the
Horse enclosure.	sport of kings.
Elegant people seen in fancy suits and dresses watching.	And you came because you had wealth and leisure and wanted to show off your mistress.
Other working-class types, drinking beer and eating hamburgers and dressed in jeans and old trousers.	Now the sport of kings has become the pastime of the proletariat.

As you can see, although the commentary is fairly detailed, the visuals are only sketched in. What you are trying to do is give the director a broad idea of what you want from the visuals, leaving the rest up to him or her. Obviously, some pictures will call for more details. Thus, for a scientific or medical film you may have to describe precisely the handling of a technical shot. But usually a brief suggestion is enough. A rough sketch will also suffice for "idea" scripts. Usually I don't bother to set out my ideas in long, elaborate sentences—just a few words to suggest the main ideas.

Does the script have to follow the divided page format? Not really. It's just that we're used to this convention. However, if you want to write your visuals across the full page and follow that with the commentary, then go ahead. The only criterion is clarity: will the ideas in the script be clear to those working on the film? If they are, then you have no problem.

When you start writing the actual script it may help you to jot down a few notes under the following headings:

1. Main ideas
2. Logical progression
3. Visualization
4. Opening
5. Rhythm and pace
6. Climax

This kind of analysis works well for me, though many of my friends plunge straight into writing without any such breakdown. It has become second nature for them to consider all these things in their mind, so they do not need to formalize their thinking. It is important to remember, though, that every script writer, formally or informally, consciously or unconsciously, has to consider most of the issues set out above.

Your first aim is for the script to present your key ideas in the most interesting and fascinating way. Furthermore, you want them to be seen as a whole rather than as a diverse collection of fragmented thoughts. And you want the ideas to move forward through the film with an easy and seemingly effortless logic and progression.

The problem boils down to this: What ideas will you use and how are you going to present them? Your research has churned up a hundred ideas. Now you are going to have to sift them, focusing on some and eliminating others, always keeping in mind the main goal of the picture. If, for example, you started researching the university film your overall list of ideas might include the following:

What does the university represent?
- originally for religious and legal training
- status: Oxford, Cambridge, Harvard, Yale
- a waste of time
- a focus of resentment for non-university people
- a generator of ideas
- a featherbed life for pampered faculty
- a hotbed of political unrest
- a marriage market
- the ivory tower
- a center for intellectual stimulation
- abundant sex.

The first task is to winnow out your ideas, concentrating only on those you deem of major importance. In the process some great ideas will be thrown out of the window, but that can't be helped. From the list above perhaps only three ideas will find their way into the script.

At this point it is useful to keep your audience in mind. Will they be interested in or able to understand all the issues you want to deal with? How much detail should you provide on each idea? Should you go into depth? Many executives in the American networks tend to believe their audiences are idiots capable of understanding only a few ideas, and then only if they are presented in the most superficial way. I disagree. I think most audiences can quickly grasp a great number of ideas, even complex ones, provided the film is attractively made.

At this stage it is also useful to remind yourself that no matter how many ideas you have, there must be one binding thread running through the film. Often this idea will be framed in the form of a question that the film will attempt to answer. Are universities good or bad for the country? Has Kennedy been misjudged by history? Was Irving Berlin the greatest popular composer of the century? Who was the real Hemingway? Does this sound familiar? It should: this statement of the main idea was the first thing you did when you wrote out your proposal all those months ago.

Having decided on the main ideas, the next task is to arrange them into logical blocks or sequences that lead easily and naturally from one to the other. By *sequence* we mean a series of shots joined by some common elements—a series of ideas, a visual setting, a series of actions, a musical motif—that make one or more specific points.

The shots in a sequence may be unified by

1. *A central idea:* We see children playing football in a park; a woman throwing a javelin; a professional baseball game; a wrestling match. The sports motif is the obvious unifying element, but the central idea that the writer wants to make might be that sport originates in war.
2. *Setting:* We see the Rocky Mountains. Tremendous mountains, waterfalls, and streams. Immense forests. Impenetrable jungles. Here the common element is the setting and the grandeur of nature.
3. *Action:* A student leaves her house, goes to the university, greets her friends, has coffee, then finally enters class. All the actions up to the class entry make for a certain unity, whereas a classroom shot would probably begin a different sequence.
4. *Mood:* War has begun. Tanks are advancing. Women are weeping. Destroyed buildings are seen in silhouette. Men are talking in groups. A small boy wanders forlornly along a street. Here the binding element is not just the start of war (idea) but also the gray, bleak mood of the people and the setting.

Obviously there are more categories and they overlap considerably. Ideas, actions, setting, central characters, mood—all these things may join together to unify a sequence. Another way of looking at it is to think of groups of ideas, images, and information that suggest a totality, a unified block. This will give you the sequence, and later you can see where the sequence fits into the whole.

You must continually ask yourself

- What is the *point* I want to make in this sequence?
- What can I *show* to make that point?
- How will *sound*, whether music, dialogue, effects, or commentary, help make the sequence more effective?

In practice you will probably be using your narration to unify the sequence and show the viewer where you want to put your emphasis.

When you start thinking about putting your sequences in some kind of order, keep two points in mind. First, remember that there is a tremendous difference between film logic and mathematical logic. The former is much more elusive, emotional, and insubstantial. It is a logic that is often felt through the gut rather than through the head. I recently saw a film about the world-famous cellist Jaqueline du Pré, who died very young. The writer-director might have started the picture with du Pré triumphant in concert and then gone back to her childhood. Instead, the film opens with Elgar's cello concerto being heard over soft, warm shots of autumn, with views of the sun sparkling through red and orange leaves. The director had opted for a gentle, poetic opening and it worked, even though the real entry into the subject was somewhat delayed. The second point is that the progressive logic of the ideas has to parallel the visual and emotional development of the film. Emphasis on one at the expense of the others can ruin the film.

The simplest and most natural ordering of ideas is chronological, but one might also want to consider a spatial development. The main thing is to find an order that gives a sense of growth. In his excellent book on scriptwriting for feature films, Dwight Swain suggests thinking about movement from the simple to the complex, from the specific to the general, from the familiar to the unfamiliar, from problem to solution, or from cause to effect. The important thing is the suggestion or illusion of inevitability, of natural movement.

The chronological progression, the oldest form of storytelling, is the most frequently used because it satisfies our natural curiosity to see what happens next. If we are introduced to a gifted child, we want to know what becomes of that child in adulthood. We want to know what happens when the sheltered girl who has been confined to her family circle takes her first room alone. We want to see the nun in the cloisters, then follow her progress when she gives up her vows and returns to the secular world. Jon Else's Academy Award-winning film *The Day after Trinity* tells the story of Robert Oppenheimer and the events leading to the creation of the atomic bomb. The basis is the simple chronological story of Oppenheimer's life from childhood to maturity to the supervision of the Los Alamos atomic project. Similarly, Don Pennebaker's *Jane* starts with Jane Fonda arriving for her first Broadway rehearsals and concludes with the arrival of the reviews after the disastrous opening night.

Another progression is the crisis, conflict, and resolution structure discussed earlier in reference to *The Chair*. At first glance this progression looks similar to the chronological structure, but there are quite a few differences. For example, one of the familiar strategies of the chronological film is to show the development of character or the growth of a career in politics, business, or the arts such as that of Oppenheimer in *The Day after Trinity*. The same may happen in a conflict documentary, but in the latter case we are generally more interested in the conflict resolution than in the character change.

The action in *The Chair* takes place over five days; time passes, but there is no character change. Instead, the tension concerning Paul's fate propels the film forward. Will he live or die? That's the answer we are waiting for. In *Mooney versus Fowler*, by James Lipscomb, we follow the lives of two extrovert football coaches and the struggle between their two teams for the local championship. Once the game is over and the conflict resolved, the film ends.

A good example of another film based on the progression of a fight is the BBC film *Whose House Is It Anyway?* In England most people cherish the myth that their home is their castle, sacred and inviolable. But evidently it isn't. If the local council wants the house for a good reason, it's theirs. Billy and Gordon Howard had owned and lived in Rose Cottage for years, but one day the local council placed a compulsory purchase order on the house and assumed ownership. The eccentric bachelor brothers, aged sixty-five and seventy-three, refused to recognize the validity of the purchase order, saying that when the bailiffs came they would shoot them rather than give up their birthright. The conflict is established in the first few seconds of the film, and the next hour shows us the stages and progress of the fight. It is a subject that touches all of us, and we are immediately drawn into the film, curious to see how the conflict will be resolved.

The chronological progression and the conflict progression are the two most common documentary threads, followed closely by the *search* motif, or the hunt for the solution of the mystery. Hence the popularity of the "Discovery" series, which investigated everything from the origins of the Dracula story to archaeologist Schliemann's search for Troy.

James Burke's series "Connections," mentioned previously, is really a variation on the search theme. Instead of filming a deliberate search, his aim is to show us how technological discovery is often achieved in the most unexpected ways. His films progress from surprise A to surprise B and so on. Watching the series is like watching a magician astonish an audience, pulling wonders out of a hat. Burke's secret is to stimulate our curiosity into following a strange series of technological changes. For amusement I charted the progress of ideas in Burke's film about the invention of rocket propulsion:

1. The film opens. Burke stands in a modern factory and talks about the many uses of *plastic*.
2. This leads him to talk about *plastic credit cards* replacing money.
3. We now slip into a discussion of *financial credit*.
4. That subject takes us back to the fourteenth century. While the film shows us knights and ladies playing around in castle grounds, Burke starts telling us how the *new idea of credit* in those days helped finance the small army of the Duke of Burgundy.
5. Because of *credit* the *army can grow* from a few thousand to sixty thousand—that is, credit allows bigger armies.
6. As armies grow new weapons come into fashion. The pike is used in a new way, but then it gives way to the blunderbuss, which gives way to the musket. Then the pike joins the musket in the form of the bayonet.
7. We return to the idea of the *ever-growing army* now two hundred to three hundred thousand soldiers strong. But armies need *food*.
8. Armies like that of Napoleon grow so large that they cannot live off

the countryside. They need food that can be eaten even if not fresh. This leads to the *development of canning*.

9. This in turn leads to *ice-making machines*, which in turn inspire the invention of chemical and gas *refrigeration* and *refrigerators*.
10. The growing emphasis on food preservation leads to the invention of the *vacuum flask*.
11. The principle of the vacuum flask allows gases to explode in a vacuum. Do this on a large scale and you have the invention of the V-2 rocket by Werner von Braun.

One is a little staggered at the end of the film to find that food for armies has led to rocket propulsion. You wonder how the trick was done. The answer is the fascinating but logical thread of ideas that Burke has woven for the viewers.

Burke's film was built up of about eleven sections that seem to lead inevitably from one to the other. I say "seem" because on close examination we can detect a terrific sleight of hand. But what do you do when the film has no superficial logic? The answer is to build up blocks of associated ideas, then segue smoothly, with the help of visuals and commentary, from one distinct section to another.

When I did a film about automobile accidents, I knew I wanted to concentrate on four things: the accidents as they happen; the reactions of the victims; the causes of accidents; and road engineering. There seemed to be no compelling arguments for placing one topic before another. So what were the reasons behind the final arrangement of the script?

I put road engineering first because it raised some interesting issues but lacked the emotional interests for a film climax. On the other hand, I thought I could get some highly moving and dramatic material on drivers that would work well toward the end. The section on cars would then slip into the middle. The script was written that way until I turned up some fascinating material on cars of the future that I thought would lead easily into the question of where we will go in the twenty-first century. That seemed a good way to end the film, so I reversed the sections on cars and drivers. The first and very rough draft of ideas and sequences was as follows:

Visual	Ideas
Cars on the road.	The trauma of the accident.
Crash, police.	
Ambulance.	Title: *Always Someone Else*
Hospital. Patient's subjective view.	
Patients interviewed in hospital.	Victims' reactions.

	Accident background
Urban congestion.	City crowding.
Mases of traffic.	The problem of movement.
Inside police lab. Police tests at scene of accident.	How police investigate accidents.
	Why Accidents Happen
Bad road engineering. Death spots. Blind Spots. Discussion with road engineer.	(a) *Bad road engineering.* The state of the roads.
	(b) *The driver.*
Talk to bus and taxi drivers. Training course for bad drivers.	Not taking care.
Training new drivers. Specialist training.	Driver training.
Bad visibility. Crowded car. Bad signs. Psychological pressure.	Pressures on drivers.
Sports car. Racing. Big cars and beautiful women.	Car as extension of the psyche. The psychology of cars and driving.
	(c) *The car itself.*
Impact tests on cars. Cars on test courses. Safety belt tests.	Building the car. Its faults. New safety measures
Innovative car designs Cars with reverse seats and periscope mirrors.	The car of the future.
Animated film with new cars and well-designed, car-accommodating cities.	The world of the future.
Wrecks of cars in a salvage yard.	Need for concern now.

What I have set out above was actually fourteen pages long. Very much a first sketch, it nevertheless set out clearly how the visuals and ideas would work together. I knew that later scripts would require much more detail and that the shooting itself would suggest new patterns and variations. However, I needed to put some ideas on paper so that I could react to them and see whether the order made sense, at least in theory.

It is also worthwhile pointing out that certain sections were included not because I thought they were logically necessary to some thesis I was developing, but because I thought they were visually interesting and might be fun to shoot. The scene in the police accident lab, for example, did not contribute much by way of ideas, but it was a marvelous place to poke around and look at lie detectors, secret camera units, methods of metal testing, and so on. The jazzy sequence, with a beautiful blond on top of a Rolls-Royce, also was not strictly necessary, but I thought it would give a certain visual relief.

What is important is that the first draft suggested a tentative order and connection between sequences that were really quite disparate. It was a beginning. In the end the editing suggested quite a radical reordering, but that's a story for the editing chapter.

Typical Problems

In looking for logic in your scriptwriting, you will often find yourself being pulled in different directions by the variety of possibilities. The most common problem is trying to decide whether to proceed chronologically, intellectually, or spatially. What is all this about in practice? Let's consider a chronological progression versus an intellectual progression.

You are doing a film about World War II and want to bring in the subject of civilian resistance. Your general story has taken you to 1942. You then find four or five stories you want to use about resistance, one in 1942, one in 1944, and one in 1945. In terms of ideas, you probably want to tell all the stories in one sequence to prove a certain point about resistance. But that will carry you to 1945, whereas the main part of your film has only reached 1942. So you have a problem.

In the same film you are showing the D day invasion of June 1944. Your idea line suddenly pulls you into a discussion of other successful and less successful attacks in the war, such as the Dieppe raid and the Italian invasion. Do you branch out and show those incidents, or do you stay with the scenes on the Normandy beaches?

There are no easy answers. I tend to ask myself a few questions: Will what I am doing confuse the viewer? Will it aid or spoil the dramatic and emotional telling of the story? Will it affect the overall rhythm of the film? In nine cases out of ten I find it best to keep within a chronological progression and to stay with one physical location until the information about it is exhausted. There are exceptions, but these guidelines seem to be the most helpful in practice.

8

Completing the First Draft

Visualization

You have worked out a story line and idea line. Now comes the fun as you start considering how to put over your ideas visually. Every sequence has a point or a number of points that can be put over by visuals, by commentary, or by a combination of both. Your aim is to find the most powerful way to use the joint forces of both picture and word. As the film proceeds it makes a series of assertions. Today the car is god; the famine in Ethiopia is tragic beyond all belief; the youngsters of today are crazier than their parents ever were. These statements need illustrating in order to prove their truth. They can be illustrated in comic or serious ways, but they must be proved. So one of the first jobs is to choose the pictures that will prove your points in the most imaginative and interesting way.

The job of visualization is shared between the writer and the director. The writer will suggest the action and visualization but knows that the director, on location, may add to or alter the suggestion or think of a better way of putting over the idea. But the script visualization is always the starting point and is usually a tremendous help to the director.

In my automobile accident film one of the points I wanted to make was that the car often becomes an extension of one's personality. It can represent power, sex, virility. In the film the point was made visually as follows:

Visual	*Audio*
Very low shots of the road surface rushing past. The road blurs at speed. We cut to racing cars speeding round a track. Women wave the cars on.	In my car I feel like a real guy. There's power in my hands. My girl's at my side. Put my foot down and I can get from San Francisco to Monterey in an hour. In my car I get really turned on. You're just not a man without a car.

> Cut to a man looking through the window of a car showroom. Inside two beautiful women in bikinis are sitting on the hoods of a Mercedes and a Ferrari—and smiling.

The commentary was in my own words but based on a number of interviews I had done during research. What I wanted from the visuals was not a parallel of the commentary, but a visual sense of the *meaning* behind the commentary. What the visuals had to do was express the machismo that drove the man who was talking.

In another part of the film I wanted to talk about all the pressures on the driver. My notes show my first thoughts on the subject. Pressure could be shown by the following sequence:

1. A mass of road signs that block each other and give confusing directions. The driver's brain is overloaded with information.
2. The windshield is blurred, rain-lashed.
3. Inside the car kids scream and nag.
4. The traffic is getting very thick. The roads are icy and night is falling.
5. The oncoming drivers are using their brights and the lights are dazzling, going in and out of focus.
6. It starts to snow.

Sometimes you are thinking of visuals to illustrate a process or an evolving action, and that's quite simple. But sometimes you need to find visuals to illustrate something a little more abstract or a little less obvious, and here you can often really let go. In our proposed university script we might want to make the point that today's students are tremendously politically involved. We might write the scene like this:

Visual	*Audio*
A student lies on the grass and reads a book beside a river	Once the student lived what was almost the life of a monk. Solitary and studious, devoted and disciplined.
Student riots in Berkeley, 1965. Student anti-Vietnam riots in 1969. Students battle with the police.	That idea seems just a little bit strange today.

Here the whole argument is made visually, with the commentary providing the lightest of frameworks. This point needs stressing because it is one of the most important things in scriptwriting: you can write with words, and you can write with pictures, but very often the pictures will make your point much more powerfully.

I wrote earlier that there were few laws for scriptwriters. I was wrong. There is one immutable law: the good scriptwriter must be visual as well as verbal. Failure to attend to the visual side of things accounts for many boring documentaries.

One of the pleasures of visualization is the fun you can have finding the pictures to match an open text. Let us assume that we are making a film about the brain and need to put over a simple statement in the commentary. "One of the main differences between humans and animals lies in the development of speech. We have it and, except in a primitive way, they don't. And what we do with it is incredible." This comment is very simple to illustrate, and we could do it in a hundred ways. A random choice of visuals might include

- Chaplin singing a nonsense song
- A man on his knees making an eloquent proposal of marriage
- An Italian and a German yelling at each other in their respective languages
- Laurence Olivier reciting "To be or not to be"
- Hitler haranguing the masses
- A baby talking to a doll

Just for fun we might want to finish off the sequence with the line "Language is golden, but thank God we can turn it off."

I leave it to you what we put in there.

Visualizing sequences

In a verite or news film you normally follow the action and write commentary later. Your visuals are "given" in the sense that you are following things as they happen. But much of the time in documentary you have to plan. What we did above was plan shots to illustrate commentary lines, but more often you try to visualize entire sequences. Again, your task is to think of the best situation to flesh out the script idea and then describe the elements of that situation in as much helpful detail as possible. That may mean writing notes regarding setting and characters, including the characters' dress and actions. This is standard practice for the "invented" industrial film, but it is also useful for the film based on more or less real situations. This is particularly true when you have researched a story and know what's likely to happen. Your writing helps the director see where to put the emphasis in a scene and what you want to get out of the scene.

An old script of mine called *A Certain Knowledge* illustrates some of the above points. The script dealt with a four-day encounter between two groups of teenagers from Los Angeles, one black, one white. The object of the film was to show that stereotypes could be broken and that suspicion and antagonism could give way to friendship if only some of the mental barriers could be removed. I wanted to go for a simple observational film, but the sponsors wanted more. They argued that the film was not simply a documentary but had the specific purpose of encouraging other schools to participate in the encounter. To that end, they wanted realistic situations written into the script.

Obviously, one had to isolate the situations, known from the past, that would reveal the initial antagonism, then indicate the change of attitudes. I explored the basic four-day program and suggested the following for the script: First, I wanted either a basketball game or a volleyball game close to the beginning, with whites against blacks. This would set up the concept of opposition, and such games often took place. Later in the film I wanted to repeat the film with mixed sides. I also suggested a closed-circuit video session in which we would show clips of police brutality against blacks in the South and other clips of Malcolm X and Louis Farrakhan railing against whites. Here I suggested recording the on-the-spot reactions of the two groups for use later as voice-overs against the video viewing. I also wrote in an open discussion to follow the viewing session.

For the latter part of the film I suggested a home visit, blacks in white families and vice versa, to be followed by a half-day hike in rugged terrain. My thinking here was that the home sessions might be awkward and tense and that we could use the hike to break the tension. The hike also served another purpose, and I wrote in some notes for the director regarding its shooting. I asked the director to concentrate on filming groups where one helped the other across rocks, where hands were stretched out in assistance, or where they sat on the grass and ate and sang together.

I wanted the visuals to be very positive but realized there was a danger of the film becoming saccharine and unreal. To counter this, I suggested we put in a number of voice-overs in the last sequence. While some would indicate a positive change in black-white attitudes, a number would still be skeptical and doubt the lasting quality of the friendships and the value of the long weekend.

Visual Resonance

No matter how many years I've been working I still find it enormously helpful to study the work of other documentary directors. Looking back, I find one director above all others has influenced my thinking: namely, Humphrey Jennings, the classic English documentary director of the early 1940s.

Jennings' greatest film is often thought to be *Listen to Britain*, and it can serve as a veritable textbook regarding visualization. The film provides a sound portrait of Great Britain in the middle of World War II. What gives the film its power is the emotional resonance of its visuals. Again and again in *Listen to Britain*, Jennings and his collaborator Stewart McAllister choose shots that have not just an immediate meaning but also cultural and emotional resonance. It is this hidden effect that makes the Jennings and McAllister films so powerful, and you can see it at work in the playground sequence from *Listen to Britain*.

1. A middle-aged woman is in her bedroom looking at a photograph of her husband in uniform. We hear the sounds of children singing.
2. The woman looks out of the window and sees, in long shot, a group of seven-year-old children doing a circle dance in a school playground.
3. Cut to close-ups of the children dancing in couples.
4. The sound of the children singing merges with the sound of a bren gun carrier (an open half-track vehicle with a light machine gun mounted next to the driver). We then cut to the bren gun carrier rattling through the narrow streets of an old English village.
5. As the bren gun carrier passes we see more fully the ancient thatched roofs and the Tudor style of the English cottages.

The images are open to many interpretations, but given the purpose of the film—to boost morale in wartime Britain—I think the intended resonances are very clear.

1. The woman looking at the soldier's photograph sets up the idea of loved ones who are gone but who are protecting us.
2. The children represent the protected, but also stand for the future.
3. The bren gun carrier asserts the immediate protection of the British way of life.
4. The background of the village, with its Tudor gables and thatched roofs, suggests the wider culture and history that is being protected. It also recalls an earlier crisis, when Elizabethan England stood alone against the Spaniards and defeated them. The parallel to England and Germany in 1939 is clear.

The sequence lasts approximately forty seconds but engenders a whole series of emotions and responses that build throughout the film.

The importance of resonance is worth keeping in mind in any documentary writing. Every visual you use may have both an immediate and appropriate surface meaning and an additional emotional resonance that can add tremendous depth. I am not talking here of obvious symbols—the American flag and so on—but scenes and sequences rooted in cultural memory: the Saturday little-league baseball game; Christmas shopping; high-school graduation. Used well, such scenes can evoke powerful memories and moods, which can obviously be of enormous help to a film.

There is, however, one point to keep in mind when going for "the resonance effect." The emotional echo of a scene may be specific to a certain region or culture and may be meaningless to other audiences. Jennings's work, which is so powerful in the English context, comes over as far weaker in the United States. Nevertheless, resonance is a tremendous addition to a writer's bag of effects.

The Opening

The opening of the film has to do two things very fast. First, it has to catch or "hook" the viewers' interest, and second, it has to define very quickly what the film is about and where it is going. These are good artistic rules and also good practical rules in a world where documentaries are seen primarily on television and have to compete with many other programs for viewers. The only real exception to both these rules is when you are dealing with well known presold subjects. If I were doing a film titled *Sherman: The Greatest General, The Real Elvis,* or *D Day: The Day That Won the War,* then I might ignore the two golden rules. In all three cases most viewers would know something of the subject matter once they heard the title. Knowing what to expect, they might not mind a slower introduction. This is exactly what occurs in the film about cellist Jaqueline du Pré.

The opening "hook" should play into the audience's curiosity. You present an intriguing situation and say, "Watch me! You'll be fascinated to see where we're going to take you." Let us imagine, say, a film that opens with a very serious, middle-aged man dressing up as a woman. In another film a rather prim and proper teenage girl is seen loading her revolver and then shooting at objects in her basement. Immediately we are struck by the strange, even bizarre quality of these situations. We want to know who the man is and what he is doing. Is he an actor, a transvestite, a spy? And what about the girl? Is she merely practicing self-defense? Does she want to commit suicide? Is she about to kill her parents? Is she the best revolver shot in the state? What is she going to do?

At this point the curiosity is piqued, the imagination stimulated. We want answers to our questions, so we decide to stay with the film for a while, but only so long as there is a payoff from the first two or three shots. They had better be leading somewhere interesting. Thus, the core assertion assures us that we are going to be treated to a fascinating topic that we would be utter fools to miss or ignore. The hook does not have to be as tremendously dramatic as are those above. In fact, sometimes we can play against the very ordinariness of the situation. For instance, a quiet man is seen in a library reading a book. He writes something down and then takes another book from the shelf. Another film opens with a frail woman chatting with a middle-aged Indian woman. Neither of these scenes is visually devastating; in fact, they are rather boring. But they take on a completely different dimension once we add commentary. Over the visual of the man, the commentary might go as follows: "He plays chess and football. He has a wife and two daughters. Not one person in a thousand would recognize him, yet he has saved millions of lives. His name is Professor Jonas Salk." The other scene is accompanied by the following commentary: "She's seventy-five. She lives in two small rooms and earns the equivalent of $2,000 a year. Yet beggars bless her, parliaments have honored her, and presidents carry her picture. Her name is Mother Teresa."

In these cases most viewers would know that Salk discovered a wonder vaccine against polio and that Mother Teresa was awarded the Nobel Peace Prize for her work among the poor of India. Even if they did not know these things, there would probably be a certain intriguing ring of familiarity about the names, so the core assertion accompanying the opening would not have to do very much. But most times the assertion and the hook have to be well fused and balanced, working hand in hand with one another.

Let's look a little closer at the *core assertion* that sets the film on its way. Sometimes the assertion appears in the form of a statement:

> At first they were heroes, and America worshiped them. Then they were villains and the world abused them. They were the most famous parents the world has ever seen. One fathered the atom bomb, the other created the hydrogen bomb.
>
> Tonight in *A Is for Atom, D Is for Death*, we discuss the careers of Robert Oppenheimer and Edward Teller and what their discoveries mean for the world today.

Obviously, there is a bit of hyperbole in calling them the world's most famous parents—after all, what about Adam and Eve—but it is the kind of exaggeration that is acceptable in scriptwriting.

In contrast to the above we find many central statements presented in question form. Using that technique, *A Is for Atom* could have opened this way. "When they split the atom, they promised a brave new world. Forty years after Hiroshima, has the promise dimmed? Will nuclear physics bring destruction or deliverance? A new universe or an abandoned planet?" Sometimes you might want to make the opening question deliberately provocative and disturbing: "He came as a prince of peace, yet his followers rampaged, massacred, and destroyed in his name. They said Jesus inspired them, but was that true? Were the Crusades a holy mission or the last barbarian invasion?" These opening sentences, whether statement or question, establish clearly where the film is going. They are the written counterpart of the visual hook, but if the visual hook dangles the promise, then the statement has to guarantee that an hour's viewing will fulfill all expectations.

If the film is about some charismatic figure, a historical personality, or even a fictional central figure in a sponsored film, it helps to introduce these characters very early and to hint at the conflicts surrounding them. You want to dangle all the goodies in front of the viewer and get their mouths watering over the intrigue and the passions that will be presented to them in the next hour. If you were doing a film based on Rommel, the German tank commander of World War II, you might open as follows:

Visual	*Audio*
German tanks firing furiously. Wildly enthusiastic German soldiers surround a small, neat officer.	In 1941 he was Germany's greatest hero. His panzer tanks had smashed the British and French forces to smithereens.
More tank battles. The same man is standing next to Hitler on a balcony, facing cheering crowds.	Soldiers loved him. Women adored him. Hitler made him Field Marshall.
Hitler's face and Rommel's face in close-up.	
Rommel stands isolated in a huge room, downcast. Close-up on his face, dejected but strong.	Three years later he was offered poison or a bullet, then given a hero's funeral by the leader he had betrayed.
A military funeral with honors	
	Tonight . . . *Rommel: The Desert Fox.*

This machine-gun-fast opening montage seems appropriate for a film on a soldier like Rommel. But that kind of explosive opening is only one approach. By way of contrast it is interesting to look at the start of *The Day after Trinity*, a life of Robert Oppenheimer directed by Jon Else and written by David and Janet Peoples and Jon Else.

Visual	*Audio*
Main title over black: *The Day after Trinity*	Narrator: In August 1945 the city of Hiroshima was destroyed in about nine seconds by a single atom bomb. The man responsible for building the bomb was a gentle and eloquent physicist named J. Robert Oppenheimer. This is the story of Robert Oppenheimer and the atomic bomb.
Hakon Chevalier reading from a letter	*Hakon Chevalier:* Stinson beach, California, August 7, 1945. Dear Oppie: You are probably the most fa-

Photograph of Robert Oppenheimer	mous man in the world today, and yet I am not sure this letter will reach you. But if it does, I want you to know that we are very proud of you. And if it doesn't, you will know it anyway. We have been irritated by your reticence these past few years but under the itchy surface we knew that it was all right; that the work was progressing, that the heart
Blast and fireball from the Trinity atomic test preceding Hiroshima	was still there, and the warm being we have known and cherished. I can understand now, as I could guess then, the somber note in you during our
Slow zoom in on Oppenheimer photo	last meetings.
	There is a weight in such a venture which few men in history have had to bear. I know that with your love of men, it is
Wide shot pan ruins of Hiroshima	no light thing to have had a part, and a great part, in a diabolical contrivance for destroying them. But in the possibilities of death are also the possibilities of life. You have made history. We are happy for you.
Hans Bethe sync	*Hans Bethe*: You may well ask why people with kind hearts and humanist feelings—why they would go and work on weapons of destruction.
Oppenheimer as a child	*Narrator*: When Robert Oppenheimer was born, in 1904, the atomic bomb was not even science fiction. He was educated at the ethical cultural school in New York City, and mastered Harvard's curriculum in three years, summa

Oppenheimer at Harvard	cum laude. He spoke six languages and had difficulty deciding whether to be an architect, a poet, or a scientist. But it was his love of physics which
Göttingen University	led him to England and Germany in the early 1920s, where the atom was beginning to yield its secrets to Einstein, Rutherford, and Bohr.

Here we have a very quiet but effective opening that is also extremely carefully constructed. The first statement beginning "in August 1945" sets forth the basic assertion: we are going to follow the story of the man responsible for building what was, until the early 1950s, the most devastating and destructive weapon in the history of the world. The film could then have proceeded easily with the narration cut that begins, "When Robert Oppenheimer was born in 1904," but it doesn't. There would have been nothing terribly wrong with such a continuation. It's a competent progression that gets you straight into the story of Oppenheimer.

Instead, the filmmaker goes from the opening statement to an excerpt from a letter. Why? Isn't this just a delaying tactic? Not really. The letter is a bold but beautiful touch. It takes us straight to the soul of Oppenheimer and humanizes him; it tells us that the creator of the atomic bomb had feelings, that he could be moved and grieved. Having shown that the man has a soul, Bethe's short comment then poses a question that will haunt us throughout the film. That done, the narration can take over and move the story forward.

One useful device is to start off with a short statement and then add a provocative comment from one of the participants in the film. The comment may be angry, even furious. Sometimes it is defiant. The common element is the passion with which these emotions are expressed. We are touched by people and their passions—whether about marriage, war, suffering, or happiness—and we want to hear more and learn more. *Haunted Heroes*, produced for the BBC in 1985 by Tony Salmon, offers an excellent example. Its subject is Vietnam veterans who have abandoned society. The opening provides just enough narration to define the subject before the director inserts an interview extract that completely grabs us.

Visual	*Audio*
Aerial shots of valleys, lakes, mountains	
	Music
More shots of forest and lakes	*Narrator*: Hidden in the for-

Trees	ests and the mountains of the American wilderness are men haunted by the echoes of a forgotten war. Lonely and tortured, they live alone, exiles
Steve hacking a tree	in their own country. Protected from people, they survive on skills learnt in the jungles of Vietnam.
	Music out These woods are sanctuary for men like Steve.
Medium shot of Steve	
	Steve: I live on a black-and-white level. I live on a life-and-death survival level and I have for a very long time. And when I'm confronted in a stressful situation, there's al-
Wide shot of Steve collecting leaves	ways a chance I'll go too far. I generally turn to the woods for peace of mind and to calm down and cool out. I'm not expecially afraid of society. I'm more afraid of what I will
Close shot of Steve	do in this society. Basically if you have a knife, some string,
Steve carrying ferns to a shelter	and maybe an axe and the clothes you're wearing that's pretty much all you need. Also pick a place that is secure. Not
Steve inside shelter	only are you not getting wet but the wind's not hitting you and you have full view of the
Steve pulling ferns across entrance to shelter	area, and if you camouflage it properly nobody can find you.
Title: *Haunted Heroes*	*Music*

Another example of an interesting opening can be seen in *Whose House Is It Anyway*, directed by David Pearson for the BBC. This was the film I mentioned earlier as a good example of the conflict situation. In this case the local council want to make a compulsory purchase of a house owned by two brothers who refuse to budge.

Visual	*Audio*
Two shots of Billy and Gordon, aged sixty-seven and seventy-three, in the dark in front of the fire	*Gordon Howard*: Here we are. Have you seen the paper, Bill, today?
	Billy Howard: Aye, I've been reading it.
	Gordon: Look at his face. He's made it and we sit here and we can't make a cracker.
Long shot of the exterior of a dilapidated house	*Narrator*: "Where there is no property there is no injustice," wrote a philosopher three hundred years ago. Owning this house has led the Howard brothers to the brink of eviction. This week they
Exterior of town hall	wait notice of arrival of the council's bailiffs.
Close-up of Gordon	*Gordon*: I'm not frightened of bailiffs coming. I'm not frightened of anyone coming. Why should I be frightened in my own home? A man's got to stand up and fight for his home. That's an Englishman's way. What they're doing they're doing a Nazi way, a Hitler way.
Title: *Whose House Is It Anyway?*	
Close-up of Ian Wood	*Ian Wood*: The Howard brothers, like the majority of the nation, think that an Englishman's home is his castle. It isn't, I'm afraid. It's his castle, but if the council wants it or the government department wants it, then it's their castle.

In 1980 Robert Kee, a well-known English journalist, appeared in and wrote the commentary for the BBC series "Ireland: A Television History."

The fourth film in the series deals with the great potato famine of nine-teenth-century Ireland. The opening is quiet and understated, yet the power of the words and the significance of the events that led to the great migration to the United States make the opening moving and effective.

Visual	Audio
A dark Irish landscape. Hills. Valleys. A churchbell tolls. Various Irish names are called out.	*Robert Kee*: A few of the names of Irish men, women, and children who died in the great famine in Ireland between 1845 and 1849. There were many hundreds of thousands of them altogether. The names of only very few are known. . . . The vast majority of deaths, perhaps as many as a million, went unrecorded.
Sync interview with Mrs. Dunleavy	*Mrs. Dunleavy*: My mother used to tell us about the famine and all the people that died because there were no potatoes. Well, of course I don't think you'd die if there were no potatoes. I think the English were in some collusion to get rid of the Irish from their lands, you see.
Hills; sun turning dark; clouds sweeping over the land	*Kee*: As with many great disasters in human affairs, there was no unmistakable signal that this one was at hand. It had been a fine hot summer, but there was a sudden break in the weather at the beginning of August 1845, with showers of sleet, lightning, and heavy rain. Reports from the counties spoke of potato crops of the most abundant yields. Then, on the eleventh of September 1845 . . .
Rain and lightning	
Freeman's Journal	Second narrator: We regret to state that we have had com-

	munications from more than one correspondent announcing what is called "cholera" in potatoes in Ireland, especially in the north.
Robert Kee to camera	*Kee*: Why was this such particularly disastrous news for Ireland? Well, because one-third of the entire population of Ireland depended wholly on the potato for survival. The Irish small farmer lived off his potato crop, so that even at the best of times life was a struggle. It had become increasingly a struggle in the past forty years because during that time the population of Ireland had doubled from four to eight million.

Kee's style is spare and straightforward. He has a strong, emotional story to tell and relates it in an unobtrusive way, letting the events and the facts speak for themselves.

Rhythm, Pace, and Climax

A good beginning takes you into a film with a bang, with a sense of expectation. The problem then is how to sustain that interest for the next half hour or hour. A lot of the problem is solved if you have provided yourself with a solid structure for the film. Even so there will be pitfalls that can be avoided if you have thought a little about *rhythm, pace, and climax*.

These are obviously not just elements of documentary films, but elements that every writer—whether novelist, playwright, or feature filmmaker—has to worry about. How often have you heard someone say, "Well, the book runs out of steam halfway through," or, "It started dragging and becoming boring in the middle and then never seemed to end." This complaint of a slow, dragging film is, unfortunately, too often made about documentaries, particularly documentaries that are determined to give you every detail of a process, every fact about a person, whether interesting or not.

And the problems occur in the best of films. *Harlan County*, by Barbara Kopple, rightfully won an Academy Award a few years ago. It was a courageous film about a Kentucky miners' fight for a decent contract. The first two-thirds of the film was brilliant, but then it became repetitive, discursive, losing all its energy. Here there was one glaring central problem: the film had a natural ending that Kopple ignored. The result was that after the natural climax, the film began again in a more boring way and seemed to go on and on forever. Points made earlier in the film were merely repeated in different circumstances without adding very much to the viewers' knowledge. My view is that Kopple, in her obsession with her subject, had ignored or forgotten the basic rules about rhythm, pace and audience demands.

What do we mean by good rhythm and pace? Quite simply, that a film should have a logical and emotional flow, that its level of intensity should vary, that it should hold our interest all the time, and that it should build to a compelling climax. Unfortunately, it is easier to point out the problems than it is to offer all-embracing solutions. Here are just a few of the most common problems:

1. Sequences go on too long.
2. There is no connection between sequences.
3. Too many similar sequences follow each other when we thirst for variety.
4. There are too many action scenes and too few reflective scenes.
5. There is no sense of development or logical or emotional order to the sequences.

Are there any hints about rhythm and pace? I can offer just a few, very personal ones. First, *get into the film fast*. Establish what you are going to do, then do it. Second, *build the film with variety* between the scenes and a gradual crescendo of climaxes.

Allan King's *A Married Couple* is an excellent example of a well-paced film. *Couple* deals with three months of a marriage crisis between Billy and Antoinette Edwards. Halfway through the film we see an extended party. Billy is wandering around with a camera, ignoring Antoinette and taking photos. Antoinette is sitting next to the fire and pointedly suggesting to a New York visitor that they could become lovers. Thus, the scene sets up a tremendous distance between Billy and his wife. The next scene, however, shows Billy and Antoinette in bed together, with Antoinette weeping on Billy's shoulder. As the audience we imagine her thinking, "Why do I have to do these things, make passes at other men? I really do love my husband." The conjunction of the two scenes is perfect.

The film also illustrates the value of establishing a series of rising climaxes. During the months of shooting, Billy and Antoinette were involved in three or four violent quarrels. In the most vicious of the arguments, which came near the beginning of shooting, Billy basically threw Antoinette out of the house. Though this was the second argument chronologically, it was the most powerful of the four, and King placed it as the climax of the film.

The need for variety between the scenes is a point that bears repetition. We see such variety in feature films, and it is just as important in documentaries. What we need is variety in the types and tempo of the scenes. *Butch Cassidy*, written by William Goldman, was one of the most successful "buddy" movies ever made. Part of the success was due to Goldman's marvelous sense of structure and his masterly sense of variety and tempo. The film is full of sequences of action, pursuit, and gunslinging, but even these get boring. So in the middle Goldman inserts an idyllic scene of Paul Newman riding his girlfriend around on his bicycle in between the trees, while the music plays "Raindrops Keep Falling on My Head." It's a light, funny scene that allows us to breathe and relax before we return to the chase.

The third hint is to put in a *definite ending*. These words of advice seem obvious but are often ignored. You do so at your peril. Many films, especially crisis films, have natural endings. When the end is not so clear, many documentarists shove in the "montage" ending, doing a fast recap of the major figures in their film. Sometimes it works, but it usually seems to me a confession of failure. If you have built your script logically, then the ending should be obvious: the completion of the school year, the gradua- tion ceremony, or the medical recovery. If you really have no ending, then I suggest a sequence that is fun and visually striking: the high-school dance, the celebrations at the end of the war, the boats arriving, the planes vanishing into the sunset. Finish with a flourish, and let them know the film is over.

What do we mean by a good *climax*? Well, just that. The film should give us a sense of finality, of completion, of catharsis (to use the old literary term). This seems obvious but isn't, and I've seen documentary after documentary that trails away with no sense of an ending. I know there is a deeper problem here. Life doesn't wrap up easily; not all stories have a neat beginning, middle, and end, and there is a grave danger in implying that it all concluded nicely. The Irish problem goes on and on after we finish our story of the pursuit and capture of the IRA man. The problems in Nicaragua continue after the refugees cross the border. And they don't live happily ever after. I acknowledge all this, but I still insist that the particular story of the film must have a strong sense of conclusion. You must resolve the issue, reach the climax, then get out fast.

All this is easier to write about than it is to do in practice. You are often uncertain about where the climax comes, whether the obvious ending is the best ending, or whether you can spare the time to wrap up the story. In 1988 I made the film *Special Counsel*, a documentary drama about the making of the 1979 peace treaty between Egypt and Israel and the public and private personalities who helped resolve the conflict. There were tremendous battles and conflicts along the path to peace, and in one sense it was very easy just to end the film with the signing of the peace accords on the White House lawn in March 1979.

That provided a very effective climax, but I felt there were still too many questions left unanswered regarding the fate of people and issues mentioned in the film. I therefore added a ten-minute section showing the actual Israeli withdrawal from the Sinai Peninsula and the battles to evict settlers forced to leave under the terms of the treaty. I also showed what happened to the main players of the film: the assassination of Sadat, the election defeat of President Carter, the death of Moshe Dayan, and the award of an honorary doctorate to one of the private but significant participants in the drama. It was a difficult choice, because this section could have come as an anticlimax. I think it works because there was both a psychological need for the information and a physical need to cool down after the rush of the great events.

What is the part of the editor in solving all these problems? As I have argued, it is the job of the writer to establish the essential solutions to problems of pace, rhythm, and climax. Obviously, the editor will also play a major part in establishing pace and rhythm. The rhythms and solutions that you as a writer put down on paper may not necessarily work when translated into the realities of filming. So, as often happens, the writer, editor, and director must work together to find an answer. However, the writer should not try to avoid tackling the problem in the first place; if you fail to provide the basic skeleton, you end up just dumping the problems in the editor's lap. But the editor must have the initial blueprint, something to react against. With that blueprint in hand, the rest is comparatively easy.

Drafts and Changes

The scripts we have considered above are final narration scripts and have to be looked at with a certain amount of care. They look good, but they may have gone through enormous changes since the first draft. Another point to bear in mind is that whereas a text such as that of Kee's on Ireland could larely be written before production, the link narration of a film such as *Heroes* is almost definitely postproduction. The draft outline of *Heroes* probably only hinted at how it should begin; it may have appeared as follows: (1) We open with a statement about Vietnam veterans living alone in the forests, surviving on skills learned in the war. (2) We then cut to a comment by one of the veterans describing that life and showing us how he lives.

Scripts also change enormously from first to last draft, and the tentative beginnings change with them as the scriptwriter searches for the perfect opening. My own film *Out of the Ashes* is a good illustration of that process. When I was working with scriptwriter Brian Winston on the film, we faced one tremendous difficulty. Though its subject, the Nazi occupation of Europe and the destruction of European Jewry, was tremendously important, some people regarded it as tired, worn-out. People had seen film after film on the subject; how could we interest them in yet another? We discussed various strategies that were eventually incorporated into the film, but one thing was clear: above all else we had to have an opening that was powerful and *different*.

It was Brian who had the brain wave: use something from Kafka, whose writings explored the evils of bureaucratic power, all the dark, shadowed corners that characterized the years 1920 to 1945. I thought the idea was brilliant. However, the chosen passages and the narration that followed them changed quite a few times. I have set out below the first draft of the opening and then the revised text as it appears in the film.

Visual	*Audio*
A window opens (stock footage from *Triumph of the Will*)	*Narrator reads from Kafka's "The Trial"*: With a flicker, as of a light going up, the casement suddenly flew open. A human figure leaned abruptly far forward and stretched both arms still further.
People at the window (from *Triumph*)	Who was it? A friend? A good man? Someone who sympathized? Someone who wanted to help?
Hitler clutches his throat (from *Triumph*).	But the hands of one of the partners were already at K's throat, while the other thrust the knife into his heart and turned it there.
Narrator sync in Prague	*Narrator*: A murder, a murder by secret policemen—the climax of Franx Kafka's novel *The Trial*. In such a century such a death has become all too common. For ours has been the age of the secret policeman, the street thug, the prison and the concentration camp—the age of that emotionless and legalized horror we now call "Kafkaesque."
	Despite all our advances we have been unable to shrug off the bestial side of our nature.
	Yet sixty-five years ago, at the end of the first Great War, it

seemed possible that the beast within had been laid to rest amidst the slaughter of the trenches. There was a new spirit; the war just ended was the war to end all wars—a war to make the world safe for democracy, to create lands fit for heroes to live in.

And no people were to benefit more from this modern world than the Jews.

Super imposed title: *Out of the Ashes*

As director I was very excited by Brian's concept and immediately sensed the pictures that could accompany the text. Brian had indicated in general terms that we use excerpts from Leni Riefenstahl's *Triumph of the Will*, the classic film about the massive Nazi rally in Nuremberg in 1934. Very specifically I imagined night pictures of storm troopers marching, flickering torches, black helmets silhouetted against moving clouds, blazing buildings, close-ups of boots, hands gripping belts emblazoned with the Nazi *Totenkopf* (an emblem of a death's head). I wanted an impressionistic feeling of dark horror rather than a concrete picture of the Nazi troops.

With this in mind, we realized that the visuals were fine, but as we looked again at this very fast first draft we found two things that were wrong. First, though the Kafka idea was good, the specific selections were not doing exactly what we wanted. They were too general and did little to forewarn us of the horrors of Nazi Germany. I therefore asked Brian to see if he could find a more pertinent extract from *The Trial* that would serve our purposes better. The second problem was that the latter part of the introductory narration undermined the opening point. We had talked of a black, brutal world coming into existence, yet finished by saying that the Jews were going to benefit enormously in this modern era. That was confusing and in complete contradiction to the mood set up by the Kafka extract. We had unconsciously set up an opening that was moving in opposite directions. Even worse, the final statement was very misleading, if not untrue. The early 1920s held superficial promise for the Jews of Europe, but that period would soon be eclipsed by a decade of unprecedented horror.

Brian saw all this very clearly and went back to his word processor. Over the next few months the opening went through several more changes until Brian finished with the text printed below, which I thought was excellent and provided everything I wanted for the opening:

Visual	*Audio*
Extract from Nazi film	*Narrator reads extract from "The Trial".* Who could these men be? What authority did they represent? K lived in a country with a legal constitution. There was universal peace. All the laws were in force. Who dared seize him in his own dwelling? Where was the Judge he had never seen? Where was the High Court?
Marching feet, silhouettes, smoking torches at night, dark helmets against the clouds	
A feeling of evil, darkness	
	He raised his hands. But the hands of one of the partners were already at K's throat, while the other thrust the knife into his heart and turned it there twice.
Narrator sync before a Holocaust memorial	*Narrator:* Joseph K., the hero of Franz Kafka's novel *The Trial*, goes to his death never knowing what his offense might have been, his enemy nothing less than the unbridled, irrational, and emotionless power of a modern totalitarian state. We have in this century too often seen in reality this legalized nightmare occur: a nightmare which we now call "Kafkaesque"—with secret policemen, street thugs, and concentration camps—where death can become an industry of the state.
We cut away occasionally to twisted, agonized figures on the memorial.	
	It is fitting that Kafka, the prophet of this horror, should have been born a Jew. For the Jews were to experience the first half of the twentieth century as a Kafkaesque ordeal, a time which promised freedom and liberty for European Jews
A dark castle broods over	

a lake.   but which brought them to the
                                            brink of annihilation.

Title super: *Out of the Ashes*

In this final version the Kafka extract is tight and appropriate to the subject
of Hitler's Germany. Furthermore, the narration flows on smoothly, enlarg-
ing the topic of "the legalized nightmare" that exactly describes the
condition of the Jews and others in Germany in the 1930s. The final
narration indicates the promise of freedom and liberty suggested in the
first draft, but it then points to the impending Holocaust.

Part II _____ *Preproduction*

9

Budget and Contract

The production contract, the agreement between you and those who are giving you the money to make the film, formalizes the terms under which the film is to be made. It is usually drawn up before the script is written, but many organizations prefer to pay for a script and then, if they like it, commit themselves to the actual production. For the sake of convenience, I am assuming your sponsor is of the second type, that they like the script, and that they want to proceed with the film.

You have probably discussed money in very vague terms up to this point. But now that you are going to sign your life away in a formal agreement, you must carefully budget the film; otherwise, your contract may not provide sufficient money to make a decent film according to the approved script.

In reality you will have thought about the production budget, at least in a general way, from your first moments in considering the film. But now is the moment of truth. My own procedure is as follows. First, I draw up a detailed production budget from which I will get a sense of the cost of the film. With that figure in mind I deal with the formal production contract, arguing terms and conditions. Because I have a very concrete idea of the needs of the budget, I am now much less likely to make mistakes in the terms I require from the sponsor.

The Budget

In budgeting we are often faced with a new version of the old question, what comes first, the chicken or the egg? Do you budget according to script, or do you script according to budget? There is no absolute answer as the conditions under which you make each film will be different. Only one thing is important: your budget must be as complete and as accurate as possible. This point is more than important; it is *vital*. If you make a mistake in budgeting, tying yourself into making a film for what turns out to be an unrealistic sum, you're likely to finish up bankrupt. My answer is to put into the budget every single need I can think of and then a few more; I always overbudget rather than underbudget. You may lose a few films if you are bidding in a competitive situation, but it's worth it in the end. A decent budget will save you many a sleepless night.

Below are the major items that appear in most budgets, and this list should serve as a good first guide. If something occurs to you that does not appear here, then shove it in, as you'll probably need it.

A. Research
    1. Script research, including travel and hotels
    2. General preproduction expenses, including travel, meetings, etc.
B. Shooting
    1. *Crew*
       Cameraman
       Assistant cameraman
       Soundman
       Lighting technician
       Production assistant
       Driver
       Production manager
    2. *Equipment*
       Camera and usual accessories
       Special camera equipment such as fast lenses
       Tape recorders and microphones
       Lighting
    3. *Location Expenses*
       Vehicle rental
       Gasoline
       Crew Food
       Hotels
       Air fares
    4. *Stock*
       Negative film
       Developing film and making work print
       Reels of quarter-inch tape
       Magnetic tape, including quarter-inch transfer
       Leader and spacing
C. Postproduction
    1. *Editing*
       Editor
       Assistant editor
       Sound editor
       Editing room and equipment
    2. *Lab and other expenses*
       Sound coding
       Music and sound transfers
       Opticals and special effects

Making titles
Narration recording
Sound mix
Negative cutting
Making optical negative
First and second answer print
Release print
3. *General*
Office expenses, rent, telephone, etc.
Transcripts
Music and archive royalties
Insurance
Legal costs
Dispatch and customs clearance
Advertising and publicity
Messengers
4. *Personnel*
Writer
Director
Producer
Narrator
Associate producer
Researcher
General assistant
D. Company Provisions
Contingency
Company profit

Ninety percent of the above items occur in most documentaries. The other 10 percent depends on the size and finances of your production. If the production is small, there may be no associate producer or general assistant, and you may also find that you are not only writing and directing but also doing all the research.

Two notes: (1) The crew is normally budgeted per day, and the editor and assistant per week. So your cameraman might appear in the budget for fourteen days at $200 per day, while your editor would be figured for ten weeks at $750 per week. Equipment rental is also budgeted per day. (2) Stock, both film and magnetic, is usually estimated at so many cents per foot—for example, 20,000 feet of film stock 7291 at eighteen cents per foot.

Besides the above, a few other items occur from time to time, and they are worth noting in your checklist:

• Studio use
• Actors
• Special wardrobe

- Special props
- Donations and presents

Some of the items in the main list are obvious and need little explanation, but others require some consideration because a miscalculation about them can have grave effects on the budget. I have discussed a few of these items below in more detail.

Stock and ratios. It is extremely important to sense at the beginning how much film stock you are likely to require for your shoot. A film that can be preplanned to the last detail and has fairly easy shooting may require a ratio of only five to one—that is, if you want a half-hour final film, you need to shoot only two and one-half hours of film. A more complex film, however, may require a ratio of twelve or fourteen to one, which is fairly standard for major television documentaries. If you are going for verite, emulating the films of Fred Wiseman, Ricky Leacock, or the Maysles, then you may be in for a shooting ratio of forty or fifty to one.

At the moment of writing, it costs about $350 to produce a twenty-minute work print, so you must be accurate as to what ratio you want to use; otherwise, your budget will be terribly inaccurate. I budget generally on a ratio of ten to one if most of the shooting can be thought out in advance.

If you are doing a videotape documentary, you have far fewer problems as your twenty-minute videotape will cost eighteen dollars or less, as compared to $350 for shooting on film.

Equipment. Some people own their own equipment. I don't, though I share an editing table with a partner. Generally I prefer to rent the equipment according to the needs of the particular film: sometimes I might want to film with an Aaton, sometimes with an Eclair. Even if you own your own equipment you should put a cost for it in the budget. This helps you at the end of the year to assess whether the equipment has really paid for itself.

Crew and shooting time. One reason for doing a decent script before shooting is that it helps you predict the shooting time needed. These days the minimum cost for a crew and equipment is somewhere in the region of $1500 a day. If you want the best cameraman and the fanciest equipment, your costs may go up to $3000 a day. If you have underestimated the number of days needed for shooting, you will be anywhere from $1500 to $3000 out of pocket per day. So again, overestimate rather than underestimate.

Another point to check out is that you know exactly what you have agreed with the crew. Is the arrangement for eight, ten, or twelve hours per day? Can you make a buy-out arrangement, offering them a flat fee whatever the length of the shooting day? What arrangements have you made about travel time? Is the crew to be paid anything on their days off when they are forced to be away from home? Do you have to deal with a union? What are you paying for a location scout? These questions must be resolved; otherwise, you think you are paying one rate, yet you finish up with an unexpectedly inflated bill at the end of the day.

The trouble is that you are dealing with a lot of imponderables. The only useful guideline, then, is to err on the generous side. This is also true concerning editing, as it is often impossible to say whether the editing is going to take eight weeks or ten.

One way around some of these problems is to agree with the sponsor on the number of shooting days and editing weeks and get them to pay extra if it goes over. This approach is discussed at greater length in the next section on the production contract.

Royalties. Royalty payments may be necessary for the use of recorded library music, certain photographs and film archives. Most of the time that you use ready-made recordings, you will have to pay a fee to the company that made the recording. The fee is usually based on the length of the selection you use, the areas where you want to show the film, and the type of audience for whom the film is intended. The rate for theatrical use or commercial television use is usually higher than that for educational purposes. Occasionally you may be able to swing the free use of a piece of music if the film is for public-service purposes.

If you are unsure of the final use of the film, it's best to negotiate the rights you want and fix a sum that will be payable if you alter the use. My policy is to get everything fixed in one go before the film is made; if you try to negotiate later and the seller knows you must have the rights, you may be in a bad bargaining position. In other words, make a provisional clearance that will stand you in good stead if you need it.

The position with photographs is slightly different. If the photographs are not in the public domain, you will have to make an arrangement with each individual photographer. Newspapers are usually fairly good at letting you use photographs for a small fee, whereas individual photographers will be much more expensive. It makes sense to hunt around for options on different photographs or to find photographs in the public domain. The extra trouble may save considerable sums later.

The main thing is that you must obtain permission before use. I know that many people don't, pinching from everybody and paying nothing. It seems a stupid policy, one that ultimately works against the film and the director. On the one hand you lay yourself open to a lawsuit, and on the other you may find that a television station will not accept a film unless you can produce written permissions.

Most of the above comments also apply to stock footage or film archive rights. Like music and photos, the cost of the rights will vary according to the purpose and destination of the film. A few years ago most archive rights were comparatively cheap; battle footage from World War II could be had for a few dollars a foot. Today, though, film archives have turned into big business, demanding immense sums for archive clips. It is not unusual to find an archive asking fifty to sixty dollars for a final used foot; this figure translates to $100 for three seconds in a completed film. Thus, if your film deals with history or a well-known personality, you may have to budget a huge sum to cover archive rights. In a film I did about World War II for a New York station, our archive payments came to over $30,000.

Part of the answer is to hunt for film in the public domain, such as film held by the National Archives. Where this is not possible, and where people are not willing to charge you nominal sums because your film idea is so great, you just have to budget adequately.

Even though archives usually publish a price per foot at which you can obtain their material, you may find it expedient to talk personally with the management. If they particularly like your film, they may arrange for you to have the rights at a reduced cost. Sometimes they will acknowledge that students aren't millionaires or big television corporations and will make allowances. It doesn't always work, but it's worth a try.

Insurance. We have insurance because of Murphy's law: what can go wrong will go wrong. If you are insured it helps you face chaos and catastrophe with a certain equanimity. Insurance should cover equipment, film, crew, properties, and third-party risk. Within reason it should be as wide as possible. You should insure the film during the shooting and up to the striking of a master negative, paying particular attention to faulty equipment and damage arising during processing. The usual compensation is the cost of reshooting.

However, insurance will not cover faulty original film stock. Therefore, be absolutely certain to test your stock before shooting. Nor will insurance cover damage and fogging by airport X rays. This is a severe hazard these days, and insurance used to be available. Unfortunately, most companies have now deleted such coverage. The only answer is to have the film hand-checked (not always possible) and/or carry the film in lead-lined bags. Most airport uathorities seem to be more aware these days of the dangers of X rays to film stock, and most machines state that they are safe for film up to 1000 ASA. That may be so, but my heart always trembles until I see a good processed film.

Sometimes you may need bad weather coverage, but this can be exorbitant. Usually I don't bother.

I always insure sets and properties as well as film equipment. I don't insure crews unless we are going on an overseas assignment. I also cover third-party risk in case the filming damages any property or any person. I didn't do this until one day my lights melted a plastic roof and almost set a school on fire. That was the only lesson I needed.

One thing to guard against is excessive insurance. It is possible to be too cautious and find yourself paying out enormous sums for risks that are hardly likely to occur except in someone's imagination. You can usually safeguard yourself on that issue by going to a reliable specialist film insurance broker.

Most insurance companies these days are unwilling to insure one individual film, preferring to work only on a yearly basis. The answer is a cooperative in which the insurance costs can be shared among various friends who between them will have several films going during the year.

Legal matters. At some point in your film, either in the negotiations with the sponsor or later, you may need to seek legal advice. This becomes particularly important if you are negotiating a split distribution deal or foreign sales. You may also need advice on the basic contract between yourself and the sponsor even if there seem to be few complications. It is therefore advisable to allow at least a token sum for this in the budget. Under the same argument you may wish to write in a sum to cover bookkeeping costs.

Personnel. Payments to the writer, director, and producer usually appear as lump sums, though the director may also be paid by the week. What should they be paid? There is no fixed rule, though many people pay the writer about 3 percent of the overall budget and the director about 12 percent. A lot depends on the bargaining position of the parties. If the writer is a member of the Writers' Guild, then you will have to pay at least union scale, and the same is true if the director is a member of the Directors' Guild of America (DGA). The situation becomes complicated if you want a DGA director, as you may have to sign a contract with the directors' union and also employ a Directors' Guild assistant.

Payment to the narrator varies according to his or her fame and bargaining power. A half-hour narration might be as low as a few hundred dollars or as high as a few thousand. If you want the best or the most well known, then you have to pay accordingly. If you have a really prestigious public service film, you may be able to get a "personality" to do your narration for free or for a token sum donated to charity.

General overheads. Overhead can amount to a surprisingly high proportion of your costs, and adequate allowance should be made for it in the budget. Thus you must think about office rent, telephone bills, secretarial help, transcripts, messengers, duplicating services, and any general help you will need. If you are shooting abroad you must add not only general travel costs for the crew, but also possible costs for film dispatch and customs clearance. Even if you bring the film back home by yourself the customs authorities may require an agent to clear it with them. So that's another item on your list.

Contingencies. However well you budget, you may find that the film costs are running away with you. The usual problems are that you need more shooting days than you thought or that the editing goes on longer than you reckoned. But the problem can be something else entirely. A few years ago, for instance, the Hunt brothers tried to corner the world's supplies of silver, and for a few months the price of silver rose astronomically. As a direct result film stock prices also suddenly rose. This meant that contracts signed before the rise did not adequately cover the real price of stock.

The contingency element in your budget shields you from the unexpected;

it's a hedge against overruns. I usually budget about 7.5 percent of the total budget as contingency. This sometimes leads to arguments with sponsors who fail to see why a budget cannot be 100 percent accurate. In that case I usually omit the contingency but specify in my contract with the sponsors a fixed number of shooting days and a fixed amount of stock. If more time or more stock is needed, then I get the sponsors to pay for these items.

Obviously, you have to use a certain amount of common sense and discretion in all this. It's no use arguing your rights, feeling your position is totally justified, and then losing the contract. This means that the contingency sometimes becomes mostly a matter for internal consideration: you budget, then add the 7.5 percent to see what a really comfortable budget should be. You then know both the preferred and the bare-bones cost for the film.

Profit margins. Should you put in a figure for company profit, and if so what should it be? People, and sponsors in particular, have a funny attitude on this score. They reckon that if you are the writer, director, and producer, then you should be satisfied for the amounts paid in these roles and should not ask for a company fee. This is nonsense and applies to no other business. If I run a garage, which is mine but registered in a company name, I expect both to be paid as manager and for the company to make a profit. The same reasoning is absolutely true in filmmaking. You may spend half a year making a film and the other half writing scripts, chasing down other projects, and trying to get various ideas off the ground. Meanwhile, rent has to be paid, taxes accounted for, and electricity and telephone bills settled. It is only the company profit element written into your film that allows you to exist the other half of the year.

That answers the first part of the question, but what should the profit margin be? This is hard to answer, but 15 percent is certainly within reason. However, that 15 percent is taken on the total budget *without* the contingency. Similarly, the contingency is taken on the original budget without the profit margin.

Videotape. There are a few differences, and most of them fairly obvious, between a budget for a film and a videotape. Clearly stock costs will be different, and items such as developing and printing will disappear. Your major changes will appear in postproduction. On some things you will save—no negative cut, no first answer print, etc.—but other costs can be exorbitant. On-line editing, one-inch work, and special effects can be very expensive, so check those elements thoroughly before signing on the dotted line.

The Production Contract

Once you have done a realistic budget breakdown you are in a good position to negotiate or finalize your contract with the sponsor. You may have made an informal agreement with them, but it's better to have a short memorandum in writing that records the basic terms of the agreement.

This is much safer in the long run. It's also wise to exchange contracts before you begin shooting, though a surprisingly large number of people plunge into the film on the assurance of a mere handshake. I wouldn't unless I knew the sponsor extremely well or if there were some compelling reason for starting in a rush, such as a necessary but one-time film event.

As I mentioned earlier, you may be dealing with the production contract before script or after script. In the following discussion I am assuming that the script has been approved and paid for and that we now need a production contract to enable us to go ahead. This may run to three pages or thirty, but in reality there are only a few points to consider, with all the rest being elaboration. I have set out below the main elements of most contracts and have tried to bring to your attention some of the points that you should consider in detail.

Definition of length and purpose. The contract will generally define in its first few paragraphs the kind of film you are doing, its object, its maximum length, and the gauge in which it is being shot. So it may read, "This is a one-hour, 16mm color film on the treatment of deafness for use in specialist schools," or it may say, "This is a half-hour videotape on frog jumping for educational television." These first few paragraphs may be surrounded by "whereases" and "wherefores," but that's just legal jargon that you need not worry about. The main thing is that you understand clearly what you are contracting to deliver.

Time and manner of delivery. The sponsor will try to get you to commit to a specific delivery date. Here you have to be careful because of the immense number of things that can go wrong, causing you to miss the deadline. I prefer to put in a definition of intent rather than commitment: "The filmmaker will endeavor to deliver the film by such and such a date," or, "The filmmaker understands that the film is due for presentation on 15 July 1990." Avoid being penalized for late delivery. This is important as, even with the best will in the world, many things cause delay. Normally the sponsor understands why the film is delayed and is sympathetic, but not always. So watch out.

The contract may also specify how many prints are to be delivered. I usually put in one, with any others to be paid for by the sponsor. I also ask for the CRI (the combined reversal internegative, used in making multiple prints) to be paid for by the sponsor.

If you are doing a videotape, the sponsor may require not just the three-quarter-inch cassette but a one-inch master.

In some contracts the sponsor asks for all the rushes and the negative to be handed over at the conclusion of the film. This is fine in most cases, but if you have film that may be valuable in the future as stock footage, then try to hang on to the negative.

Personal responsibility. Some contracts may demand that certain people do specific jobs; this usually concerns the writer and the director. The clause is fair enough, especially when the film is the very special baby of one of those two. However, you should allow yourself an escape hatch in case of unforeseeable factors such as illness.

Film cost and payment schedule. The agreement should state clearly both the overall sum that the sponsors will pay for the film and the times of payment. In most cases payment will be made in stages, and you should try to ensure that those payments come at convenient times. A typical payment schedule on a $100,000 film might look like this:

1. $10,000 on signing the contract
2. $10,000 on script approval
3. $30,000 on commencement of shooting
4. $20,000 when shooting is completed and editing starts
5. $10,000 on approval of fine cut
6. $10,000 on completion of mix
7. $10,000 on delivery of print

Sometimes the number of stages is reduced to only three or four, which might be (1) signing contract, (2) commencing shooting, (3) approval of rough cut, and (4) delivery.

There is, of course, a rationale behind the timing of the payments: you should have all the necessary money at hand when you need it. Your big costs are going to be shooting and editing, so you need money in advance to cover these stages. You also need money for your own salary and living expenses; hence, I like to receive about 20 percent by the time the script is approved.

One common bugbear is the sponsor who procrastinates on approvals. This can happen on approval of the fine cut or of the final narration. Unless you are careful you can find yourself in an exasperating situation, waiting weeks for payments while the sponsor plays around with small changes. One way around this is to put in specific dates as well as film points for payment. Thus, you could specify $10,000 payment on approval of the fine cut or on 5 February, whichever comes earlier. The sponsor may or may not agree with this point, but it's worth battling for.

Can you ask for extra payments besides the principal sum? The contract usually stipulates a total fee for the delivery of the film, and once that sum is on paper, that's it. Hence the importance, as I have stressed before, of very accurate budgeting.

If I am doubtful about the number of shooting days or if the sponsor argues for the inclusion of something that I am not sure about, I try to put in a clause covering additional payments. The clause might read, "The sponsor will pay for any additional days shooting at the rate of $1000 per day and will also pay for any film stock used on that day at cost." I am not fond of this kind of additional clause, and neither is the sponsor. But sometimes it may be the only way to safeguard your neck or your pocket.

For videotapes, you have to watch very carefully to see if the sponsor wants you to employ all sorts of cute video effects. They may, as I have mentioned, turn out to be horrendously expensive, and you want to be sure your contractual sum covers this. If you think the sponsor may suddenly dump on you the idea of high-cost DVEs (digital video effects) when you are nearing the end of the film, then protect yourself with an item regarding extra payments.

Approvals. The contract should stipulate someone who can act as the sponsor's agent and give approval at various stages of the film. Try to make sure this is someone you know (it usually is) who understands the film and whose judgment you value. In most cases the person giving the approval is the person with whom you have been dealing from the first discussions of the film, but not always. Sometimes the sponsor decides that some top executive has to give approval. From then on it's all a matter of luck. Get somebody who is intelligent and sympathetic and understands a little about film, and you're home and dry. Get the opposite—and it happens—and you're in trouble. So keep your fingers crossed, or better, insist that the person giving approval is someone you know.

Insurance. I have listed insurance as an item in the film budget itself and one of the responsibilities that you, as filmmaker, have to take care of. Sometimes, however, you can get the sponsor to take care of the subject or at least to share responsibility. Many companies and television stations have insurance policies that may cover your filming. Your task is then to make sure the company includes your film on their insurance list. Even if that is not the case, the sponsor may have so much at stake in your film that it will take out insurance on the film itself, up to the making of the master. This will still leave you to insure crew and equipment, but it will save you quite a lot of money.

Ownership. You need to establish from the start what rights you have in the film. Even though you are the contracted producer-director, you may be able to argue that the sponsor should share eventual ownership with you. There are also questions of ancillary rights and extra-payments for foreign sales. The Directors' Guild of America, for example, has stringent clauses regarding residuals that directors must receive on certain distribution deals relating to their films.

If you enter into a coproduction deal with a PBS station, then the station itself will probably provide their standard contract. This usually calls for joint raising of the production funds, an equal share of the profits, and for each PBS member station to show the film four times within three years.

Miscellaneous contract clauses. The above items take care of the most important points, but there is no limit to the things people will dream up to put into a contract. So what else can arise?

Contracts are drawn up by lawyers who try to protect their clients from every catastrophe, real or imagined. Their answer is to put in the necessary, the unnecessary, and then some. There may be a discussion of publicity. You may be asked to take stills. You may be requested to refrain from immoral conduct. You may be asked not to hold yourself out as an agent of the sponsor. You may be told that though the film is being made and edited in England, it will be governed by United States law. You may be told that all notices to the sponsor have to be written in red ink and hand-delivered to the office before ten o'clock in the morning.

I have already stressed the points that are vital for you, the filmmaker, and they are covered above. As for anything else the lawyers write in, look it over carefully and try not to laugh at the more nonsensical points. Then use common sense. If you feel that an obligation is unfair, reject it. You may have to explain your objection at some length, but don't accept the clause just because someone has written it in.

Remember one thing. At this point the sponsors want you to make the film as much as you do, so don't be afraid of arguing controversial points with them and looking after your own position. If you don't, no one else will.

Finally, if a lot of money is involved and you feel uneasy about your obligations or uncertain as to what you are really committing to, get yourself a lawyer—not one who merely sells real estate, but one who understands something about the entertainment business. It's costly, but the advice will probably pay for itself.

10
Preproduction

Once you have signed the production contract you are ready to begin the film. You are now in for a period of work that can take any where from two months to a year or more and falls into three distinct sections: preproduction, production, and postproduction. This chapter deals with the problems and tasks you are likely to encounter during the preproduction phase and all the arrangements you have to make before shooting. It assumes the script has been approved and you can move into action. This is a tremendously important period. Time and effort invested here in coherent planning, which is the essence of preproduction, pays off immensely when you come to the actual shooting.

During preproduction you have to attend to the following matters:

1. Reviewing people and location
2. Selecting the crew
3. Selecting equipment
4. Drawing up the shooting schedule
5. Obtaining permissions
6. Dealing with problems of foreign locations

Preproduction is also a good period to look a few more times at the script. In writing it one of your key considerations was that it be accepted by the sponsor: you are now beyond that stage, and you should probably reconsider the script as a plan of action. Preproduction is a useful time to stand back and ask yourself, "Does it really say something? Does it have vision? Does it have a point of view? Are the main ideas still valid?" This questioning is not a once-and-for-all process. It should be something that goes on at least subconsciously through all the film stages. But the preproduction period is an especially good time to do this because you can still change a lot of things, whereas once you start filming such changes become much harder and more expensive.

Reviewing People and Location

During preproduction, try to revisit all the filming locations and talk once more to the main people who will appear in the film. The location review (on which I often take the cameraman) helps first of all to refamiliarize you with the subject matter. A few months may have passed since you did the scouting and research, and things may have changed. The review also helps you sort out practical questions such as parking and security. You are also now looking at the locations from a slightly different perspective, with a director's eye rather than a writer's eye. When you come with the crew what will be the best shots? Which direction does the sun come up? Should you plan to shoot that building in the morning when it's in shade, or in the afternoon when it's sunlit?

This is also a time to meet again with your key film participants and anyone else who is going to help you. The meetings serve both a psychological and practical purpose. First, it may be beneficial to talk over the film in a little more detail with your on-camera interviewees and explain to them what you want to do. It's a time to put their minds at rest about how difficult it will all be and about how much their lives will be disturbed. This is also a time to get to know them better: to explore who they are, what they will say, how they might appear on camera, and if anything new and important has happened to them since you last met. You should also work on establishing a real trust between yourself and the participants or the interviewees. I cannot stress enough how important this is; it has always seemed to me that documentary directing is more about trust than finding the right camera positions. You should also use this time to examine scheduling possibilities. When are your participants free? When do they do those particular operations at the hospital? When do the main business meetings take place? What is the actual date of the school graduation? Who do you have to contact when you come to film? How many days in advance do they need to know?

One particular point that calls for your attention is future lighting options. For example, it was only while doing a preproduction "recce" that I noticed that the hospital where I wanted to film used electrical outlets totally different from those normally used. Had that been overlooked we would have been in serious trouble. Again, check how much power is available and how accessible it is.

Selecting the Crew

A tremendous amount of any film's success depends on the selection of the crew. Pick the right crew for the job and you start with a tremendous plus. Select the wrong crew and you're heading for disaster. You need to consider three factors in selecting your crew: size, function, and temperament.

Size. Should you use a large or a small crew? My own preference is for the smallest crew possible, at least in shooting intimate human situations. At such a time a large crew gets in the way of the subject matter, distancing people and disrupting privacy and human connections. Most people are tremendously wary of filmmakers. So when you come into someone's home asking questions of a personal or painful nature, the fewer people around the better.

What is a few? I would say director, cameraman, assistant cameraman, and soundman. Often in intimate situations you can get the assistant cameraman to do lights. If that's impossible, then the electrician or gaffer can complete the crew. If you really want to cut down the crew, then you as director can handle the sound. Similarly, the director can take over the job of production manager and the driving can be shared. If that's impossible, the production manager and driver should keep their distance during the filming. Obviously, at some point cutting the crew doesn't make sense. If you have a big production job, with a lot of organization and on-the-spot problems, you will probably need to add a production manager, general assistant, grip, perhaps an extra electrician, and a driver.

One thing to sort out right at the beginning of the film is whether it is being done with a union or nonunion crew. Sometimes you may have an option, but if you are doing your film for television or within a television station you may not have the option. If you are doing the film with a union crew, then you must familiarize yourself with the appropriate union rules. These cover working procedures, hours, breaks, food allowances, and the like. They also often cover travel conditions, such as first-class flights over a certain distance.

If you are acting as producer, then the choice of the crew will be in your hands. If you are director, with a producer over you, you must make sure that the crew is selected, as far as possible, according to your directions and instructions. Here the battle is often for a crew of the right size, with the producer trying to save money by giving you an inadequately small crew or low-cost personnel who are not equal to the job.

Function. Naturally, you want the best people for the crew, with each job clearly defined. I try to work again and again with the same people, whose work I know and trust, but this can't always be done. When you are taking on unknown personnel, try to check them out with people who have worked with them. Try to find out both the professional factors and the human factors. Can they do their jobs not just competently but creatively? What are they like under stress? What are their best points and their faults? If I am taking on a new cameraman, I want to see examples of previous work and talk to other directors who have used him or her. And invariably I will want to sit and chat with the prospective cameramen to get my own overall impression before committing myself.

The main problems I have had with personnel have occurred when I have worked for television companies and have had to accept staff cameramen. Sometimes they have been terrific, but a few times I have had cameramen who were bored, burned out, just waiting for retirement. In those cases the film suffered by having to use someone who was uninterested in the film and the job.

The functions of the different personnel are usually well delineated.

The soundman looks after the sound quality of the location recordings. He or she needs to be an expert on equipment and microphones and also a person of taste and sensibility, with a sensitive ear for what is being recorded.

The *assistant cameraman* is usually picked by the principal cameraman, since the two must work closely. Among other things, the assistant will check equipment, lenses, and filters, will change magazines and keep the camera clean, and will generally set up and carry the equipment. As the key assistant to the cameraman, he or she will often act as focus changer on difficult scenes and will assist with lights on a small shoot.

The *electrician* or *gaffer* is in charge of the lights, a job that carries both heavy artistic and technical responsibilities. Although it is the job of the cameraman to define the lighting style, on a documentary film the gaffer often has considerable leeway for decisions. Gaffers may be told specifically what lights to rig and where, but they may also be told very vaguely, "Key light from here, back light from there," and be on their own to carry out the job. Besides being experts in lighting styles, gaffers must also know everything about kinds of lights and their maintenance and about electrical systems. Does the small house have an adequate power supply? Should a special electrical board be brought in for the filming? What will the use of twenty-five kilowatts of electricity do to the supplies in the concert hall?

Besides letting the cameraman choose the assistant cameraman, I also consult with him or her on the choice of a gaffer. The two will be working hand in hand, and if the gaffer knows the cameraman's style and method of work, that's a great help to the production.

The *grip* is the muscle of the group, with the task of helping with all the heavy jobs. Grips may carry equipment, help with the lights, or drive. They handle the odd jobs and may be called on to help in many undefined capacities. On a small production the assistant cameraman may also function as a grip; on a larger production, that will be a separate job.

I rarely take a *production manager* (or PM) on a small shoot; instead, I do most of those jobs myself. But when the job is quite arduous I do take a PM—if the budget allows it and if the extra person doesn't disturb the shooting. The PM is the general manager of the shoot. Together with the director, he or she draws up the shooting schedule and points out any problems that may be involved in the plan. The PM will handle advance preparations, take care of travel, hotels, and food, and look after the money. One of the tasks of the PM is to spot difficulties in advance and troubleshoot when they happen. The PM goes into action when the camera breaks down, when the rental company doesn't have the right van, when officialdom gets difficult, and when the spare stock fails to arrive.

Obviously we are looking here for someone who is highly intelligent, organized, and fast—a man or woman of action. These super people do exist, and they are worth their weight in gold.

Choosing the right *cameraman* is your most important crew selection decision. Though the film's success depends on many people, the cameraman's work is crucial. Together with the director, he or she is responsible for shot selection, lighting style, and all the camera movements. It goes without saying that the cameraman has to have a creative eye. But he or she also needs to have fast reactions for news or verite style shooting and the strength to carry and use a heavy shoulder camera if there is extensive hand-held shooting.

In recent years films have often credited the "cameraman director," and some of the best documentaries have been made by this double-functioned personality. But is the combination of cameraman and director good policy? In some films not only does it make sense, but it may be the only way to get the film made. This is particularly true of cinema verite and observational cinema. On *Salesman* Al Maysles had to be both director and cameraman, and the same was true when Jon Else shot his film about the de Bolt family of California. I prefer, however, to have the two jobs done by different people. When a cameraman's eye is on the lens, he cannot usually be aware of all the nuances in a situation. The director has more distance, is less involved, and can be more aware of the overall scene rather than the particular detail. The director can also listen more carefully and see how the conversation is going to affect action.

I don't believe that there is an ideal cameraman, but I do believe that there is an ideal person for each film. However, the cameraman who is ideal for film A may be disastrously wrong for film B. It's all a question of style and situation. Some years back I shot a film on art and artists. We had ample shooting time and a very controllable film situation. We also had a heavy lighting job. As lighting cameraman I chose a friend of mine called Robert. Bob was marvelous at composition, provided he had plenty of time, and he was also an artist with light. Exactly what I needed. Six months later I shot a sports film and Bob was the last person I thought of contacting. On the sports film I needed someone who was fast and decisive, someone with both news and verite experience, someone who would essentially be picking the shots without my help. Although he was a superb cameraman, Bob just didn't have the skills or the temperament for that situation.

More than any other crew relationship, the director-cameraman relationship is that of partnership. Together they will plan the style of the film, and once the filming starts they become almost inseparable. Sometimes there will be difficulties and divisions of opinion between the director and cameraman (more of that later when we discuss directing), but the more the two understand each other, the better the film will be.

One last point is that it makes sense to take the cameraman on a location scout before filming starts. The cameraman's eye will be able to spot production difficulties, and he or she will also be able to advise you on the kind and amount of lighting you need for the shoot.

Temperament. Making a film tends to be an all-consuming operation, at least during the shooting. For many people nothing else exists during that period except the film itself and the other members of the crew. Although this is particularly true for features, it also describes the conditions on many documentaries. During filming, whether for one week or seven, whether in New York or New Guinea, your crew tends to become your family. Therefore, when you choose your crew it is worthwhile looking at their temperament as well as their skills. I always hope that the filming will be interesting and fun, and I want people to join me on the crew who share that attitude.

Often the filming is done under tremendous pressure, in frightful conditions, and far away from home. All that tends to bring out both the best and the worst in people, so you look for people in whom the first comes out and not the second. I am generally wary of morose, silent types, however good their professional skills. On location I want someone with me who is cheerful, bright, and has at least an elementary sense of humor. I don't necessarily need someone who is going to be my bosom friend for life, but I do prefer people with whom I can comfortably relax and have a drink at the end of a difficult day.

Though I think informality is necessary among small crews, it is also extremely important that there be a clear working structure, that everybody knows what they have to do and when, and that the ultimate decisions are made by the director.

One thing that is always interesting to see is how the separate individuals gradually bond into a cohesive team. That usually happens on the third or the fourth day of shooting, or after some mishap has been solved and can be laughed at. When that bond comes, the film stops being just work and becomes a real pleasure.

Sometimes, however, even with the best-selected crews, tension suddenly arises. And it can happen for all sorts of silly reasons, such as one member of the crew feeling that a second isn't pulling his or her weight. Once you become aware of that tension it needs to be settled immediately, or it festers. Usually a private talk will do the trick; if not, try to get the matter out into the open, discussed, and assigned to the past.

Selecting Equipment

Although this is not a book about equipment, it is a subject with which every director must deal, so a few short notes are appropriate. Equipment choice should be a matter for crew discussion rather than the sole decision of the director. The function of the director is to tell the crew all he or she can about the film's style, shape, difficulties, and objectives and then make decisions about equipment with them. The goal should be to use the simplest but most effective equipment compatible with the nature of the film and the size of the budget.

In selecting a camera, you need to discuss whether your shooting is basically static or mobile and whether a lot of hand-held shooting will be required. Will you need a single-frame option or variable speeds? Do you require special lenses? What about filters? Does any of the shooting require dolly tracks? And since you are going abroad into the jungle, should you perhaps take a spare camera?

You will also need to discuss stock. Since you have gone on a preliminary "recce" with the cameraman, he or she will know whether to recommend normal or high-speed film, Kodak or Fuji, and whether to work in negative or reversal. The cameraman will also know whether your preference is for shooting with available light whatever the conditions, or whether you want plenty of light to give a feature quality to the production. Again, that discussion will influence the choice of stock.

The soundman needs to know who and what you want to record and where. Given that information he or she can choose a recorder (probably his standard Nagra) and, very important, the appropriate microphones. If you are going to film a concert, the sound technician will know to bring microphones of types X and Y, and if you want to do interviews without a boom, he or she will also know to bring microphone A and B.

Lighting equipment must be thoroughly planned in advance because it is often too cumbersome or bulky to be replaced in a hurry in some remote outback. In most cases the lighting will be chosen by the director, cameraman, and gaffer in consultation. Lighting is the bane of most directors because it takes so much time to set up and can be such a pain once it's standing. I like to go for the simplest and the lightest. This often leads to arguments with cameramen who fear for the quality of the filming. My counterargument is that I want to go in fast and film the family while they are all fresh and haven't waited hours for the crew to get ready.

Equipment always goes wrong; that's why I go for the strongest, the simplest, and the most reliable. I also try to cut down on all the extras which the technicians swear they need to bring but which experience has proved to be unnecessary. On the other hand, certain items always seem to be scarce—spare lamps, connection cables, and pin boxes. Here I bring more than is necessary and have never regretted that decision.

Drawing Up the Shooting Schedule

When all the preliminaries are over, you are finally ready to draw up the shooting schedule. This is normally the work of the director and the production manager together. The main responsibility is the director's, but the PM is there to double-check all the ideas, to ensure that the schedule is feasible, and then to put the first scheduling decisions into action.

The shooting schedule is a plan of work for the shooting. Theoretically it should take all the problems involved in the shooting and solve them in the simplest, most practical, and most economical way. The schedule tells you what to film, who to film, and when and where this should all take place. Before you can do this you need certain information at your fingertips. Assuming you have fourteen days of shooting starting 1 June, you will probably need to know

- anticipated weather at your locations
- people's availability (checked out on your second visit)
- distances between locations
- any public holidays
- any special happenings such as school graduation, etc.

With this information, you can begin to break down the script and juggle the shooting to maximize shooting freedom.

The first thing to do is to go through the script and list all the filming that has to be done in one location and the people involved during the filming. You may finish up with something like this:

New York: Leon's house, scenes 3, 5, 21, 33, 45
           Leon's office, scenes 7, 10, 18
           Mayor's office, scenes 9, 24
           Joe's party, scene 1
New Jersey: Diana's garden, scenes 2, 8, 14

You will go right through the script in this way, listing who is in each scene. At this stage I also like to list all the photographs and any stock footage that I will need. My list will also include any special requirements for a scene, whether technical, such as special lenses, or practical, such as ordering drinks and food for a party.

Once you have the script breakdown you start adding other considerations, and then the complications start. Personally I like to start off the shoot with a few easy days. This allos the crew to assess each others' pace and working habits and also allows you to see how the equipment is performing. With this in mind, you start drawing up your daily shooting list. At first this is very tentative because you have to juggle so many elements. Let's say on your first day you have five scenes in mind. If you want to see whether it's feasible to do them, what questions should you be asking?

- If we want to start in the office at ten, what time will we have to leave the hotel?
- How long will it take to set up lighting?

- Once the lighting is up, how long will the shooting take?
- If we finish at eleven, can we be at Lincoln Center by twelve?
- When should we break for lunch?
- Can we do three scenes by five, get the stuff from the hotel and be at the airport by seven to catch the seven-thirty flight to Atlanta?
- Will the crew eat on the plane or expect a meal in Atlanta?
- We will probably be working form 8 A.M. until 10 P.M. Isn't that too long for a first day?

Depending on your answers, you may stay with your first tentative schedule or juggle it to allow more freedom. Your considerations each time are fairly simple: how much time do you need for preparation, lighting, meals, breaks, travel, and shooting. If you are unsure of the way your crew works or the difficulty of the scenes, it's best to be pessimistic rather than optimistic, allowing more time rather than less time for the shooting. I am always wary of beautiful schedules that look magnificent on paper but fail in practice. Something always goes wrong on a shoot. A camera breaks down; an interviewee suddenly has an urgent appointment. You overcome these difficulties in two ways. First, you make your schedule flexible rather than rigid: if you suddenly cannot film Diana in the morning, you can substitute the library sequence and film Diana in the afternoon. Second, every third or fourth day you should leave a couple of hours in the schedule totally open for fill-ins and emergencies. If there are no crises you will always find something to film, but if you have lost time or lost an interview, then the open periods in the schedule come as a godsend.

Obtaining Permissions

If you have not done it before, you must, at the point of scheduling, begin to consider the question of permissions. Are there points in the shooting where you will need permission to work? Have you discussed that permission, and do you have it in writing? If you are interviewing people in their homes or offices, then their word is probably enough (but watch for higher officialdom wanting to get into the act). Most public places, however—such as parks, museums, railways, and official institutions—require written permission.

One thing to watch is that you have asked for *all* the necessary permissions and not just some of them. For example, a few years ago I wanted to film a concert rehearsal. I spoke to the manager of the theater and the manager of the orchestra and all was well. When I came to film, however, the orchestra at first refused to participate. No one had asked *their* permission directly or explained the filming to them. In the end we went on with the shoot, but there were a few anxious moments.

Another point to check is that, as far as possible, your permission is flexible regarding date and time of shooting. Sometimes you arrange to shoot on a Monday and then have to shoot on a Tuesday. Obviously, you try to tell the authorities in advance this will happen. Sometimes you can't, and then it's tremendously frustrating to find yourself confronted by some petty official who takes pleasure in wielding power and stands by the letter of the law that you have permission only for Monday.

Though this strictly comes later, you should also consider the *personal release form* under the heading of permissions. This is a piece of paper, signed by a film participant, allowing you to use the footage in which he or she appears. Normally you ask orally permission to shoot, and then get the signed release when the shooting is completed. Such a release is usually a matter of safety rather than necessity. Few states or countries have rules about privacy, and filming someone on the street is not a basis for legal action. If such a person wants to take you to court, he or she must prove harm. That's normally quite difficult, but it can happen. You shoot a man kissing a woman who turns out not to be his wife, and he then claims your film implies that he is an adulterer. But that's the rare case. So why does one bother with a release? For safety's sake!

The release stops someone you have filmed from making trouble for you at the most inopportune moment. You have filmed a woman talking very frankly about her boss. A week before broadcast the interviewee gets frightened and goes to court to stop the broadcast, claiming that she has been harmed and never gave her permission. The judge cannot possibly hear the issue in one week, but in order to protect the plaintiff's rights issues an injunction to stop the broadcast until the case has been decided. The plaintiff's weapon, used to obtain money or out of genuine fear, is that injunction, because in practice she could probably never win the case. Showing the court the release form stops any threat of an injunction against the film.

Some people insist that you should pay one dollar for the release to make it legal. I don't hold with that argument. The dollar is necessary as consideration if your whole aim is to make a contract. But what you are really doing is getting proof of agreement, which is different. My own feelings are that offering money leads to more complications than it solves, and I have never done it.

Many people use releases on every occasion. I don't. If I am filming a street scene I don't get releases from passersby or from the people I talk to casually. Again, if I am filming in a home and it seems clear that the interviewee has given permission (otherwise why would they appear?), I don't ask for permission. This has been my practice when I film privately, and so far I have never come to grief. Most television stations, however, will insist that you produce releases for every interview; they prefer to err on the side of caution.

Obviously, it's valuable, perhaps even necessary, to get releases when you are filming in a very tricky, painful, or potentially embarrassing situation. For example, I always ask for releases when filming in hospitals, schools, or prisons. In those situations you may really be at risk without the releases. Even with releases you sometimes have to beware. Fred Wiseman obtained permissions from the superintendent of prisons and commissioner of correction when filming *Titicut Follies*, yet he still ran into trouble.

Many cities require that you receive police permission if you want to film in the streets and have to put down a tripod. The theory is that you could tie up traffic or cause a nuisance. The permission also soothes the cop who approaches and wants to know what you are doing. Many times you don't have time to get permission so you just shoot, and nobody will give a damn. But you are at risk, so the time spent getting permission is usually time well spent.

Shooting Abroad

When you want to shoot abroad a tremendous number of extra problems arise, from different weather to extricating yourself from a revolution, and you must try to consider all the difficulties in the preproduction stage. Your aims are to shoot all you need, stay healthy, and come back with all your footage and all your crew. In most cases you won't have a chance to retake, so your planning has to be especially good. The first thing to do is to hire a special production manager familiar with all the ins and outs of the country you are going to and listen to him or her very carefully. Your main questions will involve the following:

- What can you shoot and do you need permisson?
- What is the state of officialdom? Do people expect to be paid off for their help?
- What is the political state of the country?
- Do you have to declare what you are shooting?
- Is your film open to censorship?
- What is the weather like?
- Are there good medical facilities?

In other words, a good part of your questioning will relate to bureaucratic practices in the country you're visiting. A second series of questions relates to stock, equipment, and crew:

- Is raw stock available?
- Are there good labs?
- If equipment goes wrong, can it easily be replaced or repaired, or do you need to bring spares?
- How does local weather affect film stock?
- Are there facilities for sending the stock home?

My experience in shooting in Eastern Europe is that most of these countries will insist that you have a government official with you during all the filming, and some countries also insist that you use a local crew. The question of crew is also important in budgeting. If, for example, you are an American shooting in England or France, it may be worth your while to pick up a local crew rather than bring one from home.

One of the main questions you will be faced with is customs arrangements and getting film and equipment in and out of the different countries. Here forewarned is forearmed. Many countries make tremendous problems when you try either to bring in film and equipment or to take it out. Rules and regulations are often produced out of thin air, and confronted with them you feel like committing murder.

Your two best solutions to these problems are a highly efficient local agent and a PM who knows everything and everybody, and a *carnet de passage*. A *carnet de passage* is a customs document that you obtain in your own country, usually from your local chamber of commerce, for a small sum. It has a page for each country you are going to visit and lists in detail all the equipment and stock you are carrying. When you arrive in a country, the local customs will check your baggage and stamp the form, and will do the same when you exit. The forms act as a guarantee that you won't leave film or stock in the country, thus relieving you of the necessity of paying duty when you enter or leave. The *carnet* also serves another useful function: it relieves you of most of the problems with customs when you return to your own country as it proves that all the equipment not only returned with you, but also departed with you.

A word on excess baggage: this problem always confronts you, whether you are filming abroad or in your own country. Given the amount of equipment you are carrying—camera, tripods, lights, and so forth—you almost always finish up very heavily loaded. If you are traveling by train or car, that doesn't matter. But if you are traveling by plane, overweight means extra payment. Knowing this, talk to the baggage master before the flight. Point out the frequency with which your company or the television company uses the airline. Bring a letter from the airline's public relations division promising you help for a small mention in the film. In other words, anticipate the problem and use every stratagem to get the excess payments reduced or even ignored.

If shooting time and travel time are difficult to assess at home, they are doubly difficult overseas. This is particularly true of Africa, India, the Far East, and South America. Trains due to depart in the morning depart in the afternoon, if at all. Often you can't get a guaranteed departure on a plane, and even then the plane develops strange ailments, like chickens flying through the engine, which happened to me in India. If you are aware in advance that such problems will happen, you can prepare your shooting schedule accordingly. Your headaches may be no less, but your emotions will be calmer.

Once you have thought through all your problems, you are in a position to prepare the final shooting schedule. When this has been done, give a copy to every member of the crew and discuss it with them to see whether it really is practical or if you have left out anything. Besides saying what you will film and where, the schedule should also contain all the travel information regarding planes, hotels, and the like, and also all the addresses and telephone numbers of where you will be and local contacts. As you can see, a tremendous amount of thinking and energy will have been expended before the shooting schedule is finalized. Believe me, it's worth every drop of effort. Plan well, and half the battle is over.

Part III
Production

11

The Director
Prepares

The purpose of this and the following two chapters is to look at the attitude and working methods of the documentary director, offering a few hints to ease a path that is difficult but ultimately tremendously rewarding.

Up to production and location shooting, many of the director's responsibilities could, in theory, be shared. When shooting starts, however, the full responsibility for the film falls on the shoulders of the director. His or her job is to create or find the pieces that will come together in the editing to make a complete film. If a director fouls up in a feature film it may be possible to reshoot. If a documentary director makes a mistake on a one time event, there may be no film to speak of. So the responsibilities are quite high.

It is not so difficult to define the image of the documentary director, which has changed tremendously since the days of Robert Flaherty and John Grierson, as it is to clarify the role. In certain films the role of the documentary director will be similar to that of the feature director: setting up shots and telling people how to move and what to do. The similarities to the feature director's role are, however, superficial. The substance of documentary differs vastly from that of features, since you are dealing with reality, not fiction. Because the quest of the documentary director is different from that of the feature director, different qualities are called for in directing. While both share the necessity of understanding film language and film grammar, the vision, purpose, and general working methods of the documentary director diverge radically from those of the feature filmmaker.

Demands on the Director

What are the demands made on directors? What kind of people should they be, and what skills should they have?

First, the director must obviously have excellent technical skills. This kind of knowledge is absolutely essential. Most books that purport to give instructions on directing are really talking about technical problems of shooting and maintaining continuity. I assume that the first thing film students do is read these books, so I don't want to waste much time going over familiar territory. I prefer to use this book for discussing how one *thinks* about film. However, it seems worthwhile to set out a checklist of technical points and elementary directing.

1. *Camera movement.* We are talking here of pans, tilts, crabs, tracks, and dollies. You should know what they are and what motivates their use.

2. *Continuity.* The main problems here are maintaining correct screen direction between shots and proper continuity between sequences. Any good book on editing will tell you all you need to know.

3. *Motivating the viewer.* This is the first rule in directing. You guide your viewer into almost demanding certain shots. A man raises a knife and looks down. Obviously the audience wants to know who he's looking at, so your next shot is the victim.

4. *Cutaways.* These are shots that help you condense time and shift point of view in a sequence where you might have a problem with screen direction. Most beginning documentary filmmakers tend to take too few. They realize this error when they come to edit.

5. *Shot impact.* Are you paying attention to the emotional impact of the shot, such as moving in close for intensity and emotion? And do you remember those old guidelines about shooting from below when you want a character to dominate the screen and from above when you want to diminish him or her?

6. *Lenses.* Do you know the impact on the film of using different lenses, such as the long lens to slow down action and pack things together?

All of these points are elementary but worth review.

My own attitute about technical matters and guidelines for directing is simple. First, I want to know as much about the subject as possible because the rules reflect long experience. Once I have the knowledge I can decide whether to stay with the rules or break them. Second, I want to know as much about technical matters as possible because only then am I really in command and not subject to the whims and wishes of my crew, however much I love them. The more you know about filming, whether technical or human, the better position you will be in as a director.

In addition to technical knowledge, the documentary director must also have the vision and attitude appropriate to the genre. The point is that although we use the word "directing" of both features and documentary, for half of the time we are talking about two different things. Many documentaries can be written, set up, and shot as if they were features. But a sizable number of documentaries require an entirely different mind-set and mode of work. And there begins the problem for the director. In these documentaries—and they are not confined to news, current affairs, and cinema verite—there may be no script at all and hardly anything that you can plan in advance. With luck you go into the film with a series of notes and a rough idea where you want to go and how you want to proceed; you plunge in and hope for the best. Things will happen unexpectedly. You discover the film as you proceed. As events unfold, you try to understand their significance and grab their essence. You try to see the important details and how they will build to a significant whole.

This is what half the world of documentary filmmaking is like, and it resembles feature filmmaking as much as a lion resembles a mouse. More important, it makes tremendously different demands on the director. Given all that, what do we require of the director?

Clarity of purpose. As a director, you must be absolutely sure where you want to go and how you want to get there. You must know clearly what you want the film to say. In short, you must be sure of your focus. If the focus isn't there, the film is heading for trouble.

A friend of mine made a film about her family, which had five thousand members. The family had come to California four generations previously and had helped develop the state. The family name had become a household word, but this fame was not always welcomed by the family members. A few of them felt burdened by the name and history and wanted independence. My friend Jane came to me when the family was planning to hold a massive reunion in San Francisco, which she wanted to use as the backbone of the film. That made sense, but as Jane continued talking I grew more and more uneasy because she resisted committing herself to a definite focus.

The film was potentially interesting in many directions: it could have been a story about maintaining family links in the late twentieth century; it could have been a story about the development of California; it could have been a story of two or three European immigrants who made good. But it had to be one story. Jane refused to see that this was a problem that had to be resolved before filming; instead, she just plunged in, shooting a bit of this and a bit of that. Once editing started it was clear that there was no point of view and no rationale behind much of the shooting. In the end, the film was passable and fairly entertaining, but if Jane had made some stronger decisions in the beginning, it might have been superb.

Style. Similarly, it is important for the director to establish the style of the film at the beginning and then maintain consistency throughout the work. The style may involve action, flashbacks, humor, satire. It may be moody, poetic, evocative, or bright, harsh, ultrarealistic. The main thing is that the style should be consistent and that the director should be aware of what he or she is doing. Obviously, you can take risks and change style midway, but this often confuses the viewer. Novelists like John Fowles do this all the time; *The Magus*, for example, changes style and direction half a dozen times. Such changes are a much riskier proposition in film, though they can be done.

One of the best examples of a sudden change in style appears in a film I mentioned earlier, *The Road to Wigan Pier* by Frank Cvitanovich. Three quarters of the film evokes the 1930s using George Orwell's text and archive footage. The last quarter of the film shows the film's symbolic worker-singer watching television footage of British politicians. It's a drastic shift in style, but it works because the underlying theme is strong enough to sustain the change of place and mood and because the film itself suggests from the start that its style is experimental and humorous.

The lessons are simple. Consider at length what style you want before you begin filming, then stick with it. If you want to break or change your style, think through the pros and cons very carefully. What you should avoid at all costs is shifting styles without reason.

Ability to listen. As we know from so many books, many feature directors tend to talk and order rather than listen. The image of Otto Preminger, for example, was that of a martinet who commanded rather than directed and who would listen to no one. Perhaps that will do for features, but it just does not work in documentary. The documentary director must maintain authority and command, but above all else he or she must be able to listen—to observe, absorb, and pay attention. This stricture applies to both people and scenes. You are trying to understand complex human beings, their behavior and motivation, their pain and their happiness. On a wider scale you are trying to understand a scene, a group, or a society. You are trying to understand so that ultimately you can pass on your observations to a general audience. In order to do this you have to listen. There is no other way.

Decision-making ability. Decision making is the essence of directing. The difficulty in documentary is that many of the decisions have to be made with little preparation and no forewarning. Decision making on documentaries that can be prewritten and preplanned is relatively easy. The exploration of a university, for instance (discussed earlier), calls for decisions of a fairly simple type. You know in advance who, where, and when you want to film, and then it becomes basically a managerial and technical job. You make sure that you have enough shots to edit and that you have pulled the essence out of the scene.

The difficult decisions come in unplanned films, where no event can be foreseen and the situation is constantly changing. There you need your wits to establish immediately what is important and where or on whom the camera should be focused. Everything is unexpected, and you have to be able to move and roll in any direction.

Such situations don't demand much intelligence to shoot, but it does require intelligence to shoot the right thing. And that only you can know. The cameraman may consider the burning house and the wreckage the important elements; only you can tell him or her that the real story lies in the indifference of the onlookers.

All the points we have been discussing now begin to come together. If you know what you want the film to do, and if you have thought through its central point, then you have a clear guide to your decision making. If you have not done that homework, then you have no basis for your decisions.

It goes without saying that most of the time your decision making has to be done at speed. If you are uncertain what is happening, then consult the crew and listen to their opinions. What is fatal is abandoning the decision-making process and just hoping that your crew gets something. They will sense the indecision, and you will be lucky if it does not negatively affect their attitude toward you for the rest of the film.

I have stressed the necessity of knowing where you want to go with the film, but sometimes something happens during filming, something completely out of your hands, that negates your original idea. When this happens you have to make some fast decisions in order to save the film. Here the decisions are very hard because you may be bending the film ninety degrees in order to salvage something. That happened on Mike Rubbo's film *Waiting for Fidel*, made for the National Film Board of Canada. Rubbo's mission was to accompany two Canadians to Cuba and film their interview with Fidel Castro. In the end, though, Castro was never available, even though the duo waited around several weeks. With the central idea for the film aborted, Rubbo turned his cameras toward the two Canadians, one a right-wing media millionaire, the other a left-wing politician. The film became a study of the two men's views and conflicting personalities, set against the background of Cuba. This was not the original film, but it was a salvage job par excellence. And it works because Rubbo had the courage to decide on a new direction in the middle of filming and reconcentrate his energies on a more feasible subject.

The Director's Eye

Many books list qualities required by a director. By the time you have tallied off wisdom, intelligence, patience, an IQ of 200 and a summa cum laude from Harvard, you realize that you are looking at the requirements for God and not for a mere humble documentary director. The one serious asset I would list besides basic intelligence, patience, and a capacity for hard work is a good visual eye. Film is a visual medium, and the good director is one who knows how to use all its potential.

This point may seem so obvious as to be trite, yet the custom the last few years has been to treat documentary, in many cases, as if it were radio with pictures. Thus we see interview after interview, all filmed in the most boring way and interspersed with meaningless visuals that seem to have been put in merely to pass the time. It seems to me at such times that the director has forgotten the very basics of the medium. Obviously some all-interview films do work, but in many interview films one senses a director who is more interested in the polemics of the printed page than in the excitement of a visual medium.

So the director must have a good eye. We accept this as a given in feature films and look to the work of Ford, Von Sternberg, Peckinpah, and Russell for examples. A good sense of what is visually important is just as essential in documentary, but the eye is subservient to purpose. You first determine what you want the film to do and say, and these decisions will then determine the visual style. You can work the other way, determining a visual style regardless of subject matter, but that can be a recipe for disaster: witness the later work of Ken Russell.

You fix your style and discuss it with your cameraman. Again, the more the cameraman knows about your thoughts and feelings, the closer he or she can interpret your approach on film. When you actually shoot the film, there are a few obvious things the cameraman should know or be considering. What should a particular scene do, and what is its place in the film? What is the mood of the scene? Is it to be frenetic, calm, dramatic, poetic? Is the scene to be viewed from a distance, or is there to be a participation effect?

This last point is extremely important. If you are shooting on a tripod your shots will normally appear to be calm, third-person observations of the events. You will be the aloof spectator at the political meeting, the outside observer at the college graduation. By contrast, shooting from the shoulder and moving with the action enhances the first-person, participatory quality of the scenes. Instead of observing the crowd at the disaster, you become one of them, moving in their midst. You will, of course, have to decide whether you want to aim for the third-person or first-person point of view.

Finally, the cameraman will also want to know the degree of intensity you want in your shots. Are you going to go for close-ups or extreme close-ups, or do you prefer to maintain a greater distance from the subject?

When we talk of a director having a good eye, we are actually talking about two things. First, we mean that he or she should have a good sense of framing and composition and should be able to see the best angle from which the story can be told. But "a good eye" also signifies a sense for the telling detail. Sometimes that significant detail is written into the script. Thus, you shoot the employees busily at work, and then the script tells you to shoot the boss with his feet up on the table perusing a *Playboy*. However, many of the most telling sequences happen without any warning, and the job of the director is to see their significance and get the camera to film them. I mentioned earlier doing a film on a music teacher and his work in various villages. For the last scene of the film I had the teacher telling the story of the Firebird to some eleven-year-olds and then conducting an imaginary orchestra as the ballet music swelled upwards. Suddenly I noticed that while David, the teacher, was waving his arms with the imaginary baton, a very sweet eleven-year-old in the first row was carried away and was conducting alongside him. It was a nice shot in itself—the two of them conducting, arms just inches apart. But it was more, because the shot accidentally symbolized the continuity of the generations. Had I tried to set up the shot it would have looked very kitschy, but happening naturally it was tremendously useful.

Again we are back to the director hunting for the symbolic shot. The technique can be overdone, but used well it can be highly effective because in a few seconds it encapsulates what the film is about and what you want to say. The most famous example comes from Humphrey Jennings's masterpiece *Listen to Britain*. All the shot shows is a small man in a dark suit, carrying a gas mask and walking jauntily along a street. But the street is bombed-out, the windows of the shops shattered. In itself the shot is nothing. But what the shot symbolized to British audiences in World War II was the courage of the ordinary Londoner to face life in spite of the worst the Nazi bombing could do.

The Director-Cameraman Relationship

The relationship between the cameraman and the director is probably the most crucial working relationship of the whole film. If the cameraman fails to capture the material in the way the director wants, the very basis of the film is flawed.

As mentioned above, the first task is to find the right person for the particular job. Once you have found that person, you must get him or her to understand and translate your vision to film as accurately as possible. Of course, there's more to it than that. You hope that the cameraman will take your vision, add his or her own creative skills and imagination to the dream, and make something superb that neither of you could have done alone.

Visions tend to be insubstantial while scripts are concrete. Therefore, the first thing to do is give the cameraman the script or the proposal to read and digest. The next thing is to talk over what you hope to do with the film. The script will offer a partial explanation that will be amplified by your discussion. This is also a time to discuss style, objectives, and difficulties and his or her to answer questions. Some will relate to your filmic ideas, and others will be practical questions regarding equipment, time for shooting, crew, and lighting. You must gradually build a relationship of openness and trust, a relationship where each values and respects the other's creativity and judgment. And this relationship and trust had better be there, because half the time you will be entirely in the hands of the cameraman, who will be working without your control.

Generally I like to work with a familiar team and with a cameraman who has been on location with me before. When I am going to work with a new person I like to do three things: I want to see examples of previous work; I want to meet over a drink and get a sense of the person behind the work; and I want to talk to people who have worked with him or her in the past.

Most cameramen will bring you a demonstration roll if you ask for it, but it has to be viewed warily. You are looking at the best work, the best extracts, which may not be typical. That's why you should check with a few people who have worked with the applicant to see what he or she is really like. The personal meeting is necessary because you need to get a sense of personality and temperament. No matter how good the technique, if the person is dour and morose, lacking a sense of humor, he or she will find no place on my crew. Equally important, you need to assess whether the cameraman is open to direction. Some are all sweetness in the beginning, then refuse to take directions on location. They become prima donnas, demanding the sole right to select what is being shot and how it is being shot. Usually you can sense this attitude in the first meeting or through your background check. When I face an attitude like that, I just get rid of the cameraman.

But this does raise another point: Who selects the shots? The simple answer is that you both do, with the director retaining the final judgment. If I am working with a new and unfamiliar cameraman, I will, at least in the beginning, select most of the shots and also check the shots through the viewfinder. If I am working with an old friend whose judgment I trust and who knows my style, I will let him or her choose the shots and merely check the viewfinder when the framing is crucial.

Let the cameraman know clearly what you want from the scene and what specific shots are vital to you. Shooting a riding scene, I might say, "I want some wide shots of the woman riding against the trees, some close-ups — real close — of her coming towards us, and some cutaways of the spectators. You can also give me close-ups of the horses' hooves by themselves, and a few shots of the other riders waiting their turns." If I know the cameraman well I might leave it at that, but if he or she is unfamiliar to me I will probably set up a few shots to demonstrate the kind of framing I want. I will also be very precise on my crucial shots — for example, specifying that in the close-ups I want the subject's head to fill the frame.

Generally I leave a good deal open to the cameraman's judgment. Most cameramen are creative artists in their own right, with years of experience and a superb visual sense. Most probably neither need nor want a director breathing down their necks the whole time. I also like him to feel that I am open to any suggestion of how to improve the scene.

Keep one thing in mind: however much you trust the cameraman, the responsibility is yours. You must be aware the whole time of what he or she is doing, and you must not hesitate to ask that the shot be done over again if you think it has not been done properly.

From time to time problems arise even with the best of cameramen, and you have to be prepared to argue them through. In some cases the cameraman gets overwhelmed with the beauty of a particular shot and fails to see (a) that the shot doesn't convey what you are looking for or (b) that the shot has nothing to do with the film at all. I was doing a film on architecture and wanted to shoot the fancy new wing of a certain museum. My cameraman came up with one of the most artistic shots I have ever seen. The museum was framed through branches, with beautiful patterns of sky above. The only problem was that you couldn't see the building for the branches. This being so, there was no point in turning on the camera.

Not only do you have to guard against shooting beauty for the sake of beauty, but you sometimes have to remind the cameraman that, unlike stills, the shot doesn't stand by itself. It has to be edited into a sequence, and if it doesn't contribute to the sequence it's useless.

Occasionally the battle becomes one of art versus practicality. Most cameramen will try their utmost to give you memorable and artistic shots, but if they take too long the shot may not be worth the effort. As a director you know that, but trying to convince the cameraman to relinquish the shot is something else. Why does one bother to argue? Because time is money, and the effort spent on one shot reduces the time you can spend on another.

A few years ago I was directing an industrial documentary for which I needed a six-second shot of someone working with a laser. In this case my cameraman decided to go to town on the sequence. He set up inkies (very small lights), soft lights, and reflectors, generally having a ball. But all this took an hour and a half, and when I told him it wasn't worth it for a six-second shot we almost came to blows. My argument with him was simple. We had a great deal to do in very little time, and the laser shot was not terribly important to me. Given the circumstances I didn't want to waste an hour and a half on an artistic six-second shot. I preferred a simple shot that could be executed in fifteen minutes. He knew rationally that I was right, but his sense of artistry was terribly offended and he wouldn't talk to me all the next day.

Another problem concerns fatigue. Even under the best of conditions shooting can be a tremendous strain. Very often a lot of physical activity is called for, as well as high concentration. Ultimately this affects the cameraman's performance; the energy dissipates and the shots lose any flair or distinction. Focus and exposure will be all right, but the ultimate result will be very flat. This situation usually occurs on the fifth or sixth day of a continuous shoot, and you can often predict its coming. When it happens the best thing is just to pack up for the day and get a good rest.

Most of the remarks up to now relate to the way the director and the cameraman handle the controlled sequence, but many documentaries involve shooting developing, news, action, or intimate sequences. In many of these cases the cameraman has to act alone, so where does the director's job come in? As director, the main thing you have to do is indicate in advance how you want a scene shot and where the emphasis should be. The more the cameraman knows what you want from a scene, what the point is, and where the emotional center is, the easier it is to shoot it.

In 1969 Richard Leiterman shot *A Married Couple* for Canadian director Allan King. This was an intimate family portrait shot verite style over the course of a few months. King was rarely present at the shooting but analyzed the rushes every few days with Leiterman so that the latter knew fairly precisely what King wanted.

In cases like this the director's job is to get the fullest preliminary information possible, think it through, and pass on directions to the cameraman. Occasionally the director is present during the filming but is wary of disturbing the cameraman. Here it helps to work out a few directional signs, such as a light tap on the shoulder for zoom in, two taps for a zoom out. If I want the cameraman to pay attention to a particular shot or to some evolving action, I wait until the current shot is finished and then whisper directions in his or her ear.

The guiding rule for working on uncontrolled sequences is simple. Assess as fast as you can the essence of the scene, let your cameraman know that, and make sure you get it. At the same time keep in mind that you will have to edit the scene, so be certain that you have enough shots to enable you to do so.

12

Directing the Interview

We use interviews at two stages of the film—during basic research and during the filming itself. The problems arising during research have been dealt with earlier. This section deals with the preparation and conduct of the film interview.

Before the Shooting Starts

At some point you will have lined up a list of potential interviewees for the film. Once you have decided who you want to interview and they have agreed to appear, it's vital that someone meet with the interviewees and go over the nature of the interview and the way the filming will be conducted. And the right person to do all this is the director and not an assistant.

There are a number of objectives to this meeting. The most obvious is to get to know the interviewees better and to explain, without all the pressures of the camera, what you want from the interview. It's also a time to let the interviewees get to know you and put to you any questions about the film or the interview. In short, it's a time to build confidence between the two of you.

What is important at this stage is that you establish a few ground rules. These rules may cover anything from the way you want the interviewee to dress to questions that are off-limits. Such rules are generally minor, but occasionally they can be very important. For example, the interviewee may want a list of questions in advance and may agree to answer only those questions. Is this a limitation you are willing to accept? Again, the interviewee may demand to see the interview at the editing stage or may want to have the right of censorship afterward. You may or may not agree to all this. If any of these things are likely, it is much better to discuss them before you come to the filming than at the filming itself.

This pre-interview "getting to know you" does not have to be terribly formal. Obviously, half the time it will be conducted at home or in the office, but I have also gone fishing with the interviewee while discussing the filming, and in another case I discussed matters while helping strip an engine. The time taken in the pre-interview session can also vary. It can be half an hour over a business cocktail, or it might be a matter of days. There are no rules. The simple object is to know the interviewee well enough to get the maximum out of the meeting.

The most important thing in interviewing is to know what your objectives are and what you want to get out of the film session. You may want some very specific answers to very specific questions. You may want someone to talk generally about a mood or a situation. You may want someone to detail their childhood, their divorce, the importance of their research, or why they committed a murder. The main thing is that your questions must have focus and direction. This means you must do your homework. Normally this will have been done in the research or the pre-interview meeting. But if your filming is actually the first meeting, then make sure you know as much about the interviewee as possible. Know who people are, where they come from, their likes, dislikes, political attitudes, and biases. Obviously, I am setting up an ideal. Many of the documentary interviews you do will be spontaneous, with no time for preparation—in which case you just plunge in. Where possible, though, your questions should be thought out in advance. The interview itself may lead in all sorts of directions and open up interesting new paths of inquiry. That's fine, but make sure you have the main lines of your questioning preplanned.

Your choice of location for the interview depends on two factors, which you hope will mesh easily. First, you want to choose a site for the shooting where the interviewee will feel totally at ease. This could be home, work, or any quiet place. You have to be a bit careful because the most obvious may not always be the best. The father of five who is on the dole might be ashamed of his home and feel more comfortable talking to you in the park. The businesswoman may feel awkward talking to you in the office, where she knows people will tease her afterward, and may prefer the comfort of her home.

The second point to consider is the importance of background. If the story is about research, then you probably want to go for the laboratory background. If you are talking about the development of the modern university, then a dynamic campus backdrop is probably better than a dull home location. Some stories will impose the location on you. Thus, you take the general back to the French beaches to tell you about the D day invasion of the Normandy coast. Or you take Boris Becker back to the Wimbledon courts as he tells you about the first major tennis triumph of his life.

At this point you are asking yourself three things. Will the background add to the mood and drama of the story? Will the interviewee feel at ease in the location, with the possibility of numbers of people around to interfere and distract? And is there any danger of the background being so strong that it distracts from the interview?

Wherever possible I try to do the interview outside on location. This often eliminates lights, which make people nervous, and I think it gives them a certain physical looseness that is often missing in a room interview. Other advantages of the exterior location are that interview cutaways make more sense and you can have the interviewee participate in the scene. I also like to get the interviewee to walk and talk at the same time, instead of filming him or her sitting passively in an armchair. This is difficult and doesn't always work, but it can add dynamism to the scene.

Should other people be present during the interview? Every case differs. The only criterion is whether another person's presence will help or hinder the interview. Somebody is talking about the end of a happy marriage and is obviously upset and on edge. I would sense that the interview should be done with no one else around. Someone else is talking about the loss of a father in a war. She is equally upset, but it could be that in this case the interviewee needs the comfort of a family member whose eye she can catch and whose hand she can hold.

However much you have discussed the film, people are always wary about being interviewed. Yes, they have talked to you before about their experiences, but that was in the privacy of the home. Now, suddenly, four or five other people are present. There are lights. There is a rather large camera on a tripod. There is a person going around taking light readings, and someone else who wants to affix a small microphone to the subject's dress. In this situation your main task is to make the interviewee feel relaxed. I try to do this by introducing the crew, briefly explaining what all the technical equipment is about, and then taking five or ten minutes to chat over a cup of coffee or tea.

The warm-up is the culmination of what you have been trying to do in all the previous meetings—that is, make the subject feel that he or she matters, that you are concerned and involved in what they have to say, and that you care about their opinions. You are trying to build empathy between the two of you, and the more the other person feels this, the better the interview.

Normally you are the one trying to put the interviewee at ease, but this won't always be the case. Sometimes you'll be interviewing presidents or prime ministers or the like, and it may be your turn to feel awkward or shy. Even in such cases I'm not sure the rules change that much. The main danger here is that you may become too deferential and back away from the the hard, awkward questions.

In most cases it will be easy to create an atmosphere of trust because the interviewee knows that you are on his or her side. However, with the political or controversial interview trust may not come so easily. In the difficult cases you have to convince the interviewee that you are interested in his or her point of view and that you are going to be fair and nonjudgmental.

Besides breaking the ice, you should also use the warm-up time to let the interviewees know how the session will be conducted, running over the main topics and letting them know that if they make a mistake you have plenty of film and can shoot the question again.

Filming the Interview

There are three basic setup possibilities for the interview.

1. The interviewee looks, or appears to look, directly into the camera.
2. The camera catches the interviewee obliquely, so that he or she seems to be having a conversation with an unseen person off-camera left or right.
3. The interviewer is seen on-camera with the interviewee so that we are quite clear who is the second person involved in the conversation.

Each of these setups has its own rationale.

Position 1, in which the interviewee looks directly into the camera, adds a certain authority to the interview. In effect, the subject is making direct contact with the viewer, and the straight-on look tinges the shot with the magisterial conviction we associate with the World War I posters that proclaimed, "Uncle Sam wants *you!*" It's the direct-contact pose that politicians give us when they want to assure us they are our friends and not a pack of liars.

Position 2, the oblique angle, relaxes the quality of the interview, making it less authoritarian and more anecdotal, informal, and friendly. This is the interview position I prefer.

Position 3, the two-person interview, is used mostly for news or when a documentary series is being conducted by a famous host such as Bill Moyers, Ted Koppel, or the late Ed Murrow. The two-person setup is also used when you are deliberately aiming at or expect a confrontation.

When considering which position to choose, keep one elementary point in mind: How far do you want the viewer to be drawn into the film? Normally this is a function of the tightness of the shot and the directness of the approach. If the shot is tight and direct the viewer will usually be more involved than when the shot is oblique and the subject framed in a looser way. Once you have decided which approach you want, direct or oblique, then you arrange the seating accordingly. If you want the interviewee to appear to be looking straight at the audience, then you, as interviewer, should sit slightly to the side of the camera lens. If you want the oblique shot, you move further away from the camera.

Though much documentary filming can be left to the cameraman's judgment, I think you are wise to check the suggested interview frame. Does the person appear as you want them to appear? Are the clothes in order? Is there anything disturbing in the background? If the interviewee gesticulates frequently, is the frame wide enough to take in all the gestures? It is also necessary to tell the cameraman not just what frame you want at the beginning of a shot, but whether you want any camera movement in the middle of the answer. You have to indicate that at the beginning, because after your question is asked all your attention will be focused on the interviewee and not on the camera.

The experienced cameraman who has worked with you for some while should know roughly what to do even without your instructions. He or she will know that you can afford to take a camera movement in or out on a change of topic, that you probably want to vary the size of the subject in the frame with different questions, and that you probably want to zoom in slowly on an intense answer.

Besides considering whether you want the interviewee to appear directly or obliquely in the frame, you also have to consider *how* you want the interviewee to appear. Do you want them to appear formal or informal, serious or funny, relaxed or uptight? Because your very framing will induce a certain attitude of acceptance or rejection on the part of the audience, your capacity to manipulate the interview, deliberately or accidentally, is very high.

In the early 1970s Susan Sontag made a film called *Promised Lands*. A large part of the film rests on two interviews and it is interesting how Sontag, consciously or unconsciously, directs those sections. One interviewee is filmed in an open-necked shirt, sitting very relaxed on a sofa in a pleasant living room. His gestures are wide and open, and even before he speaks we feel we like him and trust him. The second interviewee is filmed in a dark suit and tie, standing up with his arms folded in front of dead-white, sterile walls. This time we feel an instant dislike even though the man has said nothing.

The lesson is simple. Your interview is not going to make its impression merely by what is said, but also through all the film techniques you use, from closing in on bad teeth to making the interviewee look like Dr. Strangelove. So be careful!

During the filming all your attention and eye contact should be on the interviewees. You are the person they are talking to, and you must make them feel that you are interested and completely with them. You are the friend to whom they are unburdening their souls about the revolution, the battle, their first love or their last fight, and you had better be interested if you want anything to come alive on the screen.

One thing you have to do before the interview starts is decide whether your questions will be heard after editing. If they are to be cut out, you must ensure that the interviewee gives you statements that are complete in themselves. If you ask: "Where were you when the Japanese attacked Pearl Harbor?" and he answers, "Walking with my girl in the woods, wondering whether we should get married," then the answer, without your question, will make no sense by itself. Instead, you should have told the interviewee that you need a self-contained answer; for instance, "When the Japanese attacked Pearl Harbor I was walking with my girl in the woods." Should you interrupt an interviewee? I try not to, even if I realize the answer won't help the film. If the answer is going nowhere, I try to terminate it gently. Sometimes I try to warn the interviewee in advance that I may want to cut occasionally if I think we are going down the wrong trail. But I say this with caution: although most interviewees will understand the necessity to cut here and there, others may find their pride offended and turn off. Many interviewers set out with an elaborate list of questions to which they keep referring during the interview. I hate that technique because it breaks any spontaneity between the interviewer and the subject. Instead, I try to get the questions well planted in my head and take everything from there. When the interview ends I glance at my list to make sure that I haven't missed anything vital.

What do you ask first? It's best to start with a fairly simple question that will ease you into the interview but that will require more than a one-sentence answer. For instance, "Tell me where you were and what you were doing when you heard the news that you had won the lottery, and what was your first reaction?" Or, "What was the reaction of your friends and family when you came back from Vietnam? Were they sympathetic to what you had been through, or did they blame you for all the killings? And what was it like with the girlfriend who had stopped writing to you?" I have in fact put several questions here, but they are all just variants of the question "What was it like when you returned?" But putting the question in different forms allows various ways into the interview.

Keep the questions clear and down-to-earth rather than philosophical. Don't ask about the problems of humanity in the twentieth century; instead, ask what it felt like to be thrown out of work on a day's notice after forty years. Also, don't bother too much about the order of your questions, unless there is something you particularly want to build up to, because you will do all your final ordering in the editing room.

Remember that you are not just looking for facts, but trying to bring out drama and a story. You must therefore encourage the interviewee to give you details of sights, tastes, recollections, smells, feelings. Usually the more specific the interview, the better it is. If you ask, "What was it like being a child in World War II?" the interviewee might answer, "It wasn't very nice. We didn't have many things. My father was away and then I was sent away. When the German planes came over we went into a family shelter." That's vaguely passable, but not really very good. With a bit of encouragement you might elicit the following:

> We didn't have anything. No sweets, no meat, no eggs. I didn't even know what an egg looked like because they gave us dried eggs. The only bananas I saw were made of wax in the fruit stores. My father was away in Africa fighting, so they sent me to stay with an old farmer in the country. He had this shelter, we called it a Morrison shelter, and it was like a table, but made of steel. When the German bombers came over six of us slept under the table, like sardines.

A good method is to start with straightforward questions and move into the more complex and emotional questions. In a program on divorce you might start with questions about the couple meeting, the attitude of the parents, and the difficulties of the first years. When you are well into the interview you can try the riskier questions: "Tell me about the night she said she was leaving."

One of the most difficult things to assess is how far to press the questions when you are getting into intimate and sensitive areas. One way to overcome this difficulty is to acknowledge from the start that you might be venturing into dangerous areas and that if the questions are too painful or too sensitive you will leave them aside. But you may risk self-censorship if your questions are too restrained from the start.

Silence itself can be a tremendous prod and encouragement in an interview. Rex Bloomstein, an English filmmaker who specializes in films about prison life, uses this technique to great effect. Rex has interviewed single murderers, mass murderers, and all types of criminals from the gentlest to the most violent. He gets them to say the most amazing things, and his weapon is silence, as on the following interview:

> I saw the old woman lying in bed. When she wouldn't give me the money I hit her with the brick. [Rex stays silent for ten or fifteen seconds and the prisoner continues.] Well, actually she looked like my mother, so I hesitated at first, and then she said, "Call yourself a man, you're just a child," and that's when I hit her. I'd already bruised my knuckles on my girlfriend earlier that evening, so that's why I used the brick.

Another filmmaker who knows when to keep silent is Kate Davis. Her 1988 film *Girl Talk* is about the experiences of three teenage girls who leave home. Davis established a tremendous bond of confidence with the girls so that the interviews are fresh, intimate, and tremendously poignant. Many of the interviews are quite long, more like monologues than interviews, but clearly show Davis's ability to get her subjects to talk. As an example, I have extracted Davis's interview with one of the girls, Mars, as she talks about her life and her work in a striptease club:

> He asked whether I wanted to stop by a mutual friend of ours 'cause he wanted to pick up some cocaine. I said sure and he asked me whether I wanted to go up. . . . He parked the car and we went up and he had six of his friends waiting for me. I remember them like having sex with me. I don't remember them hurting me, like physically beating me up. I guess after the third or the fourth one I passed out, and when I came to they had put me in his wife's running path in the park and left me there. She loaded me up in her car and took me to a hotel room and one of her friends was a doctor and he checked me out. She

got round-the-clock nurses and bodyguards for me. Three weeks later my eyes got to where I could see. They were still all black and blue, but they weren't swollen shut any more.

She asked me if I wanted lawyers. I told her about my step-brother and how when my mom had gone to court they had said that I had led Michael on and it was my fault . . . that you couldn't put the star of the track team on trial for rape.

Though you know where you want to go, strange things happen once the camera turns on. Some people freeze, and others become very free and eloquent. In the latter case you may find an area opening up you hadn't even dreamed about. If it's interesting, take a chance and go with it. The freshness of this new area may well compensate for any problems you have fitting the answers into your well-laid film plans.

Problems and Cautions

Good interviewing is the hallmark of all the best documentarists; indeed, some have taken interviewing into the upper realms of filmic art. In England one of the best practitioners of the form is Alan Whicker, whose series "Whicker's World" was essential and delightful viewing for years. Whicker was the urbane, soft-spoken, dark-suited interviewer who could go anywhere and ask the most outrageous questions. He got away with it because his questions were witty and down-to-earth, and wherever he went he seemed to show a genuine interest in his subjects. He had the knack of establishing immediate contact, disarming his interviewees and getting them to talk in the most intimate and frank way about anything from hippies, sex, and drugs to Kentucky race horses or millionaires' yachts. Like Bill Moyers, Whicker was the participatory interviewer who would do anything and try anything. He would ride in the cross-country hunt and afterward interview the master of the hounds, asking the hard questions about fox hunting being a blood sport.

What characterizes both Whicker and Moyers is that their questions are straightforward, avoiding convoluted gush. This leads me to *caution one*: Stay away from gush. Many interviewers think they have to demonstrate their wisdom and intelligence to the interviewee, so they trot out a knowledge of higher physics that would have an Einstein gasping. Not only is this not necessary, it's quite off-putting as well.

Caution two: Keep the question simple, which is not the same as asking a simplistic question. In a program on the atom bomb you could ask the following: "Everyone knows that there are tremendous intellectual and moral problems arising from the creation of the atom bomb. But then mankind through the ages has been beset by moral dilemmas. Bearing in mind the quantum leap of evil that Hitler represents, and also remember-ing the power and the influence of Japanese militarism even after the Meiji restoration, was Oppenheimer spiritually and theologically correct in forwarding the Manhattan project?" As I say, you *could* ask something like that—but I wound resist the temptation. It's dreadful rubbish. Instead, you could simply say, "What were the pros and cons of making the atom bomb, and do you think our attitude toward atomic weapons has changed over time?"

Caution three: Keep your questions open rather than biased toward a particular answer. I go crazy when someone opens a television interview with "Don't you agree with me that . . ." or "Wouldn't you say that Roosevelt was the greatest politician of the century?" Occasionally you may want to be deliberately provocative or to play the devil's advocate, but it's a tricky business and best avoided until you are fairly experienced.

Caution four: Avoid interrupting the interviewee. This is one of the most common faults in interviewing and shows that you are uninterested in the answer. It also wrecks the pace of the interview and is apt to throw the interviewee off stride.

Interview Ethics

In addition to the four warnings above, there is also the matter of the philosophy or ethics of interviewing. Here we are concerned with questions of sensitivity, fairness, politics, and propaganda.

In documentary film we use people. Our rationale is that we are using them for a higher purpose—to expose corruption, to right wrongs, to promote public welfare, and so on. And in the name of the public good we delve into people's lives, invade their privacy, and expose their souls. At the same time that we are digging into all this corruption and sin, or simply examining history, we are also using people's lives to make our living. And we know that in many cases the juicier and more sensational a story we can tell, the more exciting and profitable our final film will be. My statements may seem extreme, but an interview can affect a person's life; it can have long-term effects outside the film, and the interviewer must realize the responsibility thus entailed.

I'll give a short example. You interview a farmhand and coax from him or her a story about the terrible conditions on the farm. You retire to your comfortable motel, and a few months later your film breaks the story. You are hailed as the wonder reformer, a great crusading journalist, but as a result of the interview the farmhand gets the boot.

Another dilemma, touched on earlier, is the legitimacy or otherwise of digging into wounds and resurrecting pain. Again, we often pretend that we are doing something for the public good or because of the public's right to know, when in reality we are doing it out of the knowledge that exposed pain is great journalism.

Sometimes the question at issue is not how is the interview conducted, but how is the interview used in the finished film. I would argue as follows:

When you interview somebody, as the director you have the sole right to decide whether to use an answer or leave it out of a film. But if you use it, then the real substance of the answer must be conveyed, even if it is slightly abbreviated. It also goes without saying that in the film itself you want to portray the whole person and not a series of distorted pictures.

Sometimes, however, the shoe can be on the other foot. This happens when the filmmaker is being consciously or unconsciously used by the interviewee to make a political or propaganda point. A witness in a film tends to receive the stamp of your authority and approval. In effect, he or she is elevated to the rank of authority. Usually that's fine and all the witness's statements are true. But occasionally the statements are incorrect, and there the troubles begin. By my estimate, this problem of the unvalidated authoritarian witness creeps into 50 percent of well-intentioned American and English political documentaries.

13

On Location

Much of the approach to directing people on location has already been covered in the section on interviewing. In this chapter I will try to fill in the gaps, covering the more intricate situations.

In shooting you aim for one thing, *maximum naturalism:* your key objective is to get people to behave in the most genuine way in front of the camera. Luckily, that problem is much easier to solve these days than it was in the past. Television and the mass media have become an integral part of our public lives. We are all too familiar with the camera crew in the street, the *vox populi* interview, the filming in the park, the cameras at the football games, and so on. At the same time, cameras and video equipment have also entered our private lives. At least one member of the family has a video-camera, using it not just for weddings and parties but also for experimental filmmaking.

This increasing familiarity with the filming process undoubtedly makes the documentary filmmaker's task easier. But there are still problems, not the least because your film is intended for public exhibition, not private, and you the filmmaker are an outsider, not an insider. Documentary filmmaking often intrudes into private lives. We are saying, "Give us your lives. Trust us, and let us put it on the big screen." And for the craziest of reasons people agree, and we arrive with loads of equipment and cigarette-smoking strangers and say to them "Fine. Now *just act natural!*" The amazing thing is that, for the most part, they do. What's the secret?

A great deal depends on the bond of *trust* established between the director and the participant. The deeper the empathy and the greater the ease between the director and the people in the film, the better the final result. This is particularly true of most verite and deeply personal films. This doesn't mean that the filmmaker and the subject have to be buddies, but it does mean that time hanging around getting to know each other pays off in the end.

The second part of the secret is that people look most natural when they are performing some action, usually familiar, that takes their minds off the camera. In the Canadian film *Lonely Boy*, about the career of singer Paul

137

Anka, we get a few natural scenes and a few terribly self-conscious scenes, and it's easy to see why. In the natural scenes Paul is always involved: he is rehearsing on the piano; he's rushing to change clothes; he's signing autographs or driving a dodgem car. In the self-conscious scenes he is usually sitting with a friend or a manager, and the director has obviously said, "Well . . . er . . . just talk about anything." Paul is clearly conscious of the camera a few feet away, there is no motivation for the dialogue, and the scenes fall absolutely flat.

The best action scenes arise easily from the natural flow of the film: the mother sending the children to school, working around the house, attending to the garden, visiting the neighbor; a man dealing with an intricate job, then relaxing over a beer in the local bar. The action should be relevant, should advance the film, and should also reveal something about the characters. And, to repeat, it should be something the character feels comfortable doing.

A while back I was doing a film on aging and the distances that can grow between marriage partners after fifteen or twenty years. We shot one scene in the living room, with the husband reading and the wife knitting. It was dreadful! The scene made the essential points, but it was static, awkward, and boring. I then asked the woman what she was most happy doing. Gardening! So we filmed her among the roses. The husband was happiest alone in his room, building model airplanes. We filmed that too. Later we added a voice-over of them explaining how they retreat to their private worlds for satisfaction. We also used scraps of them talking to us as they gardened or built, and that worked perfectly. I had tried the same thing previously in the living room and it had been a dismal failure.

A common fault in documentaries is to have people engaged in actions that say nothing about them or the film. For example, a woman cooks for five minutes while the voice-over tells us she believes in women's rights, was married at seventeen, and divorced at nineteen. So what? The picture is irrelevant to the development of the thoughts and seems to have been put on the screen purely to pass the time.

Preparation

In most shoots it's worthwhile to sit down with the participants and tell them clearly what they're getting into. That sounds easy in theory, but it can be tricky in practice. Craig Gilbert, director of the verite series *An American Family*, on the Loud family of California, claims he explained everything in detail to the family before any cameras came in. However, in her own book on the filming Pat Loud claims she didn't have a clue what he was talking about, but went along out of goodwill.

Your participants must know plainly what demands are being made of them. That means they must be aware of the schedule, the hours of filming, and how long you will want them. Overestimate rather than underestimate.

If you want someone for a morning, don't say an hour. If you want them for a week, don't say a day.

Occasionally, though not very often, your participants may want a fee for appearing in the film. This is more pertinent to the "personality" documentaries rather than the average social documentary. If a fee is involved, make sure that both sides are agreed how much it is and how it is to be paid. Also, be sure that it does not contravene network rules.

If dress is important to the film, be as clear as possible what you want your participants to wear. Thus, you may want your principal character to wear a light-blue sweater in most scenes so that he or she will be clearly identifiable. If you are working in someone's house, assure them that everything will be left clean and neat at the end. Check the power supplies so that you don't plunge the whole neighborhood into darkness by overloading the electricity. And tell them not to worry about food or drink or meals as you will be supplying everything.

If you have the time and the money, try spending an acclimation period around your subjects without filming. Allan King did this with tremendous effect when he made *Warrendale*, one of the pioneer cinema verite films. *Warrendale* was shot in a home for emotionally disturbed children in Toronto, and King and his cameraman William Brayne wandered around the home for a few weeks with an empty camera before turning a foot of film. The time taken getting to know the children and letting them get used to the cameras paid off in the tremendous naturalism and authenticity achieved by the film.

Each film will necessitate different ground rules, but certain kinds of problems keep coming up. The most common ones deal with privacy, areas of questioning, involvement or noninvolvement of children, and payment. In recent years many participants have also begun asking for the right to see the rushes and for the final decision about whether the material can be used. I fully agree with the right to see the rushes, but I will not go ahead with the filming unless final-use decisions are in my hands only.

So far we have been discussing family and home situations but a discussion of ground rules also occurs in much institutional filming. In 1975 Roger Graef made the series "Decisions" for Granada Television of England. The films dealt with crucial decisions made inside various British oil and steel companies. The intimate corporate filming Graef wanted had rarely been achieved before, and Graef obtained permission only when rigid ground rules were established. These included:

1. No scoops. No information was to be released in advance, and no one was to be told about any information obtained during the filming.
2. The filmmakers would only film what they had agreed to cover.
3. No lights would be used, no interviews filmed, and nothing would be staged.

4. The companies were left with the right of veto over confidential material.

Attitude

In a novel I read recently one of the principal characters is a documentary director. At one point he goes to a hospital where he puts on a terribly sympathetic air, is shown around for two hours by the head nurse, and generally agrees with her that it is well run, efficient, a model of its kind. When he comes back to film he selects two utterly atypical wards and emphasizes their dreary, dirty, almost horrific quality. Unfortunately, the story could be true. Many directors work their way into situations by guile and then, in the interests of cheap drama, falsify the story and betray the people who have trusted them.

When we film people, we are using their lives to earn our living. Their motives for participating vary from a kindly desire to help, to a desire for publicity for their organization, to a genuine desire that their experience, their pain or joy, will enlarge someone else's vision. When everything else is said and done, there is a heavy responsibility on the director's shoulders. If at the end of the film the director and the participants are still friends, then there's not too much to worry about.

Location Checks

So far we have talked about handling the interview and working with people in different situations. In doing so we have begun to suggest certain rules or approaches for location shooting, but a few things have been left out along the way. This section summarizes what you should be doing and thinking about on location.

Schedule. You made up an overall schedule at the preproduction stage, but changes may have been made since then. Before you go out, make sure everyone on the shoot has an up-to-date schedule indicating where and what you are shooting, and the amount of time you are allowing for each scene. Make sure too that the list has the names of the participants and where they can be contacted as well as the name, address, and telephone number of your hotel.

Equipment check. Make sure your equipment is in working order before you leave your base. This is particularly necessary in the case of video equipment, as the cameras are notoriously temperamental. Sound equipment should also be thoroughly checked, particularly in regard to synchronizing functions. It is also good practice to check your cables, particularly power cables to the cameras and the sound. Where possible you should take spares. Finally, check that you have all your special equipment, and in this I would include any permissions you might need on the shoot.

Shooting list. Run over the shooting list with your cameraman. Does it still make sense in regard to the weather, mood, and so on? If, for example, you think it's going to rain, try to think of alternatives before you go out rather than when catastrophe hits. Also run over the shooting list in your own mind. Do you have a well-formed sense of the way you want to shoot the scenes? Do you know where you want to begin and roughly what your first setup will be? You will have to make some of these decisions on the spot, but many of them should be thought out before you leave for filming.

On Location

Filmmaking is a cooperative and consultative process, but it is not necessarily a democratic process. On location *you* are the boss. You can consult, you can ask advice, but you are the one in command who has to decide what has to be filmed and how everything should be ordered and carried out.

Your first problem on location is usually not what to film (that has been decided beforehand in most cases) but *how* to film the sequence. Where should your camera go? What should it frame? Should the camera pan with the people coming out of the building, or should it get them in a fixed frame with a close-up lens? You will be settling all these decisions with your cameraman, clearly defining what you want from the shot. Sometimes he or she will choose the frame, sometimes you will. Most of the time you will be standing close enough to the cameraman to whisper instructions and to have an accurate sense of what the camera is doing.

Sometimes your instructions to the cameraman will be loose; sometimes they need to be very specific. For the film's opening scene it may be enough to say, "Give me plenty of medium shots and close-ups of the students going into the university. Also try to give me a variety of types. I'm particularly interested in trying to give the impression that we have students from a dozen different countries." Another time you may say, "I want a very tight zoom into that window," because you know that in the film you want to cut from the outside of the building to a class in progress inside.

Both you and the cameraman will be looking for the best way to express the scene, but you have to be the guide because you know much better than anyone else exactly how the scene will be used in the finished film. You also know more than the cameraman does about the mood you are looking for. Discussing this matter will help, and you should also indicate very specifically the kind of shots you want. For example, you are filming in a prison. The film is about forgotten men, about harsh treatment, about antagonism and broken lives. Obviously the mood you are aiming for is one of separation, isolation, and oppression, so many of your shots will be low-angle. The harsh lines of the prison walls are emphasized. The barbed wire on the walls dominates the frames. The guard with the rifle is silhouetted.

By way of contrast, you film the prisoners from above, isolating them as tiny figures against the bleakness of the prison exercise yard. And most of the time your camera is on the tripod as you take fairly long, calm shots.

In another film you are shooting automobile racing trials, and you are aiming at a completely different mood. This time the dominant word is exhilaration. You instruct your cameraman that you are interested in movement, in low, long-lens shots of the cars coming directly toward you and sweeping around the curves. You want people running, jostling, calling. You want close-ups of watches, eyes, and flags. You tell the cameraman to get inside the action, to prowl, to be part of the scene, and suggest that most of the people shots be done from the shoulder.

One of the things that must be kept continuously in mind is the final editing process. So a key question, always, is whether or not you have enough material to give to the editor to build a decent scene. In particular, do you have enough cutaways so that you can alter your point of view or cut out of a scene easily? This failure to take cutaways is one of the commonest problems among beginning filmmakers.

Another essential thing is to maintain a clear logging of the sequences and shots for both the camera and sound. Normally this will be done by a slate that will record camera roll, sound roll, sequence, and shot. The clapboard hitting the slate will also give the editor the sync points for both camera and sound. Every time the cameraman changes a roll, the soundman should indicate that on the audiotape as well.

In some situations you will not have the luxury or the time to slate the scene properly, and you have to be careful that under pressure you don't lose sync. One way around this is to hold up fingers indicating take one or take two, and then slap your hands together. The effective sync mark will be the point that your palms make contact. Another way is for the soundman to tap the microphone on-camera, the moment of contact again being the sync point.

Besides dealing with the dynamics and mechanics of the filming itself, the director also has to think about the human dynamics of the crew. If the crew is fine, the filming benefits; if not, the filming suffers. As director, you will set the tone of the filming, and whatever you say or do will affect the crew. If you're a martinet, you can antagonize them; if you're unsure of yourself, the crew loses confidence; and if you're generally inconsiderate, the crew will get its own back. On the other hand, if there is confidence, if there is a smile, if there is consideration for the work done and the professionalism shown, then the crew will work wonders.

It sounds easy but it isn't, and this is because so much of the work is done under pressure and so many things can go wrong. The three qualities that seem to me to be essential for the good director are patience, humor, and calmness. Everyone knows things will go wrong—that the weather will be foul, that cameras will break down, that planes will be missed, that cables will be lost, that food will be lousy, and that tape recorders will go out of sync. But if you can be calm and humorous under those tensions, then things will be all right. Not immediately, but soon. And when you can continue, the problem and its solution become part of the bonding between the crew.

One thing the director must be aware of is relations among the crew. Sometimes rivalries and antagonisms develop during the shooting, and they can be deadly to the film if they are not caught and squashed. I find it helps to spend a few minutes with each member of the crew after the day's filming. Are they satisfied? Were any problems overlooked that I should have known about? Is the equipment working all right? Is there anything we could do better tomorrow? Are they enjoying themselves? The objective is simple. You start off with a crew, but you want to finish up with a team. And there is a great deal of difference between the two.

As you have gathered, much of the director's work consists of foreseeing a problem or solving it as soon as it happens. This problem solving does not have to be individual. It can, and often should be, a communal process. The camera motor has gone crazy. The soundman doesn't feel well. You have taken a wrong turn and are four hours behind schedule. You have been given the wrong lights. The equipment van has broken down. When these things happen, and they happen frequently, discuss them openly. Your crew is there to consult with, and their opinion and advice matters. But in the end you're the one who has to make the decision. With directors as with presidents, the buck stops here!

At the end of a hard day's filming it's tempting just to turn off, but one thing must still be done before you wrap. Review what you have filmed, and ask yourself whether you are satisfied or whether you have neglected anything important. If everything is fine you can complete the wrap. If it isn't, then do the missing filming immediately or fit it in the following day's schedule.

When the equipment has been packed, just check that all the film cans and film tapes are labeled and safely stored. Then go and have that drink, because you deserve it!

Part IV  Postproduction

14

Editing

Many people regard the shooting phase as an end in itself. It isn't; it merely provides the raw materials. The real building process takes place during postproduction, which is supervised for the most part by the editor. The director still acts as the captain on the bridge, but the editor now becomes the chief mate who does 90 percent of the work. Sometimes the work will be supervised by the director; sometimes it will be independent of the director. The most important thing is for the director and editor to understand each other and to function as a team as they complete the film.

Besides the overall command of the editing room, the editor's work will include screening rushes; having the film and sound synchronized and coded; having transcripts made; supervising the editing itself; discussing music and effects; laying in narration and other sound tracks; and supervising the sound mix.

The work of the videotape editor differs slightly from the above, though not very much. For the sake of convenience, I have dealt with videotape editing procedures at the end of the chapter.

This chapter discusses the way the editor and the director work together. It's not about the technical side of editing, which is outside the scope of this book. For those who want to know more on techniques of editing, I strongly recommend Roger Crittenden's *Film Editing*, while the classic on the aesthetics of the subject is still Karel Reisz's *The Theory and Practice of Editing*.

The Director-Editor Relationship

Most directors of any worth are also apt to be competent editors. Many, like Fred Wiseman and Mike Rubbo, edit their own films. So, given that the director (who is in most cases also the writer) knows most about the film, why not let him or her go ahead and edit it as well? One answer is sheer fatigue. The shooting process tends to be such a debilitating and demanding period that often there is no energy left to supervise the equally arduous task of editing. A second answer, perhaps more important, is that

147

editing is best done with a fresh eye. And that's something an independent editor has and the director lacks.

Like it or not, the director brings a tremendous number of hang-ups to editing, one being his or her familiarity with the agonies and trials endured getting the footage. Because of this the director sometimes falls in love with the material regardless of its worth. The independent editor, however, sees only what is on the screen. Everything else is irrelevant. Consequently, he or she is often a much better judge of the value of the material.

The good editor can also be a tremendous creative stimulus to the director. The editor is there not just to carry out technical directions, but also to advocate better ways of looking at the film and new and different ways of using the material. He or she is there to support what is right, challenge what is wrong, and put new energy into the whole process.

Finding the right editor is crucial to your success because documentary editing is so much more open than is feature editing. In documentary there is often no story, no script; the director dumps a bunch of rushes into the editor's arms and demands that he or she find the story. Creation and invention are vital to the very nature of the documentary editor, while such qualities may not be so necessary for the feature editor.

As a director, I find that working with a talented editor is one of the most dynamic and stimulating parts of filmmaking, and most films are better for having that person around. History bears this out over and over again. Roger Graef's films for Granada Television are superb, but their excellence owes much to the editing of Dai Vaughan. We talk of the poetry of Humphrey Jennings's films, yet again much of their success is due to editor Stewart McAllister.

The relationship between the director and the editor can be tremendously fruitful, but it can also be quite hard. In essence, you have two strong characters dissecting, analyzing, and arguing about the film for days on end. When you agree it's fine, but when you disagree the air can get quite hot. Yet when you finish you usually have something finer and better than if each had worked separately on the film.

First Steps in the Editing Room

In the best of circumstances one sees the "dailies" or "rushes" during shooting. When the shooting is finished I like to go over all of the rushes with the crew so that together we can analyze what happened. The editor is best left out of the group viewing; this is a time to look back, whereas your screenings with the editor prepare for the march forward.

After the group screening the first task is to get the rushes synchronized (or "sunc up," in film vernacular) and sent out for coding. This is usually the work of the assistant editor. Not all directors code their films, but I find it very useful. Coding is the process of putting identical edge numbers on the rushes and on the 16mm magnetic sound track. This ensures that you can easily match sound and picture, and it also makes it easier to preserve and arrange trims.

While syncing and coding is going on, the editor will also be preparing five or six logbooks for future use. One will contain the original script, the editing script, and any script changes. The second is the log of the rushes, which will show the code number, length, scene number (if available), and subject matter of the rushes. A typical series of log entries might look like this:

Code	Scene	Length	Subject
AA1–22	3	40 secs.	Students enter university
23–51	6	55	General shots art class
52–65	9	20	Students in corridors

The function of the rushes log is to help you locate material quickly. How you write it and how you subdivide it is up to you. Some people like exact descriptions of every individual shot, noting close-ups, medium shots, and even what people are wearing; all I need is a general description of a series of linked shots.

I like to set up a third log dealing only with stills, but many people list the stills in the rushes log. One reason for separating the two is that you may have to pay copyright fees on the stills, and a separate log can also include all the information on sources, and fees. The fourth log is that of the archive material ordered for the film. It is set out the same as the rushes log, but like the stills log it should include source and any copyright fee. The fifth log contains all the film transcripts, which we will discuss below. The six log lists all the music you will use in the film and its sources. It is also helpful to include a list of sound effects in this log, as that makes the final sound work on the film that much easier.

What you are doing with the logs is setting up different working aids. In the beginning it may seem as if a lot of time-consuming effort is involved, but as you go on with the editing you will see that the logs are invaluable.

The way you proceed once the material is synchronized, coded, logged, and boxed depends on the kind of film you are doing. If your editing is based on a fairly tight script, you will work one way; if the film is verite or only partly scripted, you will take a slightly different tack. For the next few pages I want to discuss editing methods on the assumption that there is a basic script at hand. The problems of verite and the unscripted film in general are dealt with at length in chapter 17.

The Editing Script

Before doing any work with the editor, you should give him or her the original script to read. This will show clearly where you first wanted to go with the film and how you thought that could be achieved. The next stage is to screen the film alone with the editor. Preferably this should be done in sync, on a large screen, so that you can feel the quality and detail of the shooting. Once you have absorbed the material on the large screen, you can review further on the editing table.

The aim of these viewings is to crystallize your own thoughts and impressions about the material. Is what you hoped for there on the screen? Has your central vision come through, or has something different emerged? Which scenes work, and which scenes appear hopeless? Which characters seem to come alive on the screen, and which seem to die? And what excites you in a completely unexpected way? Lest these impressions be forgotten, jot down a few notes or talk into a small tape recorder. Normally I don't do this until a second viewing. For the first viewing I just want the material to wash over me, and then I can ask myself a few hours later what I remember.

The editor is also taking notes, and it's useful afterward to compare impressions. As mentioned before, the editor comes unburdened by any preconceptions about the material. He or she sees only what is on the screen and views it with the critical eye of the potential audience. In many ways it is easier for the editor to see what is good or bad than it is for you, the director. After the viewing, sit down with the editor and just listen to first impressions. Just as you asked yourself what works and what doesn't, now is the time to hear the first reactions of an unbiased observer.

The first screenings show you what you have in reality as opposed to theory. Up to this point you have had an intellectual concept of the film on paper. Now the only thing that matters is the reality of the material, and there are bound to be shocks, both good and bad.

In 1988 I made a film about President Carter and the Israeli-Egyptian peace treaty of the late 1970s. The film was supposed to start with the restaging of a celebration party. On paper it was a great opening, but the party never came to life on film, and this was immediately apparent on seeing the rushes. The scene had to be cut.

About the same time I interviewed Nobel Prize–winner Elie Wiesel for another film. Here I had the opposite situation. During the filming Wiesel had given me the impression of being tired and disinterested. When the filming was over, I felt that we had nothing usable. However, when we viewed the rushes we saw that the man had a compelling power and intensity that the lens had caught but that we had been unable to see.

After a few screenings of the rushes, and after talking to the editor, sit down and review the script. Does it still make sense in view of the nature of the material? Should you lose scenes or change the order? Has any situation or character come out so well that you want to strengthen that element or that person in the film? Did the editor make any suggestions that you want to incorporate?

When the review is complete, your next move is to write an editing script. The editor will use this script as a guide, and it will reflect what is *actually* in the material. The editing script is often almost identical with the shooting script, but for the reasons given above you may also need to make considerable changes. Different scripts have different purposes. One of the aims of your very first script was to raise money for the film. The one and only purpose of the editing script is to give the editor a solid master plan on which to build the film.

And the editing script is only that: a guide to lead you into the editing. As you work on the film, building the different sequences and searching for a rhythm, you may decide to depart radically from the editing script. But that happens only when you are far into the editing and have a chance to step back and see whether the shape is correct or not.

Most editing scripts look very much like shooting scripts—that is, visuals on the left and audio or idea line on the right. As the script is only for the editor's eyes, you can afford to add any notes or comments that you think will help. For example, an editing script on modern universities might look like this:

Visual	*Ideas*
Students streaming into the campus. Sixteenth-century university buildings. Cambridge students with books.	The university as the idyllic place of higher learning. A quiet retreat removed from reality. The concept of the ivory tower.
	Probably always was a false picture.
Riots at Berkeley and at Columbia.	Today, to be a student is to be a political animal.
	[*Jim*, I think we can get the riot footage from the National Archives. What do you think about also using footage from the French protests of '68? Or do you think that would be too esoteric for an American audience?]
Professor comments on riots.	[We have two good interviews that would fit here. Either Prof. Jones or Dickson. I think Jones works a bit better on camera.]

Here Jim is the editor, and the script may be full of little notes to him or suggestions for him to consider.

Unless the original script contained commentary, it's often easier to work with an idea line rather than a commentary line in these first stages. The writing of the commentary or link narration can usually wait until the editing becomes more focused and abbreviated.

Transcripts. If your film contains interviews or long dialogue sections, these should be transcribed as soon as editing begins—a tedious process, but absolutely necessary. My rule is to transcribe all interviews but to use discretion on interaction dialogue, where it may suffice merely to jot down the main topics people are discussing. Thus, while you transcribe everything the professor says on nuclear disarmament, you may simply note, "John and David discuss the merits of various sports cars, then start talking about holidays." The simplest method of transcription is to have an audiocassette made from the quarter-inch tapes or, failing that, from the 16mm magnetic track. The cassette then goes to the typist while you get on with the film. You can transcribe from the magnetic tracks on the editing table, but that tends to cause enormous delays.

Once you have the transcripts, you have to decide what to use and where. A few readings of the transcripts will tell you roughly what you want, but you have to make your final decisions watching the material on the table. This is necessary because *how* someone says something can be as important as *what* is said. The table viewing will also give you inflections that are missing from the printed page. When you read a transcript, you might at first think that you can use merely a portion of a sentence. However, when you listen to the interview you may realize that the voice at the cutting point is too high and has clearly been caught in the middle of something rather than at the beginning or end of a thought.

The typed transcripts go into the transcripts log, and I like to keep the filmed interviews themselves separate from the rest of the rushes. Once you have decided what part of the interview you want, mark it clearly in the log book with *in* points and *out* points. A marked-up transcript log might look like this:

> New York was marvelous. Nothing I'd seen in Europe could touch it. And meeting Irving Berlin was the climax. [IN POINT] He looked old and weather-beaten, but there was a sparkle around his eyes. One evening we sat down with a piano and he played "There's no business like show business," and all the years dropped away. For a few seconds I glimpsed the genius who had written "Blue Skies" and "Alexander's Rag Time Band." Then he stopped, said he was tired, and went to bed. [OUT POINT] The next day we went on. . . .

The editing script should reflect the transcripts in whatever way is easiest for you. Thus, the editing script might refer to the excerpt above as "Mark Davis talking about Irving Berlin, interview three, page seven of the transcripts."

Obviously, it's best to get the transcripts completed before you write the editing script, but little harm is done if you have to put them in later. In that case the editing script might just say, "Various interviews commenting on Irving Berlin at age eighty."

The Editing Process

The editing process is usually split into three stages: the assembly cut, the rough cut, and the fine cut. In practice the stages blend into one another, so we are really using these terms as a quick assessment of where you are in the editing rather than absolute divisions of work.

The Assembly Cut

The *assembly cut* is the first assembly of your rushes. You take your best material, your best shots, and attempt to put them roughly in order according to your script. At this stage you are evaluating shots, selecting some and cutting others. The selected shots will probably be inserted full-length, with no attempt to shorten them. You will be overly generous rather than niggardly. You may use a variety of shots making the same point, only later deciding which you prefer.

Your interview shots will go in with the corresponding sync sound track, but apart from that you will not bother with sound at this stage. Nor will you bother with rhythm or pace; the objective of this first cut is simply to give you a rough sense of what you have and an overall feel of the film once it has been put in some kind of order. At this stage the film could easily be two or three times its final length.

The Rough Cut

The real work begins when you start working on the *rough cut*. Here you are beginning to talk about proper structure, climaxes, pace, and rhythm. You are looking for both the correct relationships between sequences and the most effective ordering of the shots within a sequence.

You should now be paying particular attention to structure. Is your ground plan for the film's development correct? Is there a smooth and effective opening? Is there a logical and emotionally effective development of ideas? Does the film have a growing sense of drama? Is it focused? Are the climaxes falling in the right place? Is your ending effective? Is there a proper sense of conclusion?

Something else you are looking for at this stage is what I call *overloading*. During the scripting stages you probably packed your film full of ideas. That may have looked fine on paper, but during editing you may find that it's all just too much to take. You are overloaded. The audience won't absorb this much information, so you may have to dump a few of your choice scenes.

What soon becomes apparent is that the material itself will dictate major changes in your first editing ideas. For example, a few viewings might suggest that a sequence would work more effectively at the end of the film rather than at the beginning.

In my automobile accident film I had a series of interviews five minutes into the picture where people talked about the effect of accidents on their lives. During the rough cut I realized that I had too much and cut out two of the interviews. One I abandoned completely; the second, in which a father talks about the loss of his son, I hung on the barrel for later use, though I wasn't quite sure where. In the middle of the film I had a good sequence but realized as we edited it that it had no climax. The sequence showed cars racing along roads, cut to cars on a racing track, and ended with a man looking at bikini-clad women decorating sports cars in a lush showroom. Meanwhile, the commentary talked about the car representing power and masculinity. Looking at the sequence, I realized that it would work more effectively if we dropped the showroom, went from the racing cars to a roll-over crash, and then cut in the interview of the father talking about the loss of his son.

You continually have to ask yourself, is the material really working where I have placed it? If not, why not? Here, the extra eyes of the editor become extremely useful in breaking your preconceived notions of order and flow. Often the editor can suggest a new order that might escape you because of your closeness to the material.

During the rough cut you are also beginning to pay attention to the rhythm *within* the sequences. Are the shots the right length? Do they flow and blend well? Are they making the points you want?

The paper cut. During the editing a tremendous amount of rethinking and reordering is going on. In many cases even the editing script soon refuses to bear much resemblance to what is on the table. How does one cope and maintain order?

One of the best methods is to make a *paper edit* of the film. Each sequence is written out on filing cards that show briefly the points being made and the intros and exits. The cards are then pinned to the wall following the first editing script. As the film goes on, a glimpse at the cards may suggest a new order. You can then juggle the cards to see what, in theory, this new edit would look like. If you follow through and reorder the film itself, the cards stay in the new order. Thus, though the editing script may be out of date, the cards always reflect where you actually are in the film. This paper edit is useful in scripted films, but it really comes into its own when you are working with verite and partly scripted material, where it becomes tremendously helpful in building dramatic structure.

The director-editor relationship. The rough cut is a process of examining, building, and tightening that can take anywhere from a few days to a few months. And the editor's role is crucial.

Some people look on their editors as mere cutters, artisans who are there to work under their control and put their great directorial decisions into effect. Such an attitude is the height of foolishness and stupidity. The good editor has honed his or her skills over the years and is probably just as good a creative artist as you are. So it helps to pay attention and learn. Most editors want to listen to you, to see where you are and where you want to go, but they then bring something creative and not automatic to the job. Sometimes they will propose radical departures from your original concept. The only criterion is artistic: will such a suggestion improve or hinder the film? Most of the time you don't know until you try.

In my film on the children's village I had a lovely sequence halfway through where the children attend the rehearsal of a major symphony orchestra. The sequence concentrated on the players, with marvelous close-ups of violinists, tuba players, and trumpeters and some especially good shots of the conductor. At the end of the film the children watch David, their teacher, as he tells them about the *Firebird* ballet, puts on the music, and then mimes the actions of an orchestral conductor.

And that was where the film was supposed to end. Suddenly my editor, Larry, suggested that we intercut some shots of the real symphonic musicians, the violinists and the conductor, as the children and David listen to the ballet music in their school shack. Initially I opposed this suggestion. I thought the audience would be confused between the scenes in the middle of the film and the scenes at the end, there was no logic behind the second appearance, and so on.

I was completely wrong. The intercutting gave the scene a magic and an extra dimension it never had in the original version. And this magic was entirely due to the creativity of the editor.

Narration. Although writing narration is dealt with fully in chapter 15, I want to mention a few points here that affect the editing process. As the rough cut proceeds it often helps to write at least a tentative version of the commentary. You can record this yourself and then have it laid as a guide for the picture editing. This will help establish the logic of the film and the flow and length of the shots. If you don't want to go to the expense of a rough guide track, you can just read the commentary to picture. However, as you will often be absent from the editing room, a guide track that can be laid in is much better.

At this point there is a certain basic dilemma. Should the words dictate the picture or vice versa? I have always believed that where possible, pictorial rhythm and flow should be the first consideration and that words should be written to picture, rather than pictures adjusted to words. That's why I have argued for the first editing to be done to ideas rather than strict commentary.

However, when you are making a film about politics or complex ideas, you may find that the commentary has to come in sooner rather than later, that you need to edit against specific words rather than ideas. In such cases write a fast commentary. There will be time to adjust it later, but it will be a tremendous help as the editor refines the material.

Music. Your film may or may not have music. In feature films we expect music everywhere, and the usual complaint is that there is too much. The music often drowns the film and leads the emotions so that there are no surprises. Documentary films use much less music, which may break the illusion of reality. However, when used well music can lift a film tremendously.

Most historical documentary series use music galore, so that Russian tanks go into battle accompanied by Tchaikovsky, while Polish partisans work wonders to the music of Chopin. Most people love it. Some people hate it. But it's all-encompassing. The interesting thing, as a filmmaker, is to see and understand what the music is really doing for the film.

Triumph of the Will, Leni Riefenstahl's paean to Hitler and his Nazi thugs, uses music to tremendous effect. The film opens with Wagner's stirring "Ride of the Valkyrie," which sets the mood of expectation and exultancy. Later the drums add passion and drama to the dark mystery of the torchlight processions. Finally, German folk songs add excitement and vitality to the early-morning shots of hijinks at the Hitler youth camp.

One of the best documentaries for learning about the use of music is still Humphrey Jennings' *Listen to Britain*, a sound portrait of Britain in World War II. It has no commentary, depending for its powerful effect on the conjunction of music, natural sound, and images. Within the film Jennings uses folk songs like "The Ash Grove" and music-hall songs like "Underneath the Arches" and "Roll Out the Barrel" to stress his faith in popular culture and the sense of the very "Englishness" of the scene. Later he uses Mozart to stress the continuity of civilized human values threatened by Nazi barbarism. The Mozart scene actually begins with a Myra Hess piano concert at the National Gallery. But the music then continues, accompanying a series of public images. As the music swells we see trees, a sailor, people boarding buses, the statue of Lord Nelson (England's savior against Napoleon), and a barrage balloon. Finally, and unexpectedly, the Mozart covers work in a tank factory, where it is gradually lost among the natural sounds of the machines.

Many filmmakers use songs in historical documentaries to give a flavor of the times, and that seems fine in moderation. Thus, the old union songs in *Union Maids* are quite effective, as are the folk songs in *The Good Fight* about the Spanish Civil War. The dangers are that the music may be used as a crutch and that the viewers may weary of Pete Seeger and his banjo.

Too often, music is used for emotional uplift alone. This is a pity, because it can also comment effectively, even ironically, on the visuals. One of the best films in the series "The World at War" was John Pett's *It's a Lovely Day Tomorrow*. The title was taken from a well-known song of the 1940s, performed by Vera Lynn. The film is about British soldiers fighting the Japanese in Burma, and the song is used sparingly to accompany shots of soldiers dragging through the mud in the monsoon rains. The song evokes a dreamy, wistful mood, a sense of regret and abandonment. But the music also suggests that there is no tomorrow, only the continuing shock and horror of today.

When should you begin thinking about music? Probably somewhere between the rough cut and fine cut. A lot of your film may actually be cut to the rhythm and beat of the music; therefore, it's best not to leave the choice until the last minute.

Your music will either be specially written for the film or taken from prerecorded albums, tapes, or compact discs. My preference, where budget permits, is to have music written directly for the film. It's not just that the music is fresh, but you can aim for a unity that is hard to achieve when your music comes from all over the place. When you are using prerecorded music, the simplest way to deal with the whole business is to record your possible music choices on cassette and then play them against the picture. You soon sort out what works and what doesn't. The effective music is then transferred to 16mm magnetic track, while the other music is put aside.

Test screenings. At some point in editing you will probably have to hold some test screenings. These might be for the sponsors or the executive producer, or to get the reactions of the intended audience. The aim of the previews is to get feedback while you can still change the film. The best time for this is toward the end of the rough cut. A critically constructive preview can be tremendously helpful to the director, enabling him or her to see where the mistakes are and to guide the film closer to the wishes of the sponsor or senior producer. But you also have to be on guard against comments that are meaningless and even destructive.

On one occasion I held a preview of a university public relations film with the university president and five of his junior colleagues in the cutting room. After the screening the president asked his juniors to react to the film. Their problem was that they didn't know whether the president liked it or hated it, and they wanted to show that they agreed with him. The result, which was rather funny, was that they all hedged their bets. "The film was fine, but . . ." "The issues were clear, the photography was good, but . . ." In the end the president, to my relief, said, "I think it's great and we don't need any changes."

Most directors of any worth know the faults and problems of their films well before these screenings. But the one thing they lack is the reaction of a test audience in a teaching or training film. Previews here are essential. What you are trying to find out is whether the film is really achieving its goals in terms of altering or reinforcing attitudes. Ideally these test screenings should be held in normal surroundings rather than in a screening room. If the sponsors are present they should be at the back so that their presence does not inhibit discussion. In the end the discussions do two things. First, they show you if you are reaching your audience. If you are, that's great. If not, you can begin to see where the problems lie. Second, such screenings often assuage the sponsors' fears. In private screenings with you they may have objected to certain scenes, characters, or language. In the test screenings they can see that the fears were baseless, with the result that you can go ahead as planned.

After the screenings, think through the criticisms. Some will be valid, others nonsense. It is useful to remember that the general tendency of these screenings is to look for problems, so don't be surprised if there is little praise. And don't revise just because a lot of people have said you should. They may just be wrong, and you may just be right. Make changes only if you think they are actually going to help the film.

The Fine Cut

During the fine cut you make the last changes to the picture and start adding or finalizing commentary, music, and effects. "Locking" the fine cut is the process of saying, "Enough. That's the film; that's its length, and that's the way it's going to go out." When you get to the fine cut, you will have expended a tremendous amount of time and energy on the film, and you will want to get out as fast as possible. You have to resist this impulse, draw a breath, and ask if the film is really working, and if not, what can be done. You ask yourself for the last time if all the issues are clear, if any of the information is redundant, if the film has the right opening and ending, the proper rhythm, pace, and flow. Does it grip the emotions? Is it interesting to an outsider? Does it fulfill your intentions?

The three elements that begin to dominate at this stage are narration, music, and effects. Some narration and music may have been added while you were working on the rough cut, but both must now be finalized. This becomes a see-saw process: sometimes the narration and music are adjusted to fit the picture, and sometimes exactly the reverse happens. Only when the picture is locked do you add missing sound effects.

Editing Videotape

Most of the points I have made about film editing also apply to editing three-quarter-inch videotape. You use slightly different technical methods, but your mind-set is the same. This being so, I merely want to comment on a few points worthy of attention.

Your initial cut will probably be done off-line in a small, low-cost studio, with the final work being done in an on-line studio, where you do your conforming and add visual effects.

In order to edit effectively, either your videotape must be shot with time code or time code must be added before editing. The time code, a series of numbers that appear on the screen during editing, later helps you find the matching point in your original master tape. They also help you dub from one generation of tape to another.

With video, it helps to lay in the commentary very early. This is both because picture changes are slightly more complex than they are in film and because many video editors argue that such a procedure helps them work much faster.

Once the picture has been cut, one generally moves into a one-inch on-line suite to lay in effects and to master the film. The object of the work in the on-line suite is to come out with a one-inch master video. The process is quite simple: the edited fine-cut dub with all the code numbers appears on-screen. A computer then finds the equivalent time code on the original cassettes and conforms the picture onto the one-inch master. While this is going on, you are also inserting all your fancy video effects: dissolves, wings in and out, cubes, wipes, and so on. The only major point here is that you should think through the effects before you go on-line, rather than working them out in the editing suite. The reason is twofold. First, the effects you are going to use will determine how you put together the off-line cut, which should be prepared with your effects in mind. The second reason is financial. On-line suites are expensive, and the more prepared you are to use the on-line time effectively, the cheaper it will be for you.

Once the picture is conformed, the sound mix can be made with your one-inch copy finally acting as your master tape for any dubs.

One final point to bear in mind is that while most European studios work with the PAL system, studios in the United States work with the NTSC format. If you have shot and edited on NTSC but your work is for Europe, you will need to go through a systems conversion. This is best done one-inch to one-inch. If you go three-quarter to three-quarter, you will find a drop in quality and subsequent picture breakup as you go down a few generations.

I have been very brief here because video equipment and video techniques seem to change daily. But not to worry. Beyond all the paraphernalia the *art* and the thinking behind the editing doesn't change drastically. If your thinking and approach is right, you can handle anything.

15

Writing the Final Narration

As the film has been progressing through its various stages, you have probably been blocking in a narration line, and sometimes the tentative narration itself. Certain films, say a historical documentary, will have demanded that you think about the narration very early on. Other films, heavily dependent on interviews and verite techniques, may have allowed you to proceed very far without thinking about the commentary. However, the moment comes when you have to write the definitive narration. That moment is usually just before or just after finishing the fine cut. It's a challenging task, but one which in the end is tremendously satisfying.

In the 1940s and the 1950s almost every documentary was accompanied by commentary. In recent years, though, a school of filmmakers has emerged absolutely opposed to the use of narration. This opposition stems from various beliefs, from a dogmatic assertion that it is a fascist practice (de Antonio's belief) to a feeling that pure verite has eliminated the need for commentary. In practice, there are some serious drawbacks to commentary that cannot be ignored. Very often it tends to be authoritarian, giving the impression of the voice of God speaking. The tone can be patronizing, with the audience treated like a child. Done badly, narration seems like a horrendous lecture forced upon the audience. Finally, instead of stimulating thought and participation, narration can produce a deadly passivity that distances the viewers from the film.

The above is true, but I think there is a much more positive side to narration. For example, though pure action films and the verite efforts of Leacock and the Maysles can work well with no commentary, the complex essay film almost always demands it if it is to have any level of seriousness. Narration can quickly and easily set up the factual background of a film, providing simple or complex information that does not arise easily or naturally from the casual conversation of the film participants. It can complement the mood of the film, and above all it can provide focus and emphasis. It does not have to judge what is seen, but it should help the viewer understand more fully the significance of what is on the screen.

161

Taking a rigid stance that no films should have narration or that all films should have narration seems to me rather stupid. Certain films work well without narration. Others are tremendously enhanced by narration. The job of this chapter is to see that when you do have to write narration, you can do it well.

The broad function of narration is to amplify and clarify the picture. It should help establish the direction of the film and provide any necessary information not obvious from the visuals. In a simple but effective way, it should help focus what the film is about and where it is going. Narration can also help establish the mood of the film, and it is particularly useful in bridging filmic transitions and turning the film in a new direction.

The first thing one learns in journalism is to let the reader know the five W's: who, where, when, what, and why. This is often the function of narration when the visuals by themselves make no sense. Let's imagine the following scene: A sunswept hillside is covered with thousands of people of all ages. Their appearance is somewhere between that of gypsies and hippies.

Some are cooking over camp fires, others playing musical instruments in the shade of hastily erected tents. In the center of the multitude is a grave surrounded by a brick wall. Fires are burning in the vicinity of the grave. All around the grave old and young men are doing Greek-style dancing, their arms linked at the shoulder, while women press notes into the cracks in the grave wall.

By itself, the above scene is fascinating but incomprehensible to the viewer. It needs some narration, not a lot based on the "who, why, where" approach, to make it meaningful.

> Once more it's May. And as they have been doing for the last six hundred years, the followers of Abu Jedida, miracle man and wonder worker, have come to this lonely spot in the Atlas Mountains to celebrate his death. Here, for twenty-four hours, picnic, passion, and prayer will intermingle till once more the crowds will disperse, leaving Abu Jedida to his lonely thoughts.

The narration lays out the essentials of the scene but doesn't describe everything. We still don't know why the men are dancing or why people are putting notes in the wall. However, it doesn't take much intelligence to assume that the first is a sign of fervor while the notes are pleas to Abu Jedida to grant favors such as a successful birth or marriage. These facts might or might not be explained as the film proceeds. The narration is simple, but there's the odd bit of flamboyant alliteration in "picnic, passion, and prayer." However, as the scene itself is fairly wild and colorful, for once the extravagant commentary can be excused.

The basis of writing most narration is finding interesting facts and presenting them in the most gripping or imaginative way to the viewer.

Facts are the raw material of commentary. The writer's job is to use them judiciously to make the narration come alive and sparkle. This is obvious. However, what is less clear is how far the writer should add value judgment to the facts. Some writers take a purist position on this matter, arguing that while it is permissible to draw attention to certain situations and present evidence about them, the judgment must come from the viewer.

That's fine as a basic rule, yet there are times when the writer feels so passionately about a subject that his or her own commitment and point of view must be expressed directly in the narration. That kind of editorializing, which can be seen in the films of Ed Murrow or Bill Moyers, is problematic, yet it is probably appropriate to films calling for action and social change. But such writing usually carries a tremendous charge and should not be used indiscriminately.

Before you actually begin writing the narration, you must consider what voice and style is most appropriate for the film. You probably thought about all these things very early on, but if not you must think them through before committing yourself to the word processor. Is your style to be somber and serious, or are you aiming at a lighter and more folksy effect? If you are doing a historical film, you will probably adopt the former. If you are doing a film on tourism or animals, you might prefer the latter. I say "probably" because there are no iron rules.

Again, you might want to try for a slightly humorous and offbeat style, the approach taken by James Burke in his series "Connections" about technological change throughout history. In program three, *Distant Voices*, Burke discusses the nature and purpose of the medieval tournaments, with their fights and jousting.

Visual	*Audio*
Slow-motion montage of knights on horseback	*Burke:* The answer to shock was a stronger horse that could take all the punishment And rearing big horses—as anybody who knows will tell you—ain't cheap.
	But the coming of the knight changed the basic structure of society.
Cheering tournament. Montage of horses, riders, spectators at castle.	The tournament was a kind of cross between the circus coming to town and a wild free-for-all, where half the time things ended in absolute shambles with whole towns getting burnt down.

Things got so out of hand that even the Pope tried to ban the fun and games. These were definitely not the days of courtly manners and fair play. But behind all the chicanery and dirty tricks there were two very good reasons for these affairs, and they both had to do with fighting on horseback.

You see, the idea of cavalry was a new thing and you needed all the training you could get to use the lance right. The other reason had to do with the prizes you won. You knocked a guy off his horse at the tournament and you took everything—his armor, his horse, his saddle, the lot.

Burke's style is really quite amazing. It's loose, conversational, free and funny. He uses colloquialisms and slang and is occasionally quite ungrammatical. And it works superbly. It looks easy but is quite difficult to imitate. In essence, it's a style evolved by Burke to suit his own personality. Burke presents the film and gives the image of a loose, easygoing sort of fellow, so the language fits the man.

This is an important point, for very often you are writing not in the abstract but for a particular narrator. Thus, if Roger Mudd or Ted Koppel were presenting the above film, your language might be more serious; if Cronkite were presenting, it might be a bit more folksy. If, however, you were writing for actors such as Laurence Olivier or Peter Ustinov, then your narration could go almost any way imaginable.

The advantage of a presenter is that he or she is always talking directly to the viewing audience, which enhances contact and involvement. If the documentary does not have a presenter, as most do not, you have to decide what perspective you want to use—first, second, or third person. The essay, the film on history or science, tends to use the formality and objectivity of the third person. The effect is rather distant and cool and runs the danger of being slightly authoritarian. Nevertheless, used well the third person can be highly effective. As suggested above, the second person helps involve the audience. It creates a sense of dialogue and conversation, of commonality with the audience.

Here is the same film written first in the third person, then in the second:

Third person

One turns the bend and sinister mountains immediately confront the viewer. On the right a dirt track is seen to ascend to a black hilltop from which can be heard strange noises. Thus the stranger is welcomed to Dracula's lair.

Or you could write it this way:

Second person

You turn the bend and immediately confront dark, sinister mountains. On your right a dirt track climbs to a black hilltop from where you hear strange noises. Welcome, my friend, to Dracula's lair.

To my mind the latter version, using the second person, is far stronger and more effective, at least in this film; here you want the viewer to feel, taste, and smell the atmosphere of Dracula's retreat. But there is another difference between the two versions. The first is essentially written in the passive voice, the second in the active. Generally, the active voice makes for more energetic and vital writing.

Your final option is to write in the first person, and this can be highly attractive for a number of reasons. It can be a gentler form that gives scope for a tremendous number of nuances. It's far less linear than the third person and allows you to be more experimental. And of course, the more personal form makes for a more human and closer identification with the viewer. In short, the "I" form breaks down the distance between the filmmaker and the viewer, which is one of the key objectives of good narration.

One of the best examples of first-person narration occurs in *City of Gold* (mentioned earlier), a film about the Klondike gold-rush town of Dawson City. According to Canadian critic D. B. Jones, "This was a film which needed an *outstanding* commentary, one that would work together with the pictures and the music to evoke the nostalgic mood that the filmmakers were after." The filmmakers' solution was to use Canadian author Pierre Berton, who had himself grown up in the Yukon, to write the commentary.

Berton uses his own childhood memories of Dawson City, then contrasts them with his father's stories about Dawson City at the height of the gold rush; thus, the personal element of the film works on two levels. At first the narration is full of comments such as, "Every summer we used to play locomotive engineer, almost on the very spot where George Carmack picked up the nugget that started it all." The writing is poetic, warm, revealing a gentle, happy childhood. Gradually the father's memories take over. "Even when my father's memory began to fail, this spectacle remained. The Chilkoot Pass. You had to pack a ton of goods up this terrible forty-five-degree slope of sheer ice—a year's outfit. Without that the Mounties wouldn't let you enter the Yukon. You couldn't stop to rest or it might be hours before they'd let you back into that endless human chain."

One of the reasons that *City of Gold* works so well is that it taps effortlessly into mood and feelings and memory. It is this ability to deal with feelings that I find so attractive about the first person.

A few years ago I was asked to write the narration for a film on the Yom Kippur War between Egypt and Israel. The film, *Letter from the Front*, was a string of hastily edited battle sequences, and I was brought in to write the commentary when the film had already been edited and mixed. The film had no line to speak of, and the task was to write to pictures and sequences that couldn't be changed and went all over the place. My answer was to use first-person narration from the point of view of one of the soldiers. That way the narration could dart all over the place and also reflect the inner tensions and feelings of someone in the midst of war. The following sample suggests my approach to the problem:

Visual	*Audio*
Soldiers lying alongside cars and in tents, absolutely tired.	You keep running, and when you stop there is this overwhelming tiredness, not just of your body but of your whole being. Where are your friends? Where are those you love? And you feel a terrible heaviness covering everything.
Soldiers playing football barefoot. Mountains behind them.	Okay, so now we have a cease-fire. Big deal! Mind you, I'm not knocking it. It's good, but I don't quite believe in it, and the silence is strange.
Soldiers talk, write letters, sleep on the grass, etc.	Now I find time completely standing still for me. There's no yesterday and no tomorrow . . . no normalcy, no reference points. There's only the immediacy of this moment.
	We are all still mobilized and plans, future, home life—all these things are vague and unreal.
	A lot of my mood has to do with the fact that we tend to share all our emotions here, both the joy and the pain . . . and of the latter there is quite a lot.

In order to write good and accurate narration you have to prepare a shot list. This means going through the film with a footage counter or seconds counter and listing the length and description of all the key shots and sequences. This is something that you the writer should do rather than the editor as each of you will view the film slightly differently.

If your film is about a university, then your first few shots might consist of groups getting off buses, students talking to each other, a cluster of buildings, more students, the occasional professor, and then a drastic cut to a lesson in progress. Your subsequent shot list might look like this:

Seconds	Picture
10	Buses arrive at campus
4	Students get off buses
8	Groups of students talking
5	A Japanese student close-up
6	A Burmese student close-up
8	Old buildings
7	New campus buildings
10	Group of students with guitars
12	Univ. profs enter campus
8	A professor looking like a hippie
15	Science classroom

The timings and groupings of the first few shots are obvious and probably would have been the same even if your editor had prepared the shot list. But why single out the Japanese student and the Burmese student? Because you suspect that at this point in the narration you may want to say something about foreign students, and these pictures are the obvious trigger.

You have also noted the hippie-looking professor for more or less the same reasons. You sense that while you may want to use the first few shots of professors to say something general about the faculty, the shot of the hippie professor may allow you to go in a different direction. Over the general shots you could say, "There are four hundred members of the faculty"; as the hippie shot comes up, you continue, "The trouble is, these days you can't tell them from the students." In other words, your shot list should help you not just make general statements, but should also give you the key pictures for making specific points.

You proceed through the entire film in this fashion until you have a shot list of four or five pages. Then you can forget the hot and airless editing rooms, take your pages, and go back to the comfort of your home to write. You don't need the editing table or the screen any more. The two essential things you need, pictures and timing, are contained in the shot list.

At this stage you know what you want to write and how to write it; you have only one problem—timing. That's where the timing section of the shot list becomes invaluable. It tells you that although you want to say something about the type of students who attend the university these days, you must be able to express everything in less than twenty seconds as you only have twenty seconds of student shot. In fact, you probably have to express your thoughts in twelve seconds as you want the film to be able to "breathe."

Some people count syllables or words, allowing themselves, say, eight words to three seconds. My own method is to take out a stopwatch and write two or three versions until I have my thoughts into the allowable time. This seems hard, but it becomes quite easy after practice.

One problem is that people read at different speeds. So while the narration may fit when you read it, your actual narrator may read much more slowly and ruin your timing. The answer is to underwrite rather than overwrite; also, keep in the back of your mind that you may have to cut certain words and phrases when you finally lay in the narration.

Style and Language

Who are you writing for?

A story is told of a broadcaster, in the first days of radio, who had a beautiful voice but kept stammering every time he confronted the cold, bleak metal of the microphone. His wife knew he loved his horse, and solved the problem by putting a picture of his horse around the microphone. Henceforth he wasn't talking to the anonymous masses, but to his horse.

When I work, I assume that I am writing for a good friend. He is sitting beside me watching the film, and in a simple but effective way I want to make the film more interesting for him. I'm not going to use pompous or superintellectual phrases, but straightforward and conversational language. However, I am going to turn my imagination loose, letting it go off in any direction that will make the film more dynamic and alive for my friend.

One thing I am definitely not going to do is describe what's on the screen. Your viewers don't need to be told that the woman is wearing a red dress or that the scene is taking place in Paris; they can see all that. But they may be interested in knowing that the dress was worn by Queen Erica on her wedding day and then never worn again after her husband was assassinated a few hours later. And they may look at the Eiffel Tower in a different way if you tell them that each year at least five people leap to their deaths from the top deck.

What I have been suggesting above are the two basic rules of narration: (1) Don't describe what can clearly be seen and understood by most people; (2) however, do amplify and explain what the picture doesn't show. Apart from these, there are no real rules to writing narration, but there are quite a number of hints about the process that may help you along the way.

Writing for the ear. The journalist writes for the eye, but when you are dealing with narration you are writing for the ear. And there's a world of difference. That generally means your vocabulary has to be simpler and immediately understandable. For instance, an article in a magazine might read as follows: "They were wed the morning after the raid on the store with the precious stones. The intruders had also sexually violated one of the shop girls." Film narration would put it like this: "They got married the morning after the jewel robbery. The thieves had also raped one of the shop girls."

You can't go back. Another essential difference between text and film writing is that in the latter you can't go back. Your writing has to be clear and make its impact immediately. This very much affects the order in which you express things. A news article might say, "Rockefeller, Louis B. Mayer, the Queen of England, Alexander the Great, and Rasputin all loved horses." A film script would put it this way: "Rockefeller loved horses. So did Louis B. Mayer, the Queen of England, Alexander the Great, and Rasputin." In the first version the meaning of the sentence becomes apparent only at the end. In the film version we know what we are talking about from the start. Of course, if you wanted the commonality of all these people to be a mystery, you could use the first version. But that doesn't happen very often.

Grammar and slang. Your narration may be grammatical and follow the normal rules of writing, but it doesn't necessarily have to be so. Your writing does not stand by itself. It is meant to accompany pictures, and the only important thing is the effect of that final combination.

Most of the time your writing will in fact be relatively standard. You will probably avoid anything too archaic or literary and keep to a simple structure. What do we mean by literary or archaic? You could say, "A million dollars sounds like a lot, but compared to the federal deficit it is an infinitesimal amount."

The problem here is that the expressions "federal deficit" and "infinitesimal amount" may be a little too complex for the film, so a simpler version might be, "A million dollars sounds like a lot, but compared to the government's debt it's peanuts!"

If we look again at Burke's script on tournaments and knights, we see immediately that he felt absolutely unconstrained about using colloquialisms and slang.

> The only answer was a stronger horse that could take all that punishment. And rearing big horses, as anyone who knows will tell you, *ain't cheap*. . . .
>
> The tournament was a kind of cross between the circus coming to town and a wild free-for-all, where half the time things ended in *absolute shambles*. . . .
>
> You knocked *a guy* off his horse and you took everything. . . .

> Well Henry had some arrows shot at *this mob* to get them to do something, because they'd been standing around *arguing the toss* who should lead the French army.

Standard English and fine grammar it ain't. But it certainly works.

Summary and rhetorical questions. I mentioned that unlike the printed page, you can't stop and go back in film. But what you can occasionally do—and it makes for greater clarity—is summarize where you are before moving on to another idea or sequence. "So there were the American soldiers in Stalag Luft Nine. Six hundred of them from all ranks. They had fought the good fight . . . and lost. The question was whether they would simply give up or try to escape. Next morning the German guards found the answer!" The above contains both a summary and a question. The occasional question is useful because it helps the audience articulate what's on their mind and also moves the film forward. "We wanted to know where they kept their war canoes, or whether their fighting ships were just myth. The chief told us we could find them three miles up the stream."

Simple, powerful sentences. Narration seems to work best using short, simple sentences with the main action verb fairly near the beginning. I am not saying that you cannot use more elaborate structures, with multiple ideas and a whole series of dependent clauses, but you have to be much more careful in your writing. Here is what I mean by the simple, strong sentence: "The American troops were young and untried. They came from Texas, from Utah, from Oregon. Few had ever been as far east as Chicago or New York. Now they found themselves five thousand miles from home, ready to invade mainland Europe. It was June fourth. Few knew it, but D day was only hours away."

Directing attention. When you write, you can make the viewer see anything you want. Although there may be a mass of information on the screen, it is your words that show the viewer what is significant. But your words do more than direct attention. They are also there to give meaning.

We are doing a film about the American South. Suddenly we see a river, trees, a paddle-wheel steamer, houses in the distance, a few horses moving around. What does it mean? Nothing until we add the commentary. "All was quiet, not even a breeze. Few knew or cared that a young man had been lynched on that tree just a day before." Write it that way and all the attention goes to the trees, and the scene takes on an aura of horror. But you could write it another way: "Once there were steamers by the dozen all along the river. They were painted like rainbows and puffed along like Delilah making a grand entrance. Now only one survives, forgotten, desolate, and soon for the breaker's yard." Write it like that and the trees are forgotten while everyone looks at the steamer.

Atmosphere. One of the challenges of narration writing is to add an extra dimension to what can be seen on the screen. We are not talking about adding information or facts, but about enhancing the mood of the film. We are trying to get inside the scene and bring it to life, so that the viewer is fully involved in the emotional experience of the film. As a writer you want the audience to feel the joy of the child who learns to walk after years on crutches, to understand the sadness of divorce, the isolation of prison, or the excitement of scuba diving.

One way of doing this is by careful use of the color words, of adjectives, of words that add texture. The words are there to complement the image, and when everything works in harmony the effect can be tremendous.

> In the bitter coldness of the night the jeeps went around collecting their burdens. Husbands said goodbye to wives, sweethearts to lovers. Faces were pale, lips cold, eyes wet. Few words were said as the last jeeps departed into the clinging mists, carrying the men to the darkness of the waiting planes, loaded bombers, and an unknown dawn.

Below are two examples from *What Harvest for the Reaper*, written by Mort Silverstein. Both show how a judicious use of adjectives can add immensely to the scene. In the first extract buses are taking black migrant workers north from Arkansas to the work camps of Long Island at the start of the summer.

> Their guide for the 1800-mile trip will be crew leader Anderson. His charge is thirty dollars. Since none can afford it, they are in debt to Anderson before the trip begins.
>
> The bus marked "special" will take them away from the indifferent towns of Arkansas, past the county seats of Tennessee into Virginia, then over hundreds of miles of sterile highway that bypass great mountains and heartbreaking sunsets, until ultimately they reach Cutchogue, Long Island.
>
> Earlier in the season Cutchogue was a resort, one of the prides of Long Island. The prim town is resplendent with schools, churches, and old homes. It also has a migrant labor camp.

The writing is simple, concise, but very effective. There aren't in fact many adjectives, but the ones used—*indifferent* towns, *sterile* highways, *heartbreaking* sunsets, and *prim* town—carry a tremendous punch.

At the end of the film the workers go back to Arkansas, somehow more deeply in debt than when they started the summer. they have been exploited by their bosses and have nothing to show for their months of sweat and grind. This is how Silverstein deals with leaving the work camp for the last time.

> The season which began in the vast darkness of night and soul is now ending the same way.

On the last day this legacy, these odors, these noises, these silences. Three men pack to go home. They have worked for almost six months on the fields of Eden, and are irrevocably mired in debt.

Eight years ago, in a memorable CBS documentary *Harvest of Shame*, the late Edward R. Murrow urged wage, health, and housing reforms for migrant workers. Eight years later, the migrant condition is still the shame of the nation.

Another interesting element of the above extract is the use of words such as "these" and "today." These words, in conjunction with words such as "here" and "now," add a sense of urgency and immediacy to the film. They can also tie the pictures to the text when there is really very little connection. Let's assume that we've found some rather indifferent pictures of war. One of the shots shows children wandering around doing nothing. As such the shot says very little to us until we add a few "heres" and "these."

Here, in the city, there is silence. The bombing has stopped. But few of these children know what tomorrow will bring. Will the fighting return? Will the slogans be repainted? Will hell reawaken in a different guise? No one knows, but today there is calm after the scream, and the city sleeps.

The particular versus the general. On the whole, particular descriptions work better than generalities. The generalities of narration are soon forgotten, whereas a striking word picture is held in the mind. We are doing a film about banking and have to tell the story of Joseph X. Smith. We don't have much to work with. In fact, all we have on-screen are some fairly dull photographs of Joseph as a young man with a cigar and some equally dull photographs of him around age sixty. One version of his life might go as follows:

He made his fortune with gambling and real estate. Eventually he was worth ten million dollars and opened his first bank. He certainly lived very well and had dozens of women. But the crash of '29 hit him hard. Eventually he lost all his money and lived the last days of his life where he'd started out, around the gambling dens of Kansas City.

Written this way you don't remember much about Joseph Smith. He is a gray character, soon forgotten. But if you particularize the details of his life everything changes.

He made his first fortune with a ten-dollar bet. He won an oil well that was thought to be dry. It wasn't, and within a year he owned half the town. Later he gambled in Europe with King George V, kept four mistresses who all had to wear the same red velvet dress, had his Rolls-Royce painted green . . . but finished up selling matches outside the gambling dens of Kansas City.

It's a bit exaggerated, but you certainly remember the guy.

The power of words. An old saying has it that pictures don't lie. Well, it's not quite true. Often they take on meaning only when the narration is added, a point we have been making throughout this chapter. This ability to provide meaning to a scene is a tremendous power, and in many cases you can bend the scene in almost any direction you want.

On-screen we see crowds of young people, yachts, a marina, and a regatta in progress. It's a happy season with everybody smiling and enjoying the atmosphere. Now let's put some words to it.

> They come once a year to celebrate Britain and boating. Soon the yachts will be out, vaunting a pride in old English workmanship.
>
> Today Nelson and Drake would be happy to see that their countrymen still rule the seas.
>
> So for the moment, and rightfully so, work is left aside as the youngsters cheer on the crews and relax in this festival of fun.

Or we could take a more critical tack.

> They come once a year to celebrate Britain and boating. But while they drink champagne and eat strawberries, the rest of the country is going to ruin.
>
> Yes, it's nice to talk of Drake and Nelson, but wouldn't it be more appropriate to talk of idle shipyards, silent factories, and men out of work? Yes, let these privileged few vent their hollow cheers, because tomorrow comes the silence and the reckoning!

Narration plus interview. Very rarely do you find a film that is all narration. Most films are a blend of narration, sync interviews, and voice-overs. It is therefore worth thinking over carefully how you can best combine all the elements. A good way is to keep the narration very factual and let the voice-overs and sync provide the emotional experience of the film. The episode *Morning* in the Thames Television series "The World at War" provides a good example on this point. Written by John Williams, the film examines the D day invasion of France by American, British, and Canadian troops. At the point of the extract the sea invasion is just about to be launched.

Narrator: Never had the channel waters seen such a mighty force. Heading for France were some six and a half thousand vessels of all types, marshaled and escorted by the Allied navies.

Glider fleets were waiting, wearing their D day markings. The first division would go in by glider and parachute, dropping behind the invasion beaches. Their losses were expected to be as high as seven out of every ten men.

Kate Summersby (voice-over): They all had their faces blackened because they were going to jump into Nazi-occupied Europe in a very short time, and you kept thinking, "I wonder how many are going to come back?" Later on General Eisenhower said, "You know, Kay, it's very hard to look a soldier in the face knowing you might be sending him to his death."

Narrator: In the last hours of the fifth of June the airborne troops set out for France.

George Alex (voice-over): Butterflies in your stomach, and you're wondering, "What am I doing here? Why did I volunteer? Am I crazy?" And everything's going through your mind, and you're worried and you know it's coming up soon. I was afraid. I was nineteen and I was afraid.

Narrator: Many men were afraid that night. They were storming Hitler's Festung Europa—Fortress Europe.

And across the water the Germans waited, not knowing when or where the blow would fall.

Problems

It's very easy to fall into certain traps while writing narration. Most of the traps or problems are obvious, but every writer falls victim to them sooner or later. Below I have listed a few of the most common pitfalls.

Lists and statistics. Although many individual shots are remembered because of the emotional force of the image, this doesn't work for narration. In fact, one of the most disconcerting things for a writer is to realize that very little of the narration is remembered ten minutes after the film has finished. If the broad details of the message are remembered, that's enough. Having said that, it becomes obvious why we avoid lists and statistics. They rarely make an impact at the time and are forgotten in five seconds.

Occasionally numbers *are* necessary, but they have to be used wisely to be effective. When the narrator in the D day script tells us that "losses were expected to be as high as seven out of ten men," it works because at that point we are eager to know those facts. However, had the writer said, "Losses were expected to be as high as 70 percent," I don't think it would have worked as well because *percent* is a more abstract term for us, while "seven out of ten men" brings us very close to the individual deaths.

The task of the writer is to make cool, abstract figures come alive for us in human terms. Brian Winston did this brilliantly while writing the script for *Out of the Ashes.* Brian needed to say that the SS troops, operating in Russia, killed over a million civilians in just over a year. How could one bring something so monstrously incomprehensible down to earth? This is what he wrote: "Close behind the front lines came the mobile killing squads of the SS. In sixteen months they and other members of the German army shot nearly one and a half million Jews—two human beings a minute for every hour of every day for nearly five hundred days." The last half of the sentence is vital, because only then do we grasp the enormity of the crime.

Wall-to-wall narration. Some filmmakers are reluctant to take up the pen; others simply don't know when to put it down. They overwrite, thus committing one of the cardinal sins of filmmaking. Your narration should be sparse and compact. Say enough to make the point, then shut up. You may think that piling detail on detail will improve the film, but that's rarely the case. More than likely you are just turning off the viewer by the sheer volume of your words. Remember that the picture needs room to breathe and that the viewer needs space and time to digest and reflect on the narration.

Another essential point is that very often narration is redundant, and you are better off letting the pictures make your point. Let us assume we are doing a film about Samuel Clemens. We have pictures of old steamers, river activity, ports, boys on rafts, and generally a rich montage of life on the Mississippi. We could write:

> As he rode up and down the river two characters formed in his mind—one a mischievous rascal called Tom Sawyer, and the other his trusted friend Huckleberry Finn. And, oh, what adventures he would give them, and what characters and sights would fill his pages. Tom would get into scrapes, meet villainous tramps, and flee for his life. And Huck would float down the river, seeing all the sights and wonders that Twain himself knew so well.

As I say, we could write it that way—but we wouldn't. Instead, we would stop the narration at the end of the phrase "and what characters and sights would fill his pages." At that point you don't need to say any more because the pictures suggest exactly what Twain is going to write about.

Clichés. Watch out for the cliché, the hackneyed phrase. At one time all the authors on feature film writing used to enjoy themselves by listing the most popular clichés: "A man's gotta do what a man's gotta do." "Yeah, it's quiet. Too damn quiet!" "There's only one doctor who can help you, and he's in Vienna." We laugh, but we do the same thing in documentary. We see a phrase that is good, and then use it so often that it ceases to have any impact.

A friend of mine used to make children's films about orphanages, resettlement centers, and good works. He chucked it when he found that the cliché factor had taken over. He had found one good phrase in his first film: "Do we want children of darkness or children of light, children of despair or children of hope?" When he found himself repeating this phrase in each film he knew it was time to quit.

Writing for different viewers. A problem that arises again and again, particularly when doing documentaries for television, is how to adjust your narration to accommodate a wide spectrum of viewers. For example, if you are doing a film on history some may know your subject well, while others may know nothing. If you give too much information you may insult the intelligence of half your viewers, telling them things they know backwards. But if you assume that the audience already has a good knowledge of the subject, you may be talking over the heads of the other 50 percent of your audience. The answer lies in finding a subtle way of presenting your information so that both sides feel happy.

Let us say we have to do a film about Peron's dictatorship. We are talking of events that happened forty years ago whose chief characters are much less familiar to us than are Churchill and Hitler. Because we know that half the audience was born after World War II, we need to establish who's who and what's what. So we could write: "Peron was an army colonel who became a dictator. He led the fascist party in his country. He ruled Argentina and gained power in 1945." All the facts are there, though expressed a little bluntly. But by the time you have recited them, half your audience has said, just before turning off the television, "Who do they think we are? Six-year-olds?" You could express facts in a less offensive fashion: "Throughout the forty years since militarism and politics swept Peron into the dictatorship of Argentina, people have wondered when democracy would return to a country governed by generals." In the second version the facts are given casually and without insulting the intelligence, and everyone is happy.

Difficult terminology. Sometimes you find yourself having to put across difficult concepts with highly involved terminology. This is particularly true of scientific or medical films. The way out of these difficulties is to simplify your language, presenting the concept visually in a manner that everyone can understand. This may require using graphics or animation or creating a scenario that demonstrates the concept.

A few years ago I saw a film on Einstein's life and work. Obviously, at some point the film had to discuss Einstein's theory of relativity—not the easiest of concepts to grasp, even for scientists. However, the writer presented the theory in an elegant fashion. He showed an airplane in flight so that we could appreciate that its speed relative to the ground was five hundred miles an hour. He then cut to two men playing catch *inside* the plane. Given this situation, it was easy to talk about the speed of the ball relative to the plane's motion to the ground. I'm not sure that everyone in the audience understood afterwards the significance of $E = MC^2$, but at least they were on the way to understanding.

Once the Writing Is Finished

Scratch track. I mentioned earlier that it's useful to write some tentative narration to help in the first steps of the editing process. You can record this yourself, and the editor can lay your scratch track against the picture. This gives you a sense of how the film is going and also allows your sponsor or executive producer to react to a more complete film. Once your final narration is complete, it is vital to try it against the film. This time you don't have to bother recording it: instead, you can just read it against the picture. This will give you and the editor a chance to see whether it sounds right and whether your timing is more or less correct.

The narrator. Your narrator can often make or break your film, so get the very best person available within your budget. When the narrator is actually going to appear on-camera, you have two additional problems to solve: how to integrate the stand-ups with the rest of the text and how to get a natural performance from the narrator.

The easiest and most efficient solution to the first problem is to write the narrator's text after you have completed the rest of the commentary. You can then see the best way to bring the narrator in and out and also judge how his stand-up text can help move the film along and solve difficult transitional points.

You have various options for solving the second problem. You can write your full text and have the narrator learn it by heart. A few narrators like James Burke can do this, but not many. Second, you can use either "dummy cards," cards placed beside the camera with the full text, or a teleprompter underneath the lens. I don't like either of these methods because the viewer can sense the eyes darting to the cards, and the performance rarely comes over as natural or spontaneous.

I prefer to go over the key points of the text with the narrator and then let him or her simply make it up in front of the camera. It may take two or three tries, but the result usually has more punch than you get with either the cards or the teleprompter.

Where your narrator is simply a "voice off," your problems are simpler. Your key concern then becomes to find the best voice to carry the message of your film. Sometimes you have exactly the right person in mind. If you don't, try a few auditions on tape. Have your would-be narrators read a few film passages and then play them back against the picture to see which works best.

Whenever possible, the narrator should see the film through with you in its entirety. After the screening you can take time out to explain what exactly you are looking for in the film and in the narration reading. Then let the narrator take the text home and read it. When you next meet, he or she will usually have some questions. Do you mind if certain words are changed so that it reads more easily? And do you mind if the narrator rephrases the text slightly because what you have written isn't very clear? This is also the time to discuss once more the style, pace, and mood of the reading—time to specify which passages you want read fast and which slow, which emotionally and which with humor. Is the narrator clear about what you are aiming for? If so, you can go ahead with the recording.

There are two ways of doing the actual recording. First, the narrator can record to picture, with you flashing a little red light every time you want a new section read. The other method is to have the narrator isolated in a recording booth and simply reading. I prefer the latter, reckoning that the narrator already has a good sense of the picture and that I want him or her to concentrate on the reading with as few distractions as possible.

Generally I try to let the narrator do the reading in one shot without interruption. At that stage you have indicated what kind of interpretation you want, and if the narrator is any good he or she should be able to hit it fairly easily. The advantage of letting the narrator just go is that with any luck, he or she will hit a good rhythm and pace and will have the time to work emotionally into the feel of the narration. Obviously, you stop the recording and go back if the reading is wrong, but if you are going to make a comment be very specific. Tell the narrator you want a passage put more dramatically or more slowly. Indicate specifically what words you want emphasized, and demonstrate what kind of rhythm you want. However, try to avoid too many interruptions in your aim for perfection, because the result may be counterproductive, with the reading deteriorating rather than improving.

In a long recording, watch that the narrator's vocal energy doesn't diminish. If it does, suggest a break. When you're finished, check the recording to see if you and the narrator are both satisfied. If not, redo any problematic sections.

The final thing is to record "presence" or "room tone." This is done by recording a minute or so of silence in the narration booth. It may sound funny to record silence, but in fact you are recording atmosphere that will fill in the sound gaps at the head and tail of the narration and occasionally in the middle.

Laying in the narration. However observant you have been during the narration recording, certain faults will show up only when you actually begin laying the track against the picture. You may find that there are problems with emphasis or intonation, that a certain phrase doesn't sound right, or that the balance between the music and narration is wrong. When you spot these points, it's usually easy to call the narrator back to make the changes. You also have to bear in mind that the sponsor or senior producer may require narration changes even at this late stage.

How do these changes affect your budget? I generally tell the narrator that I will want him or her for the main recording, but that I may also call later for minor changes. I then fix a total fee, thus avoiding awkward and costly negotiation at a later stage.

Examples

Throughout this chapter we have looked at extracts from different scripts to analyze approach, technique, and style. To finish off, we will examine a few scripts at greater length to see how writers develop their ideas.

The first example is from the Canadian film *City of Gold*, which combines personal style, memory, and evocation in a vivid portrait of Dawson City.

Visual	*Audio*
Children in park	*Pierre Berton*: This was my hometown. And my father's town before me. It's a quiet place. A few stores. A restaurant. Three, maybe four hundred people. Hard workers most of them.
Old men on porch	On the main street the old men sit on the porch of the hotel in the sunshine, and they talk about the old days . . . the good old days.
Chidren in park	The park is always full of kids.
Children and town	And after the rain there are always plenty of puddles to sail boats in.
Town views	But I must tell you that this town where I spent my childhood isn't like any other town in the world.
	This is Dawson City, the center of the Klondike gold rush. History will never see its like again.
Old buildings	Every summer, when the seeds of fireweed drifted across the valley of the Yukon River, we kids used to roam through these decaying build-

	ings. Some of them had been locked and barred for almost half a century.
Old pictures in buildings	You could buy anything in Dawson City, in its heyday, I remember my father telling me . . . anything from oysters to opera glasses. You could buy a dance-hall queen for her weight in gold, and one man did. His name was Chris Johanson, and he lived on Whiskey Hill.
Old steamboat	We played steamboat captain, too. These deserted stern-wheelers were part of a fleet of, oh, 250, that steamed up the Yukon in the stampede days.
Town, old men, atmosphere	Most of the men are gone with the steamboats. Of the tens of thousands who came here only a handful found the gold they were seeking. And yet few, I think, regretted the journey to Dawson City, for the great stampede was the high point of their lives.
Chilkoot Pass: stark, ice-covered mountains	The winter of 1897. Beyond mountains two thousand miles north from civilization, the cry was GOLD! And all over the world a million people laid plans to go. One hundred thousand actually set out.
Miners' faces	Scarcely any of these men were miners. Most were white-collar workers. My father had just graduated from university in civil engineering. All of them had no idea. They were on the way to the Klondike to shovel up gold,

and they were going to be rich
beyond the dreams of avarice.

City of Gold was written by Pierre Berton in 1956 and still remains a model of scriptwriting excellence. It looks deceptively simple, but it is in fact meticulously well planned.

1. *Introduction*. The first few sentences set the scene and the tone with short, personal, and evocative statements. "There were always plenty of puddles to sail boats in."

2. *Theme*. The theme is then stated quickly and dramatically. "This is Dawson City, center of the Klondike gold rush. History will never see its like again." This last sentence about history begins to move the film along.

3. *Particulars*. Throughout the film Berton avoids generalities, giving us instead details that heighten the sense of the craziness of Dawson City in the good old days. "You could buy a dance-hall queen for her weight in gold, and one man did." Later, although he talks about the general types who came, he very quickly gets to the specific case of his father.

4. *Personal memory*. One of the keys to the film is the fluidity with which history and personal memory intermingle. While the father's recollections move the film along, Berton's own memories play their role too. "We played steamboat captain, too. These deserted stern-wheelers were part of a fleet. . . ."

5. *Story Progression*. One of the most important moments in the script is where Berton turns from reminiscence and scene setting to actually telling the story of the gold rush. It's all done in one short paragraph. "Most of the men are gone with the steamboats. . . . few . . . regretted the journey to Dawson City, for the great stampede was the high point of their lives. . . . The winter of 1897. Beyond mountains two thousand miles north from civilization, the cry was GOLD!" It's important to note that the transition from present to past is also made pictorially, because at that point the film changes from contemporary footage to animation of the stills from 1897.

James Burke's "Connections," also tackles history, but in a very different, idiosyncratic way. Burke's subject is technological and scientific change, the mere mention of which is pretty off-putting. However, Burke makes science and technology comprehensible to the most ignorant of us in a highly amusing and entertaining way. In *Distant Voices* the subject is the development of military technology. The film starts with a tease in which you see anonymous hands packing an atomic bomb into a suitcase and carrying it through a crowd. Over this the commentary states: "This is the nightmare of the second half of the twentieth century. A suitcase with an atomic bomb inside it. Once you steal the nuclear material any physics graduate can do the rest."

Burke then slides into the issue of how changes in military technology have caused social and political changes. His first example is the Battle of Hastings in 1066. Here he argues that the Normans won because they used mounted cavalry against the Saxon infantry. However, he adds, the deadly lance of the horseman could only be used because the stirrup had been invented—a small change with overwhelming historical results.

Gradually Burke goes on to talk of other changes: the coming of the knights and the rise of the aristocracy. In the extract below Burke wants to show how the lances of the cavalry were eventually defeated by another technological change: the introduction of the long bow. As usual, Burke's language is casual, full of odd puns and jokes. The language is also directly addressed to the audience pulling you right into the film.

Visual	*Audio*
Slow-motion montage of knights on horseback	By 1250 the big league was a very exclusive club only the very rich could join, thanks in the first place to the stirrup, and the way it had led to the fully armored knight on his massive war horse. The aristocrats now made sure the club stayed exclusive: they made knighthood hereditary and took on permanent family names instead of just being "son of somebody." And because the armor covered their faces, they needed identification marks to show in battle so they didn't get clobbered by their own men. These heraldic symbols completed the separation of the aristocrats from the rest. Immensely powerful and immensely rich, the armor-plated upper crust must have felt that they had absolutely got it made.
Burke sync	By the fourteenth century the knight was a massive, expensive, complex, two-ton war machine, and at full gallop it would annihilate anything coming the other way, except of course, another knight. And then from out of the valleys of

South Wales came something that was to take away from the armored knight his four centuries of domination, like that!

Burke in Westminster Abbey, moving around the statue of Henry V

Let me tell you what happened. Henry, here, had about eight thousand men knocked out by fatigue from marching nonstop seventeen days in the rain. About a mile away across a battlefield of mud were thirty thousand Frenchmen, half of them fully armored aristocrats who'd been up all the previous night, 'cause they'd slept in their saddles because they didn't want to get all their lovely armor dirty. An arrogant, overbearing, effete lot, full of death and glory, and me first.

Pan with Burke as he walks

So when, at about eleven in the morning Henry had some arrows shot at this mob to get them to do something, anything, because they had been standing around arguing the toss about who should lead the French army, oh, since seven in the morning, the French army upped and charged straight at Henry, straight across the sea of mud, straight on to the stakes that the English had put point up in their

Burke looks at Henry's sculptured face.

path, and that was when Henry played his trump card, didn't you? He called up the secret weapon his grandfather had discovered in the mountains of Wales, and when it came into action the slaughter was unimaginable.

Montage of shots of longbow, arrows, and battle in slow motion	That weapon was the Welsh longbow, and Henry had over one thousand of them. In the hands of a master the longbow would kill at four hundred yards—and in three bloody hours the French were massacred.

Most of Burke's tricks are obvious, so only two points need be added. First, Burke uses a lot of English slang that may be unfamiliar to American ears, so a purist American television station might raise objections to the script on that ground. Second, Burke writes for himself and goes very fast, packing a tremendous amount of information into a few seconds. He just about gets away with it, but I would be wary of emulating it.

In the *Gates of Time* I was asked to write a half-hour film on the history of the Old City of Jerusalem. One problem I had was the question of the narrator's stand-ups. As this wasn't a news, verite, or personal history film, I was able to write the core narration before we started shooting. However, as we came to editing I realized that the film was a bit too loose and could do with a few stand-ups to tie the sequences together. I then went through the film choosing five or six places where I thought a very short stand-up would help. If I wasn't sure that I needed a stand-up, I still wrote one, noting in my mind that I could always discard it if it wasn't necessary or didn't work.

The stand-ups were easy to write, taking only about an hour. The only real problem was to make sure that the entrances into and the exits from the stand-ups were integrated smoothly into the rest of the script.

Visual	*Audio*
Helicopter shots of Jerusalem	When he left Palestine in the '20s, the British governor of its capital said, "After Jerusalem there can be no higher promotion!"
	For him, as for millions of others, there was no counterpart to Jerusalem in the history of the West. Jerusalem was the center of two faiths and holy to a third. It was the light. The guardian of ideals. The eternal city, the symbol of perfection.

Ground shots: many cars, dense crowds jostling, thrusting	But as well as the Jerusalem of the *mind* there is also the Jerusalem of *reality*. There is the modern city developed in the last century, and the ancient city where over 25,000 people still live and work behind medieval fortress walls.
Sync stand-up	*Narrator:* And there it is. A city that has to cope with all the pressures of the '80s as well as the gifts and burdens of a unique history.
	And therein lies the dilemma. How does one preserve and honor the spirit of the past, and the legacy of time, and yet move into the twenty-first century?
	I'm Irv Kaplan, a writer and broadcaster. In this film I want you to join me in looking more closely at the challenges and dilemmas of this city, and also some of the solutions. . . .
	(Transitional section omitted)
Medieval maps of Jerusalem	*Narrator off-camera:* Following the Crusaders, the idea of the mystical perfection of Jerusalem deepened with the centuries. Thus the British poet Blake wrote that his deepest desire was "to build Jerusalem in England's green and pleasant land."
Idealized prints of nineteenth-century Jerusalem	Again and again the prints of nineteenth-century artists show an idealized image of a Bible city where Abraham, if alive, could still walk in peace and repose.
Archive footage of beggars, cripples, dark streets, foul	After such romance the reality of nineteenth-century Jerusa-

alleys	lem came as a bitter shock.
	Lepers, cripples, and beggars greeted the traveler at every gate.
Crowded, dirty churches, filthy crowds	Baedeker's guide warned him that rubbish and filth concealed the holy places.
	When Herzl, the pioneer Zionist dreamer, visited in 1898, he wrote, "When I remember thee, O Jerusalem, it will not be with joy. The musty deposits of two thousand years lie reeking in your alleys."
British troops enter Jerusalem.	In 1917 British and Australian troops under Allenby captured Jerusalem, ending four hundred years of Turkish rule. For the allied troops, many of whom were devoted churchgoers, it was a poignant moment.
Narrator sync	After his humble entry on foot through the Jaffa gate, General Allenby stood close to where I'm standing now. Here he swore to honor Jerusalem and protect its inhabitants. Jerusalem was the *sacred trust*, and its new guardians swore to do all they could for it.

16

Finishing the Film

The Sound Mix

Once you have finished editing, you have to mix your various sound tracks. Here you may be dealing with five or more tracks, the most common ones being the narration and sync tracks, two music tracks, and at least one effects track. Ultimately you are going to mix them down into one master track.

Narration. As director you should be present as the narration is laid in to make sure that the words hit at exactly the right spot. Sometimes you may have to do this by making small changes to the picture. Other times you will have to lengthen the narration by adding pauses (blank leader) between words or phrases or by shortening the narration by taking out extraneous words. You have to take care that your editing of the narration doesn't make the text sound awkward or peculiar. For example, you don't want to take out a word and then find that the text finishes on an unnaturally high note or that the sentence ends abruptly. Also, look again and again at how much text you actually need. If you have a tendency to overwrite, see if you can lose some nonessential sentences at this point. This will help the film breathe.

Music. Music is usually laid on two tracks so that you can always fade one out, if necessary, as you bring up the other. It's also good practice to leave the picture slightly long until you have finalized the music as you may want to cut the picture to the beat of the music. If your picture is slightly long, then there's no problem; you can just cut out a few frames. But if the picture is too short, you may be in trouble.

One of the essential things to do, once the music is laid, is check how the music, narration, and sync tracks harmonize with each other. Try to avoid competition. If you have some beautiful music that is more than mood background, make sure it is not laid opposite narration. When this happens the narration always wins and the music gets lost, because narration is given prominence in the sound mix.

187

A slightly different problem exists in finding the right balance between music and effects. Many editors put in excellent music and then create very full effects tracks to enhance the film's verisimilitude. That's fine, but make sure the two blend easily. If both are laid down in the same spot, you may sometimes have to choose one or the other, but not both. Either will work alone, but mixed together they may produce a dirty or muddy effect on the sound track that is not pleasing to the ear.

Sound effects. Some of your sound effects will have been recorded in sync, but others will be wild effects recorded on location or effects purchased from a music library. You will probably lay the first as you edit the picture; the latter are laid down when you have finished the music and narration tracks. In other words, the effects track is normally the last track to be laid. Effects bring the film alive, enhancing the sense of realism. Leave them out, and you miss them immediately.

Effects are used in two ways: as spot effects and as general atmosphere. Spot effects are sync effects of doors closing, guns going off, books dropping, feet marching—effects that must absolutely match the picture. General atmosphere effects add to the mood but are not necessarily tied to a spot source. Thus, in films you often hear birds singing or a dog barking without ever seeing them.

The main question regarding effects is how much you really need. We can put this another way: not everything that you see in a film that makes a noise will require a sound effect. In fact, you may use very few. Your goals are atmosphere and realism, not necessarily authenticity. Laying sound effects is not an automatic process, but one that leaves as much scope for creativity as choosing and laying the music.

You should always record a minute or so of wild sound on every location. When you lay the tracks, this wild sound can be "looped" either to fill in gaps in the sound or to provide atmosphere.

Dubbing cue sheet. Once you or the editor have laid in all the tracks you need to make a dubbing cue sheet or mix- chart. This is a diagram that shows the entry and exit of each sound on each track, its length, and its relationship to the sounds on the other tracks. The chart will then act as a master guide for the editor and the sound engineer during the mix.

The procedure for making the cue sheet is comparatively simple. The editor puts each track on the editing table, one at a time, and then notes down from the footage counter where each sound enters and exits. This information is entered into a chart, as shown in figure 16-1. A straight line represents a cut, a chevron a fade-in or a fade-out. Two chevrons side by side, with one inverted, is the sign for a sound dissolve. To make things easier many editors color-code their charts—red for music, blue for narration, and so on.

Studio procedures. The cue sheet for the mix represents your recording master plan, and I like to have two prepared, one for the editor and one for the sound engineer. The editor is normally in charge of the sound mix and

Figure 16-1. Dubbing Cue Sheet

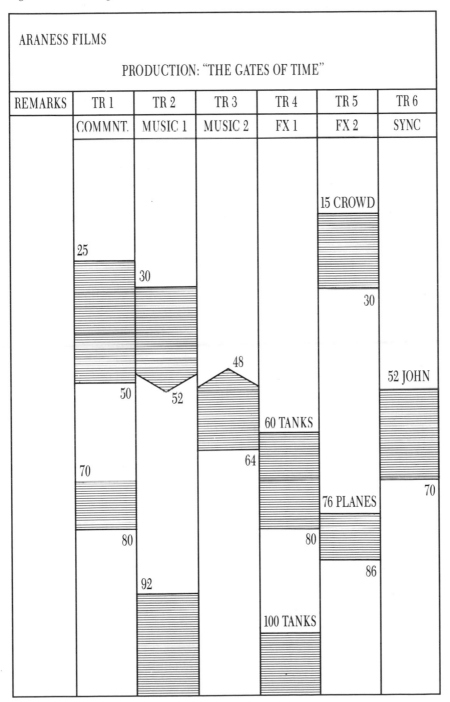

ARANESS FILMS

PRODUCTION: "THE GATES OF TIME"

REMARKS	TR 1	TR 2	TR 3	TR 4	TR 5	TR 6
	COMMNT.	MUSIC 1	MUSIC 2	FX 1	FX 2	SYNC

tells the sound engineer the desired shadings. However, you as director-producer will have the last word. At the mix the work print is projected onto a screen beneath which are running footage numbers, which you check against the numbers of the mix chart.

Projection print. One of the problems of a mix is that you are going to project your work print for the first time, running it back and forth with frequent starts and stops on the studio projector. This subjects the print to a lot of wear and tear and puts a great deal of stress on the splices. Very often splices tear, sprocket holes rip, and the film goes out of sync. Most people try to avoid the worst problems by double-splicing the film—that is, by putting splices on both sides of a join. But even that doesn't always help. The best solution is to make a low-cost black-and-white dupe print of the fine cut, using it solely for mix purposes. The extra cost is usually worth it.

Loops. Most studios carry, as standard practice, a number of background loops. These vary from bird sounds to traffic to helicopters. The better the studio, the more loops they will have available. It's useful to remember this, because in spite of all your efforts you may still find that you are lacking some sound when you start recording. Or you may find that your sound needs some additional buildup. In such a situation the loops come in very handy as they can be fed in and out of the recordings with little effort.

Mixing the tracks. Your objective is to mix all the tracks onto one balanced master track. You can do this in one go, or you can do it in stages through a series of premixes before tackling the master recording.

If you have a large number of tracks, say seven or eight, it is simply easier to premix a number of them before doing the master. Here simplicity and ease is the rationale for your actions. But there may be a second reason that is just as important: you may have to make an "M and E" track before the final mix. "M and E" stands for music and effects, and you always make sure you have this track if you think your film may be translated into a foreign language. If your film is going abroad, say to a French or German television station, they will ask for two tracks, the dialogue track and the M and E track. The station will then translate your English dialogue track to French or German, take the M and E track, and using both do a new final mix. The French or the German will then appear to be fully integrated with the music and the effects.

In what order should you do the premixes? There are no rules. Where possible, I like to do a first mix of music and effects (the M and E track), a second mix of sync dialogues, a third mix of the above two, and a fourth and final mix with the narration. If there is time and money for only one premix, then it's customary to do music and effects as a premix, bringing in dialogue and narration for the final mix.

Mixing can be a tremendously tedious process as you try to pay attention to the way all the elements blend together. Usually you will screen only half a minute or so at a time; using the mix chart as a guide, the editor will tell the engineer how the sound should be matched and recorded for that section. The recording is rarely perfect the first time: the music comes in too loudly or a certain effect isn't heard. The second time you try the same passage, everything works except that the music fade is done badly. So you bounce back and forth until you are all satisfied and can move on to the next section.

Where the original quality of sound is not very good, it can often be enhanced by the studio equipment. A filter can take some of the hum off your track, or an echo can be laid in to emphasize mood.

What you are looking for the whole time is quality of the sound and harmony between the tracks. When you have finished you must listen to the playback of the final mix. If something is wrong, now is the time to redo it. In particular you should check this final mix very carefully against the picture for sync loss caused by the picture jumping a frame in the projector during recording.

Titles and Credits

Parallel with all the preparations for the sound mix, you should also have been thinking about titles, credits, and optical effects. The usual practice is to mark in opticals, dissolves, and supers during editing. If not, they must be marked in before the film goes to the lab for the negative cut. Title and credits are another story. You may well have left your decision on these — what they are, where they appear, and how they appear — until the fine cut is completed. But again the time has come for a final decision on these matters.

There are two options for the presentation of titles and credits. You can present them white or colored on a black or colored neutral background, or they can be supered (superimposed) over a still or moving picture. The first option is simple, usually effective, and without many technical problems. The second option can look flashier and more dramatic, but it costs more than the simple title cards and can look messy if the lab work isn't of the best quality.

If you do go for the supers, you have to be careful where you place them. First, the supers should usually appear over a fairly dark background so that they stand out. It's no use having a white or yellow super over a white sky. Second, you should check that the super doesn't obscure some vital information in the picture. This may mean that your titles or credits are not always dead center, but shifted left or right according to the background.

These days, with Letraset and computer graphics, you have a tremendous choice available for titles. You may want to go for simple lettering or something very elaborate. The field is wide-open to your own personal taste and feelings. For a whimsical film you might want to try ornately decorated titles. For a medical film you may want to keep the titles very straightforward.

There are no rules except one: make sure your titles and credits are readable. This means choosing the right size for them on the screen and leaving them on the screen long enough so that they can be read easily. Usually there is no problem with pop-in, pop-out titles or with titles that dissolve into each other. Roller titles or roller credits are another story. Roller credits are often so close together and pass by so quickly that they become completely incomprehensible. Be sure to check the distance between the credits on the roller and the speed of the crawl.

Making the Print

The final work on the titles and the sound mix should more or less coincide. You can then move on to actually making the print. When you and the editor are satisfied, you can give instructions for the mix to go to the lab, where an optical negative will be made from the magnetic recording. The only thing you should do before that is make sure that you have a dupe copy of the mix so that if anything goes wrong or if the mix gets lost you won't have to go through the whole recording session again. At that point you're finished with the sound.

Once you have concluded the work on the titles and the credits, you can leave the film at the lab for the negative cut. This can take anywhere from a few days to weeks or months, depending on the length of the film.

When the first answer print is ready, check first that the film is in sync and that the sound quality is good. Second, you need to see that the lab hasn't made any mistakes in the negative cut. This can mean frames or a shot missing, opticals lost, or even, as once happened to me, a shot printed upside down. Finally, you need to check the color quality of the print. Is the color bias right? Are the blues too blue or the greens too pale? Do some scenes have peculiar tones to them? Are some scenes printed too light and others too dark? Does the film have an overall unity to its color?

You'll be asking yourself these and a dozen other questions. Normally the first print will reveal a number of faults, and it is your task to catch them. Once you see what they are, you have to sit down with the lab technicians and see how they can be corrected. The best way of doing this is to get your cameraman to sit in on the color grading and comment on the problems of each scene.

Your film may go through two or three trial prints until you are satisfied you have the best copy possible. The cost of the extra trial prints is usually borne by the lab. All this takes time, but it's worth it because now you have something to show for those months of effort. Now, finally, you have a film you're terribly proud of, and which, even in your modesty, you think might be an outside candidate for a documentary Oscar.

Part V _____ *Special Cases*

17

Cinema Verite

The previous chapters have discussed different approaches and techniques involved in making documentaries, focusing generally on the basic documentary. It would obviously be useful to examine all the documentary types in depth, from the biography and profile film to the exploration and investigation essay, but in a work such as this one there are necessary space limitations. Nevertheless, four kinds of films raise complex and acute problems that I wish to discuss in detail. The genres in question are cinema verite, documentary drama, historical documentaries, and industrial and public relations films.

Cinema verite, or direct cinema as it is sometimes called in America, is actually a *method* of filmmaking rather than a type of film of the "profile" or "nature" variety. *Cinema verite* was the name given to the radical experiments in filmmaking undertaken in the United States, Canada, and France in the early 1960s. Robert Drew, Ricky Leacock, and Don Pennebaker in particular worked furiously to perfect a system whereby lighter, shoulder-borne cameras could be used with lightweight, synchronized tape recorders. Their technical breakthroughs produced nothing short of a revolution, radically altering structure and approach in documentary.

Some of the practitioners of the new cinema tentatively suggested that cinema verite would do away with the old fiction cinema. Though their approach varied from person to person, the general method of filming necessitated the following:

- an evolving story with plenty of incident
- no prestructuring
- following the story as and when it occurred
- a tremendously high ratio of shooting, up to forty or fifty to one
- no prompting, directing, or interviewing between the director or cameraman and the subject
- minimal commentary (if any)
- finding and building the film on the editing table

The results of this approach were tremendously fresh and exciting, certainly as compared t the well-crafted but rather dull, static, and predictable documentaries of the networks. Today it is hard to recall any of the news documentaries of CBS, NBC, or ABC from the 1960s, whereas the cinema verite films of that period are still constantly viewed.

In general, cinema verite films of the 1960s examined personalities, crises, and pop concerts, with some limited political coverage. Starting from that base, filmmakers of the 1970s and 1980s helped extend the range and possibilities of the form, which is still tremendously popular. For various reasons, cinema verite seems to be the most attractive option open to young filmmakers. It is associated with perhaps the greatest films of the 1960s. It also has a veneer of excitement and seems to promise intimacy, truth, and an ability to transcend the crass barriers of old-fashioned documentary: altogether an attractive canvas. As one student said to me, "It is less manipulative. More human. It gets to the heart of things, and it's more real and direct."

I am not entirely convinced. Cinema verite may be all that is claimed above, but I suspect there is another reason for its popularity; it seems to involve less work than do the older documentary forms. You apparently don't have to do any research. You don't have to write boring scripts and boring commentary. You don't have to bother with preplanning but can just go ahead and shoot. And if you screw things up, never mind; everyone knows the film is made in the cutting room. Indeed, despite its many attractions, cinema verite also has immense problems that are underrated by beginning filmmakers. You must consider them before you race ahead.

Shooting Difficulties

Cost. When you make a cinema verite film, you are entering uncharted regions. Very often you don't know what you will shoot, how much you will have to shoot, and what makes sense to shoot. You just plunge straight in and spend your time waiting to cover the critical moments. But as you don't even know what *are* the critical moments, the tendency is to shoot and shoot, and that becomes tremendously expensive. Many cinema verite films are shot on a ratio of forty or fifty to one because nothing is preplanned or prestructured. This may mean the purchase and development of fifty hours of film stock. If the film can be shot on videotape then there are tremendous savings, though editing costs may still be very high. Stock costs are just the beginning. Crew costs then have to be added, and as the number of shooting days are indeterminate, these may be tremendously high. Students viewing the marvelous early Drew and Leacock films often forget that these films were financed by Time-Life, which is certainly not one of the poorest corporations in the world.

Postproduction costs can also be astronomical. Not only is editing time likely to be longer than on the structured film, but taking care of the paperwork, transcripts, records, and the like is also likely to be expensive. *A Married Couple*, Allan King's study of a marriage in crisis, was shot over a period of eight weeks in 1969. The estimated budget for the ninety-minute film was $130,000. The final cost, due to overruns and the need for extra shooting, was $203,000. Today the cost would be at least $800,000 to $1 million—not very much for a feature, but very high for a documentary.

Finding the film. Some filmmakers plunge into their films without the least clue what they will be about. They're just following a hunch. If you film long enough something interesting will happen. I guess the same rationale supports the argument that if you leave monkeys long enough with a typewriter, they will write *Hamlet*. It seems obvious that one must have a clear concept before embarking on a film, yet many cinema verite filmmakers ignore that to their cost. You must know what your film is about. It may change direction or emphasis midway, but without that initial clarity you are going to finish up in some very deep waters.

Don Pennebaker took a risk in doing *Don't Look Back*, the story of Bob Dylan's first English tour, but not much of one. Dylan was controversial, colorful, charismatic. Something was bound to happen on the tour, and even if it didn't the songs would guarantee a reasonably entertaining film. By contrast, the dangers were far greater in Ira Wohl's Academy Award–winning *Best Boy*. Following a brain-damaged adult for a few years could not have been the most promising of subjects. In the end the film succeeds because of the warmth of the subject and his family, the sensitivity of the filmmakers, and the riveting process of change in Philly presented by the film.

The problem the filmmaker often faces is that having weighed all the changes and come to the conclusion that the subject matter is interesting, even fascinating, the film goes nowhere. Nothing seems to happen. Nothing seems to develop. And in the end one is left with a mass of material without center or focus, and which, if the truth be told, looks pretty boring.

When the Maysles brothers started filming *Salesman*, the concept probably looked intriguing: follow four Bible salesmen around long enough and something will happen. As it turned out, although the brothers shot some amazing footage, they didn't have a clue what the final story might be about. According to editor Charlotte Zwerin, the real story was only found on the editing table.

> David and I started structuring a story about four salesmen, very much in the order the thing was filmed. Anyway, we started with the four salesmen story, and it took a long time because we started off in the wrong direction. We took about four months trying to make a story about four people, and we didn't have the material. Gradually we realized we were dealing with a story about Paul, and that these other people were minor characters in the story. So the first thing was to concentrate on Paul, and go

to the scenes that had a lot to say about him. That automatically eliminated a great deal of the other stuff we had been working on till then. (From Alan Rosenthal, *The New Documentary in Action* [Berkeley and Los Angeles: University of California Press, 1971])

What to film. What do you film when you are not sure of the story, you're not sure what is going to happen, and stock is costing you about $175 for every ten minutes of filming? This is one of the greatest dilemmas of cinema verite: when should you start shooting? In action, conflict, or performance films, the answer is relatively easy. You go for the action, the drama, the climax. You shoot the race, getting the beginning, a bit of the middle, and definitely the end. You shoot the soldiers' assault on the hill, including preparations and the moment of takeoff. When you shoot the performance, you make sure you have plenty of backstage material, first entrance, audience reactions, and highlights.

But what do you do when your film is about ordinary lives, where there are no clearly defined dramatic points? Do you just hang in and shoot everything? Obviously not. But what are the guides? First, you want to look for the scenes that reveal personality, attitudes, and opinions. This may be by talk or by action. The corollary of this is that you have to be very sensitive to what is happening, listening very carefully as well as watching.

Second, you look for scenes that will develop into something—an argument, a burst of passion, a rejection, a coming together. Even if the scene doesn't develop, are you watching something that is significant in itself for indicating mood or feeling?

Third, you look for patterns over time and try to mark out the most useful time to be around. It might be dinnertime, when all the resentments of the day begin to flare up. It might be late evening, when the kids have gone to bed and the husband and wife are left to face the predicament of their faltering relationship.

Anticipation is the key. You have to cultivate that sensitivity to know when things are going to hapen or going to break, and be ready.

How to film. Usually, filming cinema verite implies no retakes and no asking of questions again. So what do you do if the situation is jumping, but, as usual, you're in a one-camera shoot? You go for the most important sync dialogue and try to anticipate where the next main dialogue is going to come from. Afterward you try to get the cutaways so the editor will have something to work with, hoping that while doing this you're not losing too much sync. The essence of cinema verite shooting is not that much different from normal documentary. You try to understand the scene and what's going on, seize the heart of the action, and then go for it.

In the film *Crisis*, Don Pennebaker's task was to shoot a meeting in the White House between President Kennedy and his staff as they discussed the integration of two black children into a southern school. It's interesting to see how he planned to shoot, and then how he changed his strategy because of the evolving situation.

> I told the soundman, stay out of the middle of the room. Get the best sound you can but don't get in the middle because I am going to try and get a whole roomful of people. The most extraordinary things were happening in the room. It was the first time we'd ever tried to shoot a roomful of people and it was very hard to do.
>
> The usual rule is you start wide and you end up on whoever is making the scene work, whoever you're interested in, and you come in tight and you watch him—you know, you go in that direction.
>
> In this case I had to reverse all that and keep pulling back, because every time the president would do something or say something, there'd be eight people moving around or changing position, and you realized there was some extraordinary ritual dance going on, which had to do, I guess, with the way power was leaking out of the system. (From P. J. O'Connell's manuscript, "Robert Drew and the Development of Cinema Verite in America.")

The Editing Process

In 90 percent of the cases, the cinema verite film is found and made on the editing table. Often the filmmaker senses there is a story but is unsure what it is until the material has been sifted and partially edited. So the selection of a creative and thoughtful editor becomes even more crucial to the success of the film.

In a scripted film the editing process is fairly straightforward. Since the line of the film is given, it is usually easy to start at the beginning and without too much bother make your way to the end. In a cinema verite film, you often don't even know what the focal point of the film is or what it is about, let alone have the comfort of starting at a beginning and working through to a conclusion.

Where do you begin when you're faced with all these problems? I start by cutting scenes I like and seeing what makes them work and what they reveal to me. At that stage I don't bother with the placement of the scenes within the overall film. When I finish a scene, I write the details about it on a card and pin it to the wall. This work might go on for weeks or months, depending on the film. During this time a process of clarification is taking place; I am beginning to see connections, lines, meanings. Sometimes this happens in the editing room itself, sometimes when I'm relaxing. It's certainly not a linear process.

Perhaps once a week, alone or with someone else who is seriously involved on the film, I look at the cards on the wall and try to see connections and links. Slowly but inevitably, the thrust of the film emerges.

The complexity of editing a cinema verite film can be seen in comments made by Ellen Hovde, one of the editors and codirectors of the Maysles film *Grey Gardens*. A portrait of two unusual women, Edith Bouvier Beale (Big Edie) and her fifty-five-year-old unmarried daughter, also called Edie, the film was shot by Al Maysles and recorded by David Maysles. I asked Ms. Hovde if the Maysles told her what they were looking for in the film.

> No. Never. They had no idea. Just a sense of two charismatic people, and that there might be a story. . . .
>
> When the material came in we just let it wash over us. In general it was very strange. You almost couldn't tell if you had anything until you cut it, because it was so free-flowing. Very repetitive. It didn't have a structure. There were no events. There was nothing around which a conversation was going to wheel. It was all kind of the same in a gross way, and you had to dig into it, try to find motivations, condense the material to bring out psychological tones.
>
> I was always, I guess, looking for relationships. I think we were pushing in film terms towards a novel of sensibility rather than a novel of plot.
>
> I don't think we were clear at all (at least not in the beginning) about the direction we were going in. I think we all knew there was nothing in terms of "action," but what was really going on was not clear.
>
> The main themes that Muffie (my coeditor) and I decided to go with were the questions "Why were the mother and daughter together?" "Was it possible that little Edie was there to take care of her mother, and it was the demanding mother who took care that her daughter couldn't leave?" and "Was the relationship really a symbiotic one?"

Ground Rules

Cinema verite often makes more strenuous demands on the filmmakers and the film subjects than do typical documentaries. There is usually a much greater demand for intimacy and openness. The filming is frequently done in homes rather than in public places, and the filmmaking itself can take months rather than weeks. In those circumstances you need to establish a set of ground rules from the start. These help define and smooth the working relationship between you, the filmmaker, and your subjects. The rules will vary with each situation, but certain discussions come up time and time again:

- *Time of shooting*: Can you shoot at any time and on any occasion, or only at certain defined periods?
- *Prelighting*: Can you prelight the main shooting areas so that all you have to do is throw a switch (much the best way), or do you have to set lights each time you shoot?
- *Off-limits areas*: Can you go anywhere, or are certain places off-limits?
- *Recording*: Can you record anything, or are certain subjects off-limits?

Obviously one aims for as broad a permission as possible, hoping that the subject will trust your judgment when to shoot and when not to.

In the mid-1970s, Roger Graef shot a cinema verite series in England called "Decisions." The films were shot during discussions over vital decisions made by three huge business corporations, including British Steel. The films were breakthroughs, bringing cinema verite techniques to the corporate world and demystifying the way business works. This kind of filming had never been done before, and Graef's chief task was to gain entry to the corporations, win their confidence, and assure them that the films would be both to their credit and for the public good. The ground rules that Graef laid out between himself and the corporations were as follows:

1. The filmmakers would shoot only what had been agreed on by both sides.
2. No scoops to newspapers. This was essential when a great deal of confidential information was being disclosed.
3. The films would be released only when both sides agreed to it. In other words, the filmmakers weren't setting out to embarrass the subjects.
4. In return for the above, the filmmakers asked for total access to one or two subjects they had agreed to film — that is, the right to film them at any time and walk in on any conversation.
5. The filming would be done without lights and without anything being staged.

When Richard Leiterman shot *A Married Couple* for Allan King, he basically lived in and around Billy and Antoinette Edwards for two months. Here the three main rules were

1. there would be no communication at all between the filmmakers and the subjects;
2. the filmmakers had the right to come at any time, morning or evening, and film anything unless a door was closed; and
3. the subjects were to continue whatever they were doing or whatever they were talking about whenever the filmmakers walked in or started shooting.

I talked some while ago with Leiterman about that shooting, and it is quite clear that what mattered more than the rules was the confidence that the

Edwards had in Leiterman's judgment of when and when not to shoot. Severe and violent quarrels, including Billy throwing Antoinette out of the house—yes, that was all in. Billy and Antoinette about to make love—that was all right while they were playing around with each other, but out once they reached the bedroom.

Although it's easy to lay down ground rules, they have to be treated with caution. Even when you have permission to film anything anytime, you have to proceed with common sense. In 1963 Robert Drew, Ricky Leacock, and Don Pennebaker were given permission by John Kennedy to film intimate presidential staff meetings for what ultimately became *Crisis: Behind a Presidential Commitment*. Kennedy had given the filmmakers virtually free access, and yet this is how Leacock described the filming to critic P. J. O'Connell:

> Pennebaker [the other cameraman] would notice that the President would keep glancing at the camera. And then Penny would stop shooting. Because if he didn't, he knew that within minutes the President was going to say, "Stop." *Then* you would have the problem of starting again. You have to get a Presidential permission to start again. If he stopped before the President stopped him, then he could decide when to start again. Okay, you're going to miss a whole lot of stuff, but you've got the power to start again.

General Criticisms

Over the years, cinema verite has run into a barrage of criticism as a technique, and it's useful to be aware of the main negative arguments before you embark on a cinema verite film.

1. *They are simplistic and nonintellectual.* This argument has been used mostly against Fred Wiseman by critics who maintain that his films merely portray the surface of institutions; without greater sociological or economic explanations (which he avoids), the films are of limited interest.

2. *Casting is all.* The line here is that no talent is needed to make a cinema verite film; all you need is a head for casting. Find the right charismatic talent, like the Beatles, Leonard Cohen, or a race-car driver, and your film is in the bag.

3. *The portraits are superficial.* One of the early claims of verite was that it managed to dig deeper into personalities, that it would penetrate the outward veneer and find the "real" person. This claim is now under severe challenge as critics argue that, even with verite, the subject is as much on guard as in the old films.

4. *The method is unethical.* Here the main argument is that the subjects are unaware of what the film is doing and will do to their lives and their

privacy and that the filmmaker is merely exploiting them for his or her own fame and fortune.

Many of these criticisms have to be taken quite seriously. On the whole, though, I think the criticism is overdone. Looking back, it is clear that the method has been handled with compassion and sensitivity by the majority of serious filmmakers, and their works have provided an understanding of people, families, institutions, and social actions that would have been quite impossible with any other method. In short, they have enriched the whole documentary tradition and created an honorable path well worth following.

18

Documentary Drama

One of the most popular forms of television to emerge in the 1980s has been that of documentary drama, or docudrama. The form has embraced single films and series, ranging from *Skokie, Missiles of October,* and *The Atlanta Child Murders* to *Blind Ambition* and *Washington: Behind Closed Doors.*

Documentary drama has a long history, studded with some of the most famous names and films in the documentary pantheon. You could start anywhere, but you would have to include Harry Watt's *North Sea,* Humphrey Jennings's *Fires Were Started,* the work of Willard Van Dyke and Leo Hurwitz, and, more recently, Peter Watkins's *The War Game,* Ken Loach's *Cathy Come Home,* and Chris Ralling's films for the BBC. This body of work has, however, raised certain theoretical problems. Where is the center of truth in this form, and how believable or suspect is it? These are vital questions, as the basis of documentary is its relationship to truth. In docudrama, however, whole areas seem to be opening up where fiction is presented as fact, as reality.

In spite of its problems, documentary drama has a tremendous appeal to serious filmmakers. Leslie Woodhead, the creator of some of the most interesting documentaries shown on English television, sees it as a form of last resort. "It's a way of doing things where ordinary documentary cannot cope —a way of telling a story that would be impossible by conventional documentary methods." What is the impossible story? For Woodhead it has ranged from a story about a Soviet dissident imprisoned in a mental hospital to *Strike,* about the Russian invasion of Czechoslovakia.

Woodhead's aim has been to recreate history as accurately as possible, and his means—summed up by David Boulton, one of his scriptwriters— are very instructive: "No invented characters. No invented names. No dramatic devices owing more to the writer's (or director's) creative imagination than to the impeccable record of *what actually happened.* For us, the dramatized documentary is an exercise in journalism, not dramatic art."

Woodhead's *A Subject of Struggle* was about an elderly Chinese lady put on trial by the Red Guards at the height of the Cultural Revolution. In 1972, when the film was made, the nature of the revolution was a tremendous puzzle, and no film of any duration had come out of China about it. Woodhead obtained the trial transcript, talked to sinologists about it, did further research, and then used the transcripts as the basis of a docudrama. In the case of Soviet dissident General Grigorenko, the basis of the film was provided by Grigorenko's detailed diaries, which he had managed to smuggle out of prison.

One of the most famous docudramas of the mid-1960s was *Cathy Come Home*, about the plight of the homeless in England. It was shown three times on the BBC and did a great deal to alleviate the plight of those without shelter or lodging. Scriptwriter Jeremy Sandford came to the subject through the experiences of a close friend who was about to be evicted from lodgings and lose her children. Sandford did extensive background research but put his final script in the form of a drama rather than straight documentary. I was curious about this decision, and when I met Sandford in London, I asked him why he chose drama and actors over straight documentary. Sandford replied:

> Real people are often inarticulate when disaster hits them. There can be flashes of emotion in a live documentary, but these flashes cannot be sustained throughout a film. An actor with an actual script avoids that problem. Also, at this time, cameras were not allowed in the homes for the homeless. Even had I been able to get in and make a television documentary, I wouldn't have been able to do justice to the emotional reality of the people living there. Instead I saw it all in the form of a play — a situation anyone with a social conscience just had to write about.

Sandford has done a number of other docudramas, including *Edna: The Inebriate Woman*, so I pushed him a bit further on justifying the form. "The justification for it must be, as I have said, that the events portrayed are inaccessible to true documentary treatment, either because they are in the past, or because they lie in some area of secrecy or inarticulacy, such that to shoot them as straight documentary will destroy the very thing one is trying to show."

Both Sandford and Woodhead provide excellent arguments for the docudrama form. Once the choice is made, the main problems are (1) what form the piece should take to keep it as close as possible to the truth and (2) how do you inform the audience about the real nature of what is on the screen.

Techniques

Characters portraying themselves. When you have a strong human or political story, it is worthwhile considering whether the main characters can play themselves. They have been through the situation, lived the events, and can recall the emotions and the dialogue. This method is not easy, but where possible it adds tremendous plausibility to the film, as in the docudrama *Ninety Days*, directed by Jack Gold. *Ninety Days* recounts the experiences of a young, white South African woman sent to prison for political activities under the ninety-day laws. The film was based on the autobiography of Ruth First, who played herself in the film. After the screening, there was no doubt among the critics that First added a dimension of reality that would have been missing had she been portrayed by an actor.

Similarly, the National Film Board of Canada made a film in the mid-1980s about a Canadian doctor who, in defiance of the government, ran an abortion clinic out of a deep belief in the rights of women to manage their own bodies. The film shows the running of the clinic, the government prosecutions, and the three or four trials of the doctor until he is pardoned and the abortion laws amended. Again the doctor plays himself, adding immensely to the strength of the film.

Verification. Most docudramas rely on the audience believing that what they see on the screen actually happened or has a very strong basis in fact. This was the main strength of *Cathy Come Home*. At the time *Cathy* was produced, stories about the homeless were regularly making the front pages of most of the English newspapers. Thus, when the drama finally appeared it resonated against the audience's own knowledge of similar facts and situations.

Among its scenes the film shows its main character, Cathy, at a rundown trailer park. A few months earlier a radio documentary called *Living on Wheels*, which was recorded on location, had featured exactly the scene Sandford wrote into his film. Sandford then has a fatal fire occur at the trailer park. Again, the incident was based in fact, and many people were already familiar with the appalling number of children's deaths caused by such fires. As Sandford commented,

> Nearly everything in the film was founded on something that actually happened. An incident, like the fight where Cathy strikes one of the staff, was an amalgam of two real incidents. One concerned a principal who threw out one of the inmates of the homes for talking to the press. The other involved the death of a baby and the belief of the inmates that this was due to dysentery. I combined these incidents into a cameo where an inmate writes to a paper about a baby's death. (From Alan Rosenthal, *The New Documentary in Action* [Berkeley and Los Angeles: University of California Press, 1971])

Sandford's method was to take a dramatic social situation, research the facts, and then weave a tale based on the facts. A more common method is to take a historical incident and reconstruct it, as in *The Trial of Bernhard*

Goetz or *The Atlanta Child Murders*. However, in the latter method any deviation from authenticity can shake the believability and effectiveness of the whole program, as happened in Anthony Thomas's *Death of a Princess*. This film showed (via actors) the public execution of a Saudi Arabian princess and her lover for various sexual offenses against Islamic law. This incident was true and had been widely reported in European newspapers. However, the film then went on to show other elements of the behavior of the Saudi Arabian aristocracy whose basis in truth was more questionable. This inability to distinguish between truth and fiction finally made the entire work suspect.*

To keep a sense of proportion, it is necessary to distinguish between facts that are crucial to the story and incidental fictions. In *Cathy* the romantic episodes are incidental fictions, but the trailer fire has to be based on fact; otherwise, the whole film crumbles. In *Death of a Princess*, the scenes in the Arabian household can be taken as incidental and unimportant fictions. By contrast, the scenes of Arab women picking up lovers in their Mercedes make crucial political and social criticisms. As such they need to be based completely on fact, yet the perhaps-inaccurate impression of *Death of a Princess* is that they arose from the producer's imagination.

Accurate dialogue. One of the keys to making effective docudramas is to find the most accurate sources for the dialogues and commentary. Usually these sources will consist of letters, diaries, interviews, and newspaper reports. Sometimes court statements will also provide the basic materials, and this was part of Sandford's working method in *Cathy*:

> It was while I was working on a newspaper series that I came upon the actual case on which the fatal fire in *Cathy* is based. I followed the proceedings in the coroner's court, and then I more or less transferred what occurred to the sound track of *Cathy*. For instance, there is the scene where the girl describes how the caravan [trailer] was filled with smoke and how she escaped with little Gary in her arms. "And what happened to all the others?" the coroner asks. "They all got burned up," she says. The dialogue is verbatim from the court report.

Accuracy of location and characters. In feature films, the emphasis in location shooting is on cheapness, exoticism, and reasonable working conditions. Accuracy and authenticity are usually the last words mentioned. But authenticity is the key to docudrama, especially as regards period and physical setting. In *Strike*, several hundred still photographs were used to show Poland and Gdansk in the early 1970s. These provided references not only for design, wardrobe, and makeup, but also for casting

---

*In a discussion I had with Thomas (February 1990), he maintained that all his main incidents were verifiable.

the actors. In *Ninety Days* Ruth First worked with the designer so that the feeling of the cell and the South African prison would be as accurate as possible.

Obviously, you are as accurate as your budget can afford. In the 1970s the BBC made two splendid historical series, "The Search for the Nile" and "The Explorers." The first told the story of the major African explorers, such as Burton and Speke, while the second recounted the stories of Pizarro, Columbus, Von Humboldt, and the like. Both series were filmed at the locales where their stories took place. The expense was enormous, but the authenticity thus achieved was easily worth it.

The viewer's right to know. It is crucial that you let your audience know whether they are looking at fact, fiction, reenactment, or fiction based on fact. How do we tell the viewer all this? One answer, given by Robert Vas in *The Issue Should Be Avoided* and by Jill Godmilow in *Far from Poland*, is to use signposting or subtitles that clearly indicate the source of what is happening on-screen.

Another method is to indicate at the beginning of the film which characters are real and which are fictional, and which ones are portrayed by "real people" and which ones by actors. It is also worthwhile to let the audience know immediately the factual basis for your incidents and your dialogue; this means that the audience understands from the start the nature of your method and techniques. Some people put these explanations at the end of the film; however, I think they are preferable at the beginning so that the audience can put the film into perspective.

Examples

The inspiration for docudrama can come from anywhere. Often the source is a story in the headlines, as in *The Trial of Bernhard Goetz* and *The Atlanta Child Murders*. Sometimes a film has its genesis in politics, as in the films of Leslie Woodhead. Sometimes it's biography, sometimes it's history; sometimes it's public, sometimes it's private.

Letters from a Bomber Pilot, by David Hodgson, is one of the best docudramas to come out of England. Presented by Thames Television in 1985, it provides an interesting illustration of the source of ideas and is also worth looking at in terms of method.

David Hodgson's mother died in spring 1978. While David's brother and sister were sorting through their mother's belongings, they came across a pile of letters at the bottom of her wardrobe. Dated between 1940 and 1943, they were the correspondence between David's older brother Bob and his mother and father and friends. A pilot in the Royal Air Force (RAF), Bob had vanished over Europe in March 1943. The elder brother had just been a shadow of a memory to David Hodgson, who was six at the time of Bob's death. The letters, however, revealed the reality of the missing Bob. Not only that, they also conveyed very vividly the experiences of being a young airman during the early years of the war. Written with humor and honesty, they described the training, the friends, the drinking, the crashes, and falling in love. And, of course, they described the feeling of the operations.

Besides telling the story to his children, David Hodgson, a documentary filmmaker, felt the story would have significance for the general public. Using the letters as the basis of his script, he started tracing what happened to many of the people mentioned in the letters. The resulting film tells the story of just one of the 55,000 RAF pilots who fell in the war. It is a particular story of one man and one family, but it strikes resonances with anyone involved in the war and tells a younger generation about the immense personal cost of the conflict.

It's a brilliant film, but its method is simple. Narrated by David Hodgson, the film is grounded in a personal point of view. The letters, which form the basis of the script, are sometimes illustrated by library footage and sometimes by acted scenes. Occasionally an incident or mood suggested by a letter will be fleshed out in a short invented scene. Thus the talk in a letter of a friend falling in love is followed by a short scene in which two airmen tease the lovesick Hughie. What gives the film its poignancy is that a number of the people mentioned in the letters were traced down and interviewed by Hodgson. The friend will appear in an on-screen interview, which will then dissolve into a reconstructed scene with actors. At first the voice-over of the interview will guide the scene, and then the actors' dialogue will take over. These simple techniques work very well, as can be seen below:

Visual	Audio
Stills of Bob as a baby, then various family group shots	*Narrator:* My brother Bob was born on the thirteenth of January 1921 in the south London suburb of Norwood. Our mother Maud was seventeen when she met a young film cameraman, Jimmy Hodgson, and they were married in 1918. Bob was the second of their children. My sister Joan was two years older.
Bob with model boat; Bob with sister	Bob was a gentle, intelligent child who became enthralled by one of the century's most spectacular developments—flying.
Archive footage of plane taking off; aerobatics; pilot in	He dreamt of becoming a pilot, and his favorite way to

control tower	spend a Saturday afternoon was watching the planes at Croydon airport.
Stills of young Bob with model aircraft; mix to still of Bob in the RAF, with other pilots in uniform	In January 1941, eighteen months after the war had started, Bob joined the RAF. He was one of the thousands of young men who wanted to serve in what they all thought was the most exciting and glamorous of the services.
Archive footage of bomber in flight	In May he started his training as a bomber pilot.
Title: *Letters from a bomber pilot*	
Various stills of Bob in uniform with friends or with family	
Credit: A film written and directed by his brother, David Hodgson	
Close-up as hand writes letter; tilt up to Bob Hodgson (actor), who reads letter to camera	*Bob*: 16 Elementary Flying Training School. Near Derby. August 1941.
	Dear Bill, I started flying on Monday. *Music*: Glen Miller Story, "In The Mood"
Air-to-air shot of Bob learning to fly small plane, to illustrate Bob's letter	I went up first for twenty minutes to get air experience. After about an hour I went up again and was allowed to handle the controls. At first it
Mix medium shot Bob to camera	wasn't so easy (*in vision*), but after a while I began to pick it up.
Air-to-air shots	Samson said that when he saw me, six-feet-four, etc., he thought I'd be as ham-handed as anything. But I seemed quite OK.

The film continues with air-to-air shots, overlaid with extracts from Bob's letters about learning to fly. The commentary then takes over to talk more widely about the policy of the air chiefs and civilian morale at home. This is all illustrated with library footage of bombing raids, destruction, and bodies being buried. Gradually the number of scenes with actors increases.

Visual	Audio
Still of Hugh Feast	Narrator: Hugh Feast became one of Bob's closest friends. Like Bob, he came from London and was the same age, just
Still of Bob, Alf, and Hugh Feast	twenty. In November 1941 they were posted to RAF Shawbury to learn advanced navigation and night flying. Most RAF stations employed
Archive footage of WAAFS (Women's Auxiliary Air Force)	WAAFS (young women serving in the air force) in technical and ground jobs, and not surprisingly romances blossomed. Hughie Feast was the
Hughie Feast (actor) shuts door and walks to bathroom, watched by his friends.	first to be bowled over, something his friends treated with schoolboy glee.
Derek Cadman, Alf Kitchen, Bob, and Bob Wells	Bob: Now what's Mr. Feast getting dolled up for?
	Alf: He's meeting his WAAF.
	Bob: Again?
	Alf: He's got it very bad, hasn't he?
	Bob Wells: This is the third time this week. It's serious stuff, isn't it?
	Alf: Let's lock his door.
The four split; Bob goes to the bathroom. Bob Wells: Come on! Let's do it.	
Close-up of hands locking door	Bob (voice-over): Dear Joan, Hughie Feast is going out with
Medium shot of Hughie shaving. Bob peers at him from door. Lads run into dormitory, followed by Bob	a WAAF from the station sick quarters. I believe he's taking her seriously, as when we first chipped him about it he took it

Alf at table. Bob goes and lies on bed.	with equanimity, but now he loses the wool and gets chipped even more. Tubby's asked Bravington's to send a catalogue of engagement rings to Hughie's home address to give his parents a shock—just innocent fun.
Hughie brushing hair. Wipes face and exits.	
Hughie leaves bathroom, walks to dormitory door and finds it locked.	Last night Hughie had to meet his WAAF at 6:45. He went into the bathroom clad only in his trousers, and Tubby locked the door of his room, so that he
He walks back into the main dormitory, puzzled.	couldn't get the rest of his clothes.

The scene ends with the friends ribbing Hughie, holding up the room key and exclaiming, "Oh this key, the key to your heart. Ah, that one."

As the film proceeds, various people are interviewed about their memories of Bob and how they met him. The interview with Bea Couldrey demonstrates how such interviews are integrated into the film.

Visual	*Audio*
Still of Bea.	*Narrator*: At the beginning of September Bob came on a forty-eight-hour pass, and went to a local dance. There he met a girl called Bea Couldrey.
Medium close-up of interview with Bea	*Bea*: My friend Doris and I went to this dance held by the Home Guard. Not many people attended these dances, because the hall wasn't terribly
Pan with dancing couple to see Bea (actress) sitting talking. Bob and his brother and sister enter.	big. I remember sitting on the side and then I saw this very tall man coming through the door. . . .

The film alternates between Bea reminiscing over the scene and the actors picking up dialogue to show how Bea and Bob meet and dance together.

In the final scenes we learn that the details of Bob's death were discovered only recently. We also learn that all four of Bob's closest friends in the RAF were killed as well.

Visual	Audio
Still of group of forty-eight young RAF men	*Narrator*: None was more than twenty-two years old. Of the forty-eight men photographed at Bob's initial training wing,
Still as above, showing only ten remaining	it seems likely that less than a quarter survived.

I have emphasized the need for accuracy and detailed research if one wants to raise the level of the film above romanticized biography or fictitious history. To emphasize the point, I have set out below the comments of Leslie Woodhead (producer) and Boleslaw Sulik (scriptwriter) on the sources and treatment of *Strike*:

Sources

At first sight "Solidarity" might seem to have had a very public birth. Indeed, the extraordinary confrontation in the Gdansk shipyards during late August 1980 looked at times almost like a media event, unique in a Communist country, with the news crews of the world there to watch every development. Our researches have revealed a very different reality.

As the result of contact established during the making of an earlier dramatized documentary we have been able to gain an unusual access to much previously unknown material. . . .

Now after six months of detailed debriefings of dozens of eyewitnesses inside Poland and across Western Europe, and the careful examination of almost one hundred hours of private tape recordings, a quite new version of events in the Lenin shipyard has emerged. By collating all this material, we propose to reconstruct for the first time a precise day by day account of what really happened, both in the yards and in Warsaw's dissident community. To focus our research, we have also retained as a consultant one of the key "Solidarity" leaders, the woman around whom the strike began, Anna Walentynowicz.

During the crucial but uneasy first four days of the strike, no journalists or cameras got into the shipyard. We have now managed to obtain private tape recordings of vital incidents during those tense early days, made by the workers themselves at the time. With those recordings and eyewitness reports we have been able to piece together for the first time an accurate account of how the strike began, and how on several occasions fear and confusion nearly caused it to collapse. . . .

The Director and the Designer have visited Poland, gaining access to the Lenin shipyard. As a result, it will be possible to reconstruct in precise detail all the key locations inside the

yards. We have also researched and photographed the important dissident locations in Warsaw. As a consequence of this
firsthand access, we expect to be able to recreate the most
accurate settings in our drama documentary experience.

Treatment

We plan a two-hour dramatized documentary. All characters
will be real people represented by actors. All events will follow as
closely as possible the sequence established by our research. Sets
will recreate as precisely as possible the actual locations: the main
gate of the Lenin shipyard, the MKS meeting hall, the presidium,
the experts' meeting room, Jacek Kuron's Warsaw flat.

Some use will be made of actuality film events in the shipyard. Wherever possible, dialogue will be an exact translation of
the private tape recordings made at the time. Where actual
recordings are not available, the dialogue will be compiled from
the record of several eyewitnesses. We intend to indicate the
different status of these two procedures.

We aim to produce a dramatized documentary which will
stand as an historical record of an important event. We believe it
will also be compelling drama for a television audience.

The actual start of the film, when it was made, is shown below:

*Pre-credit sequence: Shaky 8mm amateur film. A murky view of
a large crowd. A loud, rasping Polish voice is heard. A handful
of leaflets is thrown up. The Polish voice fades and the narrator
comes in.*

Narrator: December 16, 1979. The Baltic port of Gdansk in
Communist Poland. An illegal demonstration is in progress,
filmed by a sympathizer with a home movie camera. On this
spot, just nine years before, striking shipyard workers were
killed in a clash with police. The speaker at this anniversary
protest asks each person in the crowd to return here next year
with a stone and some cement to build a memorial. The speaker
is an out-of-work electrician called Lech Walesa. But long
before the year is over, these people, followed by millions across
Poland, will mount an unprecedented challenge to the Soviet
order in Eastern Europe, igniting the most serious European
crisis since World War II. This film tells how it all began with a
strike, which in just seventeen days became a revolution called
"Solidarity."

*Walesa's distorted voice is heard again and continues as the
tense, grainy faces of the crowd swirl past the camera. Suddenly*

the film flashes orange and runs out. On the blank screen the title stabs out: Strike.

The title fades as factory hooters are heard, followed by muffled sounds of gunfire. Simultaneously, from the blank screen a black-and-white still takes form like a developing photograph.

Still photographs of a rioting crowd in a smoke-filled street. A crowd carrying a dead body on a wooden door. A male Polish voice starts singing and subtitles roll on.

Subtitles: Janek Wisniewski fell. They carried him down Swieto-janska Street. To meet the cops. To meet the tanks. Men of the shipyards, avenge your mate.

The stills sequence continues with images of street fighting and a building on fire, surrounded by a huge crowd. The ballad goes on.

Subtitles: Workers of Gdansk. You can go home. Your battle's done. The whole world knows and will say nothing. Janek Wisniewski fell.

The voice fades out and the narrator comes in.

Narrator: These photographs were taken in the streets of Gdansk, Gdynia, and Szczecin in December 1970. The terrible scenes were committed to the folk memory, and the photographs have been kept hidden for ten years.

A photograph of a woman bending over a body. The ballad comes back for a final stanza.

A dissident meeting; 8mm film. Several people sit in a drab, anonymous living room. The narrator introduces the group and explains the occasion.

Narrator: A home movie record of a meeting in Gdansk, early in 1980. These people are campaigners for the creation of Free Trades Unions in Communist Poland. They are the principal figures of the drama reconstruction which follows.

(Individual introductions follow, starting with Lech Walesa and continuing through Anna Walentynowicz.)
Anna Walentynowicz, nearing thirty years of continuous work in the Lenin shipyards as a welder and crane driver. Once a heroine of labor, decorated for her outstanding work record. By August 1980, in lengthy dispute with the shipyard management.

The home movie is now seen to be running on an editing machine, watched by Anna herself.

Narrator: Anna Walentynowicz has come to London to help in the preparation of this film. As a central figure in the Polish Free

Trades Union movement she has a unique inside experience of what happened. (*Anna cues a tape recorder; her own voice is heard speaking to workers.*) The voice of Anna speaking to Gdansk workers, recorded inside the Lenin shipyard during the strike.

What is interesting in the above is the attempt to show the viewer the authenticity of the sources and all the film methods used. The same approach was taken in another Granada film, *Invasion*, and again the first few minutes are used by the writer to inform the audience about technique and approach.

Narrator: On the night of August 20, 1968, the armies of the Soviet Union and their Warsaw Pact allies invaded Communist Czechoslovakia in an attempt to install a new government obedient to Moscow. They had done the same in Hungary a decade earlier. They were to do it again in Afghanistan a decade later. They called it "fraternal assistance."

Title: *Invasion*

Exterior location—day—Austria. The Austrian side of a border checkpoint with Czechoslovakia. In the background all the paraphernalia of a sensitive East-West crossing point: Soldiers, guns, lookout towers, barbed wire. Zdenek Mylnar walks up to the frontier.

Narrator voice-over: At the time of the Soviet invasion this man was one of the most powerful politicians in Czechoslovakia. His name is Zdenek Mylnar. Twelve years after the invasion of his country he is an exile in neighboring Austria. He left Czechoslovakia in 1977 after publicly criticizing the Russian-backed regime. Today he is the only man who is free to give an eyewitness account of what happened behind closed doors in Prague and Moscow when the Russians set out to force the Czech leaders to sign away their country's independence. His account, recorded for us under detailed cross-examination and supplemented by independent research in Western Europe and Czechoslovakia, forms the basis of the filmed reconstruction which follows. It is as accurate as our research can make it.

The actor who is to play Mylnar walks across to chat to him.

Narrator: All the characters in these events are real people represented by actors. Except where there is a written record, the words spoken are a dramatized recreation of what we believe to be essentially true. The personal recollections of Zdenek Mylnar are spoken by Paul Chapman.

We hear Chapman's voice as he stands with Mylnar.

Voice-over of Chapman: In Czechoslovakia, the spring of 1968 arrived in a genuinely human sense. People shared a feeling that after decades of fear and oppression, their lives had finally changed for the better

As Mylnar's recollections begin, the music and cheering crowds of May Day 1968 gradually break through.

Mix to library film of singing and dancing in the streets of Prague.

19

The Historical Documentary

History has become one of the basic themes of documentary filmmaking, especially television documentary, and with more than $4.5 million going to produce the Vietnam War series it has also become big business. The historical documentary is extremely popular and comes in many forms, including straight essay, docudrama, and personal oral histories. It offers tremendous scope and challenge to the filmmaker, but is also beset with a number of problems both practical and theoretical. The practical matters include the use of archives, the way programs are framed, and the use of experts, witnesses, and narration. The theoretical problems include interpretation, voice, and political viewpoints. And in the background is an academic voice arguing that filmmakers shouldn't even touch history.

Film History versus Academic History

Many academic historians argue that filmmakers should leave history alone. Their arguments go beyond the individual case to an overall critique of the genre. Real historians, they say, are interested in accuracy, filmmakers in entertainment. Television producers, they add, are concerned only with gimmicks and show business personalities to introduce the programs. In the end, they conclude, documentaries like Alistair Cooke's "America" are myopic garbage put out by blinkered, unlearned journalists, presenting ideological views with which few historians would agree.

Strong stuff! So what can one say?

Of course, there are bad and stupid historical documentaries, just as there are ridiculous books on history, but there are also very good ones as well. And yes, filmmakers do want to entertain (as well as enlighten), but this aim is not incompatible with historical accuracy.

Most documentary producers also work with a historical adviser. I admit that advisers are sometimes used simply as window dressing to get the blessing of the NEA or NEH, but they have a number of serious functions to perform and can be of inestimable help to the filmmaker. Donald Watt,

219

himself a historian, suggests the following ways that the adviser can contribute to the film.

1. The adviser should see that the subject is completely covered within the limits set by the length of the program and the material.
2. The view presented of the subject must be objective within the acceptable definition of the term as used and understood by professional historians. It must not be *parti pris*, or anachronistic, ideological, or slanted for the purpose of propaganda.
3. The events described, the "facts" outlined, must be accurate, that is, in accordance with the present state of historical knowledge. Hypothesis and inference are all legitimate, but only if they are presented as being exactly that. (Donald Watt "History on the Public Screen," in *New Challenges for Documentary*, ed. Alan Rosenthal [Berkeley and Los Angeles: University of California Press, 1988])

Ideally, the relationship of the filmmaker and the adviser is one of partnership. But in the end, one person has to decide on the nature of the program, and I see that person as the filmmaker. However, you ignore the historian at your peril.

Part of the disquiet of historians is that they really don't understand the difference between academic and television history. They don't understand what the filmmaker is trying to do and the limits within which he or she works. The goals and the framework can be stated fairly simply:

1. We are making television programs, not writing articles for learned journals, but we still want accuracy.
2. We are working for a mass audience that can be composed of the aged and the young; the Ph.D. and the person who left school at age fourteen; the expert and the ignorant.
3. We have to grab the audience. If they don't like what we show, they will turn elsewhere. Unlike students, they are not necessarily predisposed to what we want to show. We want to entertain, but we also want to heighten the knowledge of the audience.
4. We cannot reflect; we cannot go back. We are unsure of the audience's knowledge of the subject: some will know everything; others will know nothing. We have to be clear, concise, and probably limited in our scope.
5. Finally, our intent is to present *a* view of history, not *the* definitive view of history.

Nothing so far is particularly new to us, and I have covered many of the points earlier, but they are worth reiterating because these issues go to the heart of the making of historical documentaries. Clearly, the writer-director who wants to do a decent historical film faces a great many problems. Some of these are discussed below, and where possible I have tried to suggest a solution.

Approach

The three paths most commonly chosen for historical documentaries are the essay, the "great man" approach, and the "personal reminiscence" method, all of which overlap to a great extent. The essay form is very common and must be mastered. It can be coldly objective—like the essay on the making of the atom bomb in "The World at War"—or more subjective and personal, as in *It's a Lovely Day Tomorrow*, John Pett's film on the Burma campaign in the same series. The essay often builds itself around a compact event or episode that offers the writer a clean narrative structure with a well-defined beginning and end. Thus, if you were doing a series on the American Civil War, you might well suggest the Battle of Gettysburg or Lincoln's assassination as single film topics within the overall series framework.

"The World at War" series, produced by Thames Television in the early 1970s, covered World War II in twenty-six programs. But somebody had to decide how those programs should be allocated. The approach could have been a straightforward chronological recounting of the war. This was not done. Instead, the series was broken up into compact events and partially complete stories. Thus, the Russian campaign emerged from three films about battles, *Barbarossa* (the German attack), *Stalingrad*, and *Red Star* (the siege of Leningrad). *Pacific* covers the American invasion of Tarawa and Iwo Jima, while *Morning* deals with D day and the Battle of Normandy.

One of the great differences between "The World at War" and previous series, both British and American, is that it never uses mandarins or experts when the experiences of ordinary people can be used to tell the story. In previous films and series the revered figure, the expert, or the personality tells the audience what it ought to think. The ground-breaking work of "The World at War" was that it left space for the members of the audience to form their own opinions.

The "great man" approach works the other way. Here, the statement from the beginning (and the attraction) is that history will be seen through the eyes of one of the participants. The film admits its subjectivity and its partisan quality, but promises entry into the innermost sanctums of the high and the mighty. This approach seems fine to me since the biases are clear and open. In England, the most famous series made this way centered around the life of Lord Louis Mountbatten, uncle of the queen, a famous war hero and commander, and the last British Viceroy of India. In the United States one could easily imagine a series based on Eisenhower's diaries or Westmoreland's reminiscences.

In "personal reminiscence" films, a section of history is told through the stories of a number of people. Often these figures are not particularly famous, but their stories are sufficiently representative to define an issue or the feeling of a period. Three good examples would be *Nine Days in '26* by Robert Vas, *The Good Fight* by Mary Dore, Sam Sills, and Noel Buckner, and *Seeing Red* by Julie Reichart and Jim Klein.

Nine Days in '26 tells the story of the great general strike in England of 1926, which at one point looked as if it might precipitate a social revolution. It is oral history without pundits, told by those who participated both in making and in breaking the strike. Everyone in the film came to Vas via the same method.

> We advertised in various newspapers for people who had some-thing to say about their experience to come forward. We had a tremendous response because this was a crucial event of social history. I certainly didn't go for distortion. I strongly sensed there were different sides to the same truth. . . .
>
> We had a tremendous response, and after selecting twenty-five people after visiting and talking to at least 150 during the research we gradually realized the enormous conflicts, the gulf between the attitudes, the tension, the charge of this whole situation.

The Story

The story is of prime importance in the historical documentary. This may earn academic scorn, but in a visual medium the dynamic story is vital. Telling stories is what film does best, whereas it deals with conceptual and abstract thought only with difficulty. This approach obviously affects what you can cover. You go for the event, the incident, the intriguing tale, and may thus distort the broader canvas. The danger is there, and I am the first to admit it.

Robert Kee's series on Irish history for the BBC is a case in point. "Ireland: A Television History" covers eight hundred years of history in twelve programs. If you examine the individual films, you see that one is devoted to the great Irish famine of the 1840s, another looks at the story of the patriot Charles Stewart Parnell, while a third covers the Easter rising of 1916. These are all great stories and make superb television, but do they reveal the most important issues and trends in eight hundred years? That is open to debate, and we would have to see what was sacrificed that these topics might be chosen. But if Kee's dominant motive was to choose historical topics that made for compulsive viewing, then he chose well.

What you must do is look for the central theme and then find a concrete way of illustrating it, a finite story that will flesh out the theme.

In *Out of the Ashes* I knew that one of the major points I wanted to make was that innocent civilian populations suffered enormously during the war, and that often this was due to the brutality of the SS and their killer groups. But how to illustrate this? Suddenly I remembered the story of Oradour, a small village in France. In June 1944, an SS troup entered the village and for no apparent reason massacred more than six hundred people—men, women, and children—in one morning.

During research I visited Oradour and was appalled at what I found. A cemetery with pictures of twelve members of a family on one grave, seven members of a family on another, all bearing the same date. Oradour was never rebuilt. Instead, its ruins still stand as a grim memory of that obscene day. The Oradour story was intensely moving and I went back a few months later to film the church, the graveyard, and the silent ruins. In the simplest, most tragic of ways, Oradour summed up an evil and brutality that is still with us today.

Commentary

The general length for a televised historical documentary is about fifty minutes. This means, roughly, that you can use only about fifteen minutes of commentary, or a quarter of the program's length. In reality you are left with about fifteen hundred to two thousand words to play with, which is not a great deal, and a tremendous amount of detail has to be left out. You simply will not have time to explore all the ramifications of the Tet offensive, nor will you have time to explore in detail what happened to President Lincoln's family after the assassination. That's why good and effective narration is crucial.

What does narration do best? We have explored this in some detail, but it bears repeating. Narration is excellent for stories and anecdotes and for evoking mood and atmosphere. It is not good at detailed analysis of complex events or abstract thought. Above all, narration works best when it is related to images. It should point up certain things. It should explain. It should call attention to detail and lie in the background. The narration must not describe the images, but it should make us understand their significance.

Visuals and Archive Material

The maker of film histories is doing a *visual* history. That is what is so confining and so challenging, and what in the end makes the filmmaker's task so different from that of the academic historian. And as a visual history, the materials at hand will be photographs, location shooting, archive material, and witnesses.

The first problem is how to deal with the prephotographic era. The solutions are well known, if not terribly inspiring, and usually consist of using prints, reconstructions, and filming at historical and archaeological sites. Some reconstructions are not bad. Peter Watkins's *Culloden* managed to convey the atmosphere and mood of the last battle between the English and the Scots in the eighteenth century. Others are just awful, like the reconstruction of the siege of Cawnpore in the "British Empire" series.

Another gimmick that has found favor the last few years is "timeless location" shooting. This artifice demands an "as if" jump of the imagination. We look at today's Bedouins or fishers and are supposed to assume that that exactly reflects life at the time of Jesus or Mohammed. Sometimes it works, but usually the self-consciousness of the method is all too obvious and gets in the way of believability.

Archival problems. The visual photographic record, which begins about 1840, can be problematic as well as beneficial. A few points are worth noting, especially in regard to archive footage, because it is the basic ingredient of so many documentary histories.

The first dilemma is that the footage that is visually most interesting may also be historically irrelevant. Thus, while tank battles of World War I may be fascinating to watch, they may provide little insight into the deeper meaning of events. The second difficulty is the misuse and misquotation of archive film. This happens, for example, when stock footage of the 1930s is carelessly used to provide background to a film about the 1920s. The third, and possibly most serious, problem is the frequent failure of filmmakers to understand the biases and implications of stock footage. One example will suffice. During World War II the Nazis shot a great deal of footage of their captured populations. Much of this footage is now used as an objective news record, without acknowledging that the footage was shot to provide a negative and degrading picture of those slave populations.

The other side of the coin is that in a visual medium, the very absence of stock footage may lead to a serious distortion of history, as a subject or incident simply disappears. Because you don't have archive footage of the Yugoslav partisan resistance (which, of course, the Nazis never shot), the subject is never mentioned in the film. In other words, unless you are careful, the sheer existence of archive material may dictate the line of your film, whereas it should be subservient to it.

Visual history can often be defective not because events or actions were physically unfilmable or politically undesirable to film (such as death camp murders), but because those in a position to do so thought the events were just not important enough to photograph. One example was the failure of newsreel operators to record the famous "iron curtain" phrase from Winston Churchill's postwar speech at Fulton, Missouri.

Archive material can be fascinating, quaint, captivating, magical, haunting. But it can also be tremendously distancing and unreal. This is particularly true when you suddenly put black-and-white archive footage in the middle of a color film. So you must occasionally ask yourself whether your archive material will work to your advantage, or if there is a better way to do it.

Witnesses. The use of witnesses is one of the key methods for enlivening visual history. Sometimes the witnesses merely provide color; sometimes they provide the essential facts of the story. It is interesting that multiple witnesses are often used to recreate the sense of the events. Sometimes the witnesses are complementary, sometimes oppositional. For example, in "Vietnam: A Television History," witnesses were frequently used to contradict each other. In the episode *America Takes Charge*, a raid on a Vietnamese village is recalled by one of the attacking soldiers and by one of the Vietnamese villagers. Their accounts of the same event are light-years apart.

Witnesses are sometimes the sole authority for the facts, and therefore the choice of witnesses can be crucial when history is in dispute. One option is to use oppositional witnesses, as in the Vietnam series, but most producers seem wary of that method. Yet when this is not done, the results can seem strange at best, and biased at worst. Two series on the history of Palestine serve as good illustrations on this point. Both "The Mandate Years," made by Thames Television, and "Pillar of Fire," made by Israel Television, deal with the flight of the Arab population from Haifa after 1945. In "The Mandate Years" the incident is recalled by a former British army commander who is hostile to Israel and very sympathetic to the Arabs and who claims that the Arabs were forced to leave. In "Pillar of Fire," an Israeli witness, General Yadin, recalls how the Jews begged the Arabs to stay. Clearly, visual history is no less contentious than academic history.

People's memories are notoriously unreliable, and you must keep that point before you when making historical films. In recalling their childhood, the war, their romances, their successes, and their failures, people will invent and embroider and often not even be aware of it. But as writer and director you must be aware of this tendency. Often it doesn't matter, but sometimes it matters immensely. Watch also for what I call the "representational voice": the lovable, heartwarming character who smokes his pipe, grins, and tells you what we all felt on that day when the British attacked — on that sad, sad day for Ireland. There's not too much harm in using such characters, but be aware of the game you are playing.

20

Industrial and Public Relations Films

Probably more people are employed in making industrial and public relations films than in making documentaries. This has certainly been the case in the 1980s, when small-format video equipment has revolutionized the subject. Today industrial films are *in*, with everyone using them. Compared to the print medium they are seen as relatively cheap but effective publicity materials, with the word "publicity" being used in its broadest sense. It's a popular and lucrative field, and one worth getting to know.

Documentaries and Industrials: The Difference

Many industrial films masquerade as documentaries. They slip into the cinemas or onto television under the billing *Young Adventure* or *Head for the Sky* They purport to be documentaries on nature or flying, but we realize after two minutes that they are really promos for Yosemite or the Air Force. We enjoy them, and there's not too much harm done. They give the illusion of being documentaries because so many of their techniques are the same: location shooting, real people, natural sound, godlike commentary, and so on, but we know they are a horse of a different breed. The main difference, of course, lies in *purpose*. The documentary usually has a strong social drive. It wants to inform you, to draw your attention, to awaken your interest so that some social or political problem can be fully understood and perhaps ameliorated. By contrast, the ultimate purpose of an industrial or public relations film is to do a good sales job. Such films want you to buy something, to support something, or to do something. You cannot receive an industrial film passively. If you do, it's a failure. The film wants you to receive the message and then jump into action. This can mean anything: changing your bank, joining a health club, supporting a charity, taking up skiing, or going to Bermuda for your holiday.

The action is not always immediate; sometimes the film wants to sow an idea for the future. the Canadian National Film Board's *The Sky* may not send you off to the Rockies immediately, but the idea of their beauty and attractions will have been well planted after one screening. The Shell Oil film on historic castles of England doesn't necessarily say, "Come this moment," but the ground will have been prepared.

The sponsors for the industrial film can come from anywhere. All you need to be a sponsor is to have a message and the money to put it on film. In practice, the main sponsors are industry, business, universities, government agencies, professional organizations, and charities. And all want to put out their own distinct sales message. Their films usually group themselves under five or six distinct types:

1. Recruitment and training
2. Promoting a service
3. Demonstrating a product
4. Building an image
5. Teaching and advising
6. Raising funds

Often the categories will overlap; your film may be promoting a wonderful new medical product or machine and at the same time illustrating the special system or service under which the product is made available to you once a week.

The Call to Action

Most but not all industrial films ask you to do something, and the call to action can take many forms. Join the navy. Visit this country. Support this museum. Make yourself into a superwoman this way. Learn automobile repair that way. Your task as a writer is to search out the arguments that will support the film's message, and then find the best way of putting them over in the script.

Recruitment. Let's say you have landed a nice fifteen-minute film whose basic message is "Join the marines." Your first job, after research, is to marshal all the arguments you can to support that action. They might include:

Good pay at a young age
Good sports facilities
Camaraderie
Learning a trade
Seeing the world for free
Serving your country

Your film is then built entertainingly to put over these points. You might do it by following an eighteen-year-old recruit through his first year, but there are all sorts of ways. The film has to be realistic, and it has to be plausible, and therefore you can often allow some of the problems to come in. Thus, you can say in the recruitment film, "Yes, it's a hard life," and this point might appear in the recruit's letter home. Of course, the inverse message here is that the recruit is proud to be a real man and not a wimp.

Sometimes the recruiting film may be disguised in different wrapping. Some years ago, for instance, British Airways (or BOAC as it then was) put out a good corporate image film. You saw a flight crew in training, all the backup service of BOAC, the concern and attention given to passengers, and the crew visiting different parts of the world. The core of the film, however, was provided by watching a young pilot learning to fly, handling propeller planes, going onto jets, and finally mastering the giant 747. The film was very well done, and if shown in schools probably induced a rush of recruitment letters to British Air.

Product or service. In product or service films, your task is, once more, that of a salesperson. With luck, the products or services you are selling can be absolutely fascinating and the task of filmmaking extremely enjoyable. A friend of mine, for instance, was asked to make a film for a world hotel chain. His research took him to Hong Kong, South America, and France, staying all the time at the best hotels. Another friend did a film to boost pure malt Scotch whisky. Not only did he get to see and sample the best Highland distilleries, but he had a tremendous holiday in the bargain.

While doing the research you will be putting questions to the sponsor whose answers will underpin the script. You want to know what the product does, how it works, why it differs from its rivals, and what are its main advantages.

Corporate image. One of the most profitable areas of industrial filming is the making of corporate image films. These too are sales films, but on a slightly broader basis. Sometimes the image is that of a company such as American Express or Bank of America; sometimes that of a profession, such as architecture or dentistry. The message of the corporate image film is not necessarily to buy something or do something immediately; rather, such films tell us that the company or profession is looking after your best interests.

Sometimes the film is made to sustain an image. Thus, the British stock market put out a film in the mid-1980s showing how the stock exchange arose and what fun it was to buy stocks today. This was before the crash of 1987. The film itself was screened daily to anyone who came to visit the stock exchange. In 1988 Union Carbide felt that its image had suffered as a result of the recent Bhopal disaster in India. It consequently commissioned a film to show that it was, in fact, a company that was highly attentive to safety and that the gas escape was not its fault.

Teaching and training. Teaching and training films are another category of films that are becoming increasingly popular, particularly in health and sport. One of the most popular videos ever was Jane Fonda's exercise tape. But that was just the beginning. Now, if you want to mend a car, become a tennis champion, learn yoga, bring up your baby the right way, or do up your house—there's a tape for it.

Factories, schools, businesses, and hospitals are also big users of the training film or tape, which is an excellent demonstration tool. You can easily take someone through a process, showing the right way of doing things. You can demonstrate new machines, and you can reach your sales force in different towns and countries.

One of the things that the teaching film does very well is demonstrate safety techniques or provide a warning. Here the minidrama is often used. A few years ago Film Australia was asked to make a film illustrating the dangers of smoking in hospitals. Their answer was to stage a docudrama of a fire. A patient ignores the safety warnings in a hospital and smokes in bed. Within five film minutes the whole hospital is ablaze, with eight fire engines in attendance outside and dozens of patients being carried to safety. It was an expensive film to make, but it put across its point.

Public service. Public service films lie somewhere between normal documentaries and the sponsored corporate film. Again, they can use any technique, but their usual object is to benefit the public as a whole rather than to publicize a specific factory, business, hospital, or university. Government agencies are one of the main sponsors of the public service films, and their subjects vary little from country to country; public health and fighting racism are two of their main concerns. Sometimes the public service film will be sponsored by a private corporation or a special interest group. Some of the best public service films of recent years have been sponsored by Amnesty International and various church-affiliated human rights organizations.

The public service field is wide open and is often a good entry path for the beginning filmmaker. That is why I suggested above a film to help young children overcome their fear of hospitals. That would be a typical public service film, and also one that might appeal to a number of sponsors.

Relations with Sponsors

Working with sponsors is an entirely different problem from that of working with television stations. In the latter context, someone usually has some idea of what film and filming is all about. That is not necessarily the case at all with sponsors.

What are you really up against?

Even though the sponsor may have suggested the film, he or she may still not be sure it is a good thing. Many sponsors still think film a tremendous waste of money, and even though they have agreed to do something, they may be tremendously lukewarm about the project. That means you will be battling the whole way. Similarly, many sponsors will want to see immediate, concrete results from the film. You must then convince them to be realistic about the short- and long-term effects of the film.

Often the sponsor will tell you that he or she has to feel happy and moved by the film. That's all right, I suppose, but it misses the point: the film is made for the audience, not for the sponsor. Antony Jay, one of the best filmmakers in England, once expressed it to me this way: "You're not making a film for the company but for the people the company are going to show it to. You're not out to pat the managing director on the back or boost the ego of the chairman. Your job is to capture and hold the attention of people who don't necessarily want to be sold to or preached to, but who merely want an entertaining half hour." If the audience is moved and happy and acts—then that's really all that counts.

There are four battles that have been fought with sponsors through the ages but which rarely get immortalized in print. The first battle is for *unorthodoxy*. Try to do something different, try to be a little unusual, try to do a film in a new way, and you may find your sponsor climbing the wall. Your second struggle is the *catalogue* controversy. You are doing an industrial or hospital film and your sponsor may ask you to mention every department and piece of equipment in the hospital, or every branch or product of the firm. Resist to your last dying breath. Catalogues have a place in stamp collections, but usually only ruin films. Another major conflict is over *big shots*. Out of the best of intentions, the sponsor may ask you to put in the factory owner, the board of governors, the main contributor, wealthy relatives, and so on. Again, ask yourself whether this naming of names does any good for the film or is simply sucking up to the boss. Last but not least, you may have to wage war over the question of *committees*. All sponsors love committees. But remember one of the wisest sayings of all time: a camel is a horse designed by a committee. Stay clear of committees. Making films under the guidance of committees is the fastest route to disaster that I know.

The Golden Rules; or, How to Survive Your Sponsor

But all is not lost. Over the years filmmakers have evolved certain golden rules for dealing with sponsors, rules that enable you to survive and make good films.

1. You must find out, right at the beginning, the main message that the sponsor wants to convey. If possible, have the sponsor put in a single sentence the one central idea that the film should leave with the viewer. If the sponsor can't tell you, then you're in trouble. But if he or she does, then make sure that you can come back to that central idea throughout the film.

2. Confirm if there is anything absolutely vital to the film. If the sponsor argues for the catalogue or the big shots, try to axe the idea. Apart from that, listen carefully and weigh the sponsor's idea for its worth.

3. Find one person who is willing to take total responsibility for the film and the script. This saves you going to management and hearing a multitude of different voices, all arguing for something else.

4. Make sure your budgeting is realistic. If you have been given only $7,000 to make a film, make sure that your sponsor doesn't expect the

production values of a $70,000 film. This is vital, as many sponsors haven't a clue concerning the true expenses of filming. If they can afford only a modest house, then tell them from the beginning that they cannot expect a mansion.

5. No sponsor is realistic about timing. They all want their films done yesterday. Make sure you give them a completion schedule that is based on actuality and not fantasy.

6. Find out from the sponsor how and where the film is going to be used. Will it play before big audiences or small audiences? Will any informational literature be given out at the time? Will a speaker accompany the film? All these points help you evaluate how you should tackle the film.

Production Points

As already mentioned, many public relations and industrial films convey the flavor of documentaries but are far more manipulative. They use many of the same techniques, but they also add one or two of their own.

Identification. The technique of identification occurs again and again in recruitment or training films. The audience is presented with a character with whom they can sympathize and identify: the boy who decides to join the army is like your older brother or the kid next door, or the manager being trained is just like you. However, take care that the identification really works.

Audience. If "know your audience" is one of the commands of documentary, it is even more important in industrial films. You must know for whom you are making the film, as this affects your whole technique, approach, and style.

Real people. You can use actors in industrial films, but I don't like it. I think it is much more convincing to use real people in real situations, slightly guiding their behavior in front of the camera. This approach is also usually more practical. Engineers know how to use tools, surgeons scalpels, and so on. Put an actor in a complex job and he or she stands out like a sore thumb.

If I am shooting a film in a factory and need certain types, I try to get the manager to let me know who is the most suitable, the most intelligent, and I pick up my "actors" then and there. They are usually terrific and very cooperative. But apart from very simple direction, it is your job to learn from them and not vice versa. For me this means two things. First, I don't ask the actors to do anything they normally wouldn't do. Second, I rarely script casual dialogue. I give the actors the situation and try to find out from them how they would handle it and what they would say. I let them understand the point I want to make, but I leave it to them to put it over in their own way.

Animation and special effects. Animation, graphic or computer, is a marvelous tool for industrial films. Often you have a mass of information that you can't get over by filming in a factory or elsewhere, or a concept that is difficult to put over using a physical object. For example, if you want to compare two types of growth over time, animation can be a tremendous boon in making your point simply but effectively.

Again, video special effects, if not overused, can make all the difference to an industrial or public relations film. For example, they are very good at contrasting preparations and results. Let's say you are doing a film on agricultural and flower research. You know you have to show the scenes in the labs, people looking at microscopes and so on, and you know it looks pretty dull. But show that lab scene on one side of the screen, while the other shows a scene shot from a helicopter of dozens of fields of bright flowers, and the film is transformed. This is the simplest of video techniques; there are, of course, dozens of others. The important point is this: if you are doing video, you have at your disposal dozens of effects that would be too costly to do in film, but which can transform the look of your picture.

Humor. Humor is one of the principal tools of the public relations and industrial film, particularly in England. There the makers of industrial films constantly use John Cleese, who plays the befuddled British lawyer in *A Fish Called Wanda*, to write and star in their movies. One common approach is the nitwit who gets into an awkward situation because he or she doesn't have any sense or doesn't know the right way to approach a job. We see Laurel and Hardy try to take a piano into a house through a window; we see somebody ignore advice and build a boat that promptly sinks on its first outing. These wrong methods are then contrasted with the correct procedures.

As I have said before, humor isn't used solely in training or sales films. It can have a much wider application, and it is one of the better and more entertaining ways of putting across a message.

Voice. In documentary, we are accustomed to a commentator with a neutral voice. But what works for documentary may not be best for the industrial film, where you have many more opportunities to humanize the narrator and add more personal warmth. Once the narrator becomes a character, rather than an anonymous, faceless voice, you have much greater possibilities of reaching out to your audience and talking to them in a direct way. This was a technique that Antony Jay used very effectively in *The Future Came Yesterday*; I have given an example from the script at the end of this chapter.

Approach. The sponsor can tell you the message, but it is up to you to find the most effective and imaginative way to put it over. You probably have a wider variety of techniques available to you than in the standard documentary, but you are still faced with that old question: what approach shall I use?

From Picture to Post was a half-hour public relations film made for the British post office. It didn't have anything specific to sell but wanted us to understand that the post office is doing good work. It could have got that message across in many ways, perhaps most obviously by touting the speed of mail delivery or automated services. Instead, the film focused on the way stamps are conceived and created. We see four designers faced with different tasks: each has to design a stamp, but on a different subject. One has to do a new design for a portrait of the queen; his method is to make a clay bust and then try different photographs of the final statue. Another has to do a series on bridges, and we follow him looking at bridges in England and Scotland for inspiration. A third has to do a series based on the Bayeux tapestry, commemorating the Battle of Hastings in 1066, while a fourth has to create a number of designs around the new Concorde supersonic plane. In the last case, all the designs are based on a model.

Each artist uses a different technique, and it is quite fascinating to watch the evolution of the designs. The film is just following the old rules: get a good story, show what we don't usually see, follow process, and you can't go wrong. Eventually we see the final designs and the printing of the stamps. There is nothing complex to the film, but it offers a very entertaining look behind the scenes, and we come away with a greater appreciation of the complexity of making an everyday artifact that we all take for granted.

Tonight We Sing was also a corporate image film, but one that was also trying to do a selling job. The subject was the Glyndebourne Opera. Going to Glyndebourne is an English tradition. It is a beautiful, small opera house with its own resident company, set in country gardens in southern England. One attends in evening dress, sees half the opera, has a champagne picnic on the beautiful lawns, and then sees the rest of the opera, which is usually a Mozart or Rossini comedy. Although fairly well known in England, Glyndebourne was not familiar to American audiences. Thus, the directors of Glyndebourne came up with the idea of a film that would both publicize the opera and sell the idea of "going to Glyndebourne" in the United States.

The filmic concept is simple but effective. At the beginning of the film we meet David, a young American wandering around London. He is on vacation but doesn't quite know what to do. While in a railway station, he sees strange-looking people in evening dress board his train. In the carriage they drop tantalizing phrases about "seeing the new Duke" and "wondering how the Duchess is." David's curiosity is piqued, and when they leave the train he decides to follow them. And so, out of the blue, he stumbles onto the romantic, fairy-tale world of Glyndebourne, discovering that all the mysterious references are to the opera *The Marriage of Figaro*.

The film works because of all sorts of things, but three things stand out. First, David provides the right sort of identification for an American audience. Second, the film is very funny, with the English types portrayed as just this side of eccentric. Third, the film works because Glyndebourne has something well worth telling: it presents great music in a beautiful setting. When you have all these elements the public relations work becomes simple.

The Future Came Yesterday: An Example

Antony Jay's *The Future Came Yesterday* was made for International Computers Limited (ICL). Its subject was machine tools and electronic numeric control. To put it mildly, this is not a subject that at first glance makes your heart light up with joy. Instead, you are likely to say, "My God, what on earth does that mean?" The film came to Jay through the enthusiasm of engineering manager Douglas Hughes. Hughes had a lot of ideas about better control systems in ICL's factories but felt that he couldn't talk to the board of directors. They didn't understand his words, and his memos never got read. He felt that the only way to get through was to make the film and demonstrate concretely what he wanted to do. Jay continues the story as follows:

> Eventually we summarized the concept of the film. What we wanted to say was, "We realize that the computer can enormously simplify production control, but first of all we have to reorganize our factory to prepare to use the computer." It was as simple as that.
>
> Here it seemed to me very clear that I had to start *The Future Came Yesterday* with a sequence satirizing an existing factory setup. So I deliberately said nothing in the beginning about new ideas. Instead, I tried to make people agree that the old ones were ludicrous.
>
> When I thought I was familiar with the factory and had grasped the basic idea, I looked through my notes and wrote up a basic commentary that would run about thirty or forty minutes.
>
> Of course, being a film producer and a director, I don't write things down unless I see pictures in my mind, but the concept was very much that of an illustrated talk. It was the logic of the explanation that had to dominate, not the logic of the pictures. The pictures had to follow.

The discussions for the film, including meetings, planning, and scriptwriting, took four months. The shooting itself was done over the course of two weeks when the factory was totally disrupted. ICL, of course, was not the name given to the company in the film. Instead, Jay invented a mythical company, Universal International, and then had stamps and letterheads made with that name on them.

Below I have set out the first section from the script, called "The Adrian Sequence," which gives a very good indication of the biting and slightly sarcastic style Jay used to start off the film. It's clearly written for a character voice, and it is very much a real person talking to you.

Visual	*Audio*
Interior design office. Sketch on drawing board with hands doing details. Zoom up to Adrian sketching; he occasionally looks dreamily out of window.	*Narrator:* Have you met Adrian, our design engineer? Clever chap. University degree. Has lunch in the staff dining room. Doesn't talk to the production people very much. Well, they haven't got much in common. Except that they're going to make what he designs. But that's their problem.
	Look at that job he's drawing now. Every figure and line he puts down is full of implications for the production people. Costs. Size of machine.
Adrian writes ".0005" against a point on the drawing.	Precision of machine. Tooling. Machine loading. Tremendous responsibility? No, bless you, Adrian doesn't worry about little things like that. He's not a computer, and anyway, no one ever tells him.
Pan over to drawing on the floor. Hold, then pan to first camshaft acting as paperweight on pile of drawings on nearby table.	Look at his last job. Really beautiful design, that was. Multiple camshaft. He used that kind of shaft because he knew there was a nice bit of bar that size in the lab. He put the cams on a keyway; they made a lovely model in the lab.
Dissolve to factory interior. Second camshaft being machined in final stages; pile ready for assembly.	Trouble was, those clots on the floor couldn't repeat it. Had to go back and design it again. Now it's got the cams and the shaft all in one piece. Real bull-at-a-gate job. Oh yes, it *works* all right. But there's no satisfaction in that sort of thing.
Interior, design office. Adrian makes quick adjustment to	Anyway, off this one goes. Five hundred a year, Adrian de-

sketch. Cut to close-up of finished sketch.

Dissolve to medium close-up
of draftsman's desk with Adrian's sketch being copied by
hand.

signed that for. As it happens,
marketing already knows
they're only going to want one
hundred. But no one has bothered to tell Adrian. What's it
got to do with him?

Conclusion: Problems and Challenges

I hope that this book has given you some insight into filmmaking. I have tried to cover most of the main issues and show you how professionals deal with certain problems. However, some issues don't fall neatly within the previous chapters, and I will therefore deal with those here. They concern the outlook of the filmmaker, the question of perspective, and the challenge of the future.

The Director's Burden

We looked at some of the director's day-to-day problems in chapters 11 and 12, but there are also wider problems that you must confront sooner or later, the most serious of which are ethical. I am presenting this here as a director's problem, but it goes without saying that it is also a matter of serious consideration for the writer.

Ethics

The relationship of ethical considerations to film practice is one of the most important topics in the documentary field. The problem can be simply framed: filmmakers use and expose people's lives. This exploitation is often done for the best of motives; sometimes it's done under the excuse of the public's right to know. Whatever the excuse, though, film occasionally brings unforeseen and dire consequences to the lives of the filmed subjects. So the basic question is how you, the filmmaker, treat people to avoid such consequences. It's a hard question, not easily answered, and it has been present in documentary filming from *Nanook* through the Grierson years to the present. Now it has a new dimension added to it because of the advent of cinema verite. Here is a technique that allows a closer, more probing view of people's lives, as well as less time for reflection and consideration of one's reactions, than anything that has gone before.

Many questions lead from the main issue of how far the filmmaker should exploit a subject in the name of the general truth or the general good. Does

239

your subject know what is really going on, and what are the possible implications and consequences of being portrayed on the screen? When the subject gave you consent to film, what did you intend and what did he or she intend? When should you shut off the camera and destroy the footage? And should your subject be allowed to view and censor your footage?

Finally, there is the question of economic exploitation. We filmmakers earn a living from our work, building reputations that are convertible into economic advantage. But our subjects generally acquire no financial gain from the enterprise.

Obviously, I think that in the end most of us can justify what we do. If I didn't, I wouldn't continue as a filmmaker. But the subject of ethics is tricky, and it is one that you must, as a serious filmmaker, come to grips with sooner or later.

Legal Matters

Whether you work as a producer, director, or writer, you must be aware of certain legal considerations. I am not talking about obvious things such as theft or personal injury while filming, but about libel and slander. These two branches of the law can open up very deep traps which you must avoid if you want to survive. Both these torts deal with ruining a reputation. Broadly speaking, to libel or slander means to defame somebody or to lower his or her reputation in the eyes of the common person. If I call you a slut, a tart, a traitor, a wife beater, an abusive father, or a conniving thief, the odds are that I have either slandered or libeled you. The difference between slander and libel is that the former is a vocal defamation, the latter written.

Three points need to be made at this juncture. First, truth is usually a total defense to libel. Second, you attack someone's professional competence, you can really lay yourself open to trouble. And third, intent and malice may have some bearing on whether a libel has been committed.

Though the applicable laws differ from state to state and country to country, the penalties in most places for committing a libel can be tremendously severe. This means that you must take care, particularly if you do investigatory documentaries.

Normally you are allowed to probe public figures more severely than you can private people, but even then you have to make sure that what you are saying or showing is essentially true and fair. This is something CBS Television ignored to their cost in 1982 when they made *The Uncounted Enemy: A Vietnam Deception*. In their film, CBS alleged that General Westmoreland had, in 1967, led a military conspiracy to sustain public support for the Vietnam War by deliberately giving the White House a gross underestimate of the size of the enemy forces. Later, two journalists wrote an article alleging that there had been extreme bias in the collection and preparation of the materials for the program. In 1984 Westmoreland brought a libel action against CBS. His case was excellent, but it was eventually withdrawn because of various technical considerations and because of the nuances of malice that had to be proved.

Don't think this warning about libel applies only to subjects like Westmoreland. If you attack your local lawyer or school principal for incompetence, don't think they'll take it lightly. Libel suits are now popular, with big awards to the successful supplicant. So stay clear. Better to use that money on your next film than on legal fees and judgments.

Using Your Wits

As a director, your professional knowledge takes you quite far, but there will be times when your survival and your ability to complete the film will also depend on your wit and your scheming. Murphy's law has it that what can go wrong, will go wrong. Unfortunately, this law also tends to be true of film. Remember, "be prepared" is not just the Boy Scout slogan; it's also your motto. And when things go wrong, that's when you have to call on your humor and common sense.

I am not going to cite all the trials and tribulations of filmmakers over the years, but here are a few of the most common:

- After having agreed to talk, your interviewee balks at the last moment at being filmed.
- You fix an appointment to film somebody, and they forget to turn up.
- One of your crew angers the person you are filming.
- Your soundman gets a toothache in the middle of shooting.
- Your crew doesn't like the long hours, the bad pay, and the fact that they have to share rooms and can't bring their lovers with them.
- The camera breaks down, the wrong film is used, the sound gets out of sync, and you get caught in a revolution.

All these things have happened and will happen again. When they do, that's when you have to call on your wits, common sense, humor, and determination to carry things through.

What we are talking about is making hard, quick decisions in order to get the film done. But you'll also face the situation when the only way to get the film done is to use *chutzpah*. *Chutzpah* is a lovely Yiddish word, much used in Hollywood, which can be translated as "outrageous cheek." The best example of *chutzpah* is the lad who killed his father and mother and then asked the judge for mercy because he was an orphan. *Chutzpah* is cheek, boldness, and outrageousness, and it is one of the most essential qualities for a filmmaker. Two short examples suffice to show it in action.

In the late 1970s Emile de Antonio made a film called *Underground* in which he and Haskell Wexler talked to five Weatherpeople, self-confessed urban revolutionaries who had eluded the FBI for years. All the filming was done in secret, but then came the problem of developing the materials. The film was processed through Wexler's commercial company, but the audiotapes, which were very revealing, presented more of a problem. De Antonio explains how he solved it:

> I took the tapes to a sound house and said, "This is a new kind of transactional psychoanalysis, and I'll pay you your regular rate if you'll get out of here and let me transfer it myself. You see, I've signed a contract with this shrink, and this stuff is confessions of men and women about their inner sex lives, and the contract states that if anyone else hears it the contract is null and void." So the guy was perfectly happy to take my money and let me transfer. (From Alan Rosenthal, *The Documentary Conscience* [Berkeley and Los Angeles: University of California Press, 1980])

Another friend of mine, Abe Osheroff, made the film *Dreams and Nightmares* about his experiences in the Spanish Civil War. However, besides looking at the past, Abe also wanted to examine Franco Spain of the mid-1970s, which was still a fascist state. Among other things, Abe wanted to demonstrate the cooperation of the Nixon government with Franco and decided this could be done by showing United States strategic bombers in Spain. However, given the film's argument against current American foreign policy, it was highly doubtful that the Pentagon would release such footage to Osheroff.

Abe's answer was to establish a dummy film company and write a powerful anticommunist script designed for college students. He then sent this script to the Pentagon and told them this anticommunist film needed certain footage. The Pentagon was delighted and sent him all he needed. There was one catch. The letter giving permission for use stated that if the material was used for any other purpose than that set out in the script, the user was liable to a fine or imprisonment. Osheroff's attitude was that if the FBI busted him, it would be fantastic publicity for the film. Evidently they were too intelligent and did nothing. So the *chutzpah* paid off.

Staying Alive

It's no use being the world's greatest filmmaker if you can't get your films funded. In an expensive medium you have to be a businessperson as well as an artist. You have to find a sponsor or you're dead. By sponsor I mean anyone with money who will support your film. This can be a university department, a television station, an industrial corporation, a government agency, a church, a film distributor, and even friends.

You can interest people by telling them your idea, sending letters, proposals, and so on, but one thing is vital: showing them your previous work. Sponsors want to see your track record. They want to assess what you promise in the future by seeing what you have done in the past. This means you must have some work to show them, which is very hard if you are a student. Film diplomas are fine if you want to teach; otherwise, the more films you can finish or participate in while you are at the university, the better your chances of landing a sponsor.

As a filmmaker you have various possibilities in looking for work. The television station and the industrial corporation with its own film unit offer the safest bet. They need films, they have the money to make them, and they can sometimes offer a degree of permanence in the notoriously unstable film world. In reality, though, most of us end up as independent filmmakers. How do we raise the money for our films that will change the world?

Abe Osheroff got his $50,000 for *Dreams and Nightmares* through the backing of enthusiastic political supporters. Emile de Antonio picked up the $100,000 for *Point of Order* while having a drink with a wealthy liberal friend. *Antonia*, by Jill Godmilow and Judy Collins, was backed by the latter's concert earnings.

One way into filmmaking is to submit your idea to television. In the United States this is not easy, but it can sometimes be done in the field of public television. Occasionally PBS decides to sponsor a documentary series with marvelous-sounding names like "Great Americans" or "The Living World" or "The Spirit of the Future." This means three thousand people apply for grants to make ten films. The odds aren't great, but occasionally a newcomer slips in. Proposals can also be made to independent PBS stations. In theory, each station has a planning department that evaluates proposals. They are supposed to see whether the proposal fits the station, whether it is unusual or innovative, and whether funds can be raised on the proposal. But little of this touches reality, and I know of hardly anyone who has made a film this way.

In Europe things are improving. First, the European networks, particularly in Germany, are more open to accepting outside suggestions for productions and coproductions. Second, the English broadcast system is opening up to greater participation from independent filmmakers. Channel Four has, of course, been available to the independent since its inception and has either totally or partially funded a great number of documentaries. Connections can be made by letter, but a personal reference is better. Suggestions go through a commissioning editor and are then referred to a committee. Competition is fierce, and your odds of winning through are not high, but it's worth a try. What makes England interesting for filmmakers is that Margaret Thatcher's government has started to pressure both the BBC and the commercial networks to open their doors to independents. By the early 1990s the companies must take at least 25 percent of their output from people outside the stations.

Most independent American filmmakers I know who work in documentaries raise their funds through applications to local arts councils and foundations. These foundations have, in fact, become the chief sources of independent film financing in the last few years. The principals here are the Rockefeller, Ford, and Guggenheim foundations, the American Film Institute, the New York Council for the Arts, the National Endowment for the Arts, and the National Endowment for the Humanities. Funding is intensely competitive and dozens of applicants are turned down for every grant awarded. For example, Barbara Kopple was turned down again and again while trying to fund *Harlan County*, which went on to win an Oscar.

Foundation funding has certain inherent difficulties. Many of these relate to the writing of the proposal, a document which can sometimes reach the length of *War and Peace*. Most foundations require a proposal clearly stating the nature of the film, its objectives and limits, and a well-defined program relating to the film itself. Foundations also like to play it safe by requiring the participation of "experts" to provide academic respectability to a project. Such requirements make sense sometimes, but they are obstructionist when the filmmaker is operating in a field that the scholarly mind has not yet penetrated. What you have to do is acknowledge the basically conservative nature of foundation activities. The art film, the science film, and the educational history film pose few challenges to them. By contrast, the political, investigatory, or critical film rarely finds a place in foundation funding without a great deal of trouble.

The peculiar thing is that this setup may favor those who can write good grants over poorer writers but better filmmakers. This has been acknowledged, so many of the major arts foundations will go out of their way to offer you assistance in writing and framing your grant. Various periodicals can also help you considerably in this grant-writing business, such as the *AFI Education Newsletter*, *The Independent*, and *Foundation News*.

I should also mention that most good libraries have a copy of the foundation list put out by the Council of Foundations. This lists the names and addresses of most of the major foundations in the United States, together with a list of projects which they support. A few days perusing that list (it is immense) can be worth a good few dollars in your pocket.

The Future

The question for the future is where do we go from here? Old solutions and ideas for documentary writers and directors may not work in tomorrow's world, and the sooner we realize that the better. How do we face the 1990s? What do we want to do, and how are we going to do it? What do we want to say? Should we be putting over the old messages or saying something new? Who will our audience be? Will our films be framed according to past styles or will they be totally innovative? And will we be using the old technology or futuristic equipment we can only dream about now?

Technology and audience. The 1980s has been the age of the communications revolution. It has been the age of the VCR, the videodisc, the compact disc. Electronic editing in both film and video has taken tremendous strides forward. Cameras have become even more lightweight and min-iaturized. Interactive television has become a buzzword. Video has be-come an essential tool in filmmaking. One television cassette takes hours of material. High fidelity is the norm. The Walkman and the Watchman proliferate. The flat television screen is here, and the high-definition television screen is coming tomorrow. Cable television spreads, while television satellites orbit the earth, providing international as well as national audiences.

What it all means is that nothing is sacred: neither the technology, nor the classical concept of audience, nor the style and manner of film distribu-tion. What we have to do is try to see that the change becomes a blessing and not a curse.

The new computer chip may well cheapen and aid filmmaking. If I am right, it will be a blessing because it could mean that filmmaking will become as easy as writing. No longer will one be burdened by massive crews, horrendously heavy lights, and bulky equipment. Instead, one person will go out with a lightweight camera and do every single job. I know you can say that that is done today, but it's a hassle. What I hope to see is a one-pound camera–tape recorder that can go anywhere, do anything, record continuously for four hours, and give images as fine as anything on 35mm or 70mm film. I want to see technology simplified so that the problem becomes what to say, rather than overcoming technology.

As to distribution, everything is up for grabs. At the moment the market is heavily weighted against the filmmaker, with the main distribution options being television, cable, and commercial distributors. That may change. The spread of satellites will bring a demand for product, and one can only hope that demand will include documentaries. But leaving that aside, perhaps documentaries will be marketed by mail order. Perhaps electronic systems will enable the filmmaker to feed the documentary privately and cheaply to the viewer-consumer.

The lesson for filmmakers is simple. You must keep up with the new technologies and must also be aware how changing distribution systems might work to your advantage.

Subject and style. Subjects change fast. *Nanook* and *Chang* inspired the romance and travelogue films. *Potemkin* and *Triumph of the Will* showed what could be done with political propaganda. Grierson hit the social documentary, and Jennings's poetics boosted war morale. All were inter-esting but gave way before new trends. In the 1970s, subject matter ranged from Vietnam and the women's movement to films on the family, interper-sonal relationships, and the growing threat of nuclear war. What charac-terized these films was that many were made outside television and were made with a passion that was frowned on in the networks. Many of them also embodied new techniques and new styles. Until the late 1950s the accepted form for the documentary was the prewritten script with the visuals conforming to the narration. Cinema verite changed all that, bringing in its wake the personal, unscripted film found in the editing room. Now video in its turn is changing the shape and style of films, adding a zip, flashiness, and immediacy not often seen before.

Change doesn't necessarily mean improvement, but things will change. The objective is to absorb the lessons of the past and hope that they provide a few maps to the future.

The Challenge

In the end two questions dominate everything. What do we want to say, and how passionate are we about saying it?

If there is a subtext to this chapter, it has to do with commitment: commitment to get the film done, commitment to a certain set of values, and a commitment to share a perspective that implies the world will be a better place for the practice of one's art and craft. Somewhere in there, ethics, craft, and art meet and make magic.

And what does the filmmaker want to do with that magic?

Throughout this book, my basic assumption has been that the documentary filmmaker is interested in the real world and wants to change it for the better. And that is true whether he or she works within or beyond the domain of television.

At one time I thought the duty of the concerned filmmaker was to try to bring about social change. Now I am more inclined to see the involved filmmaker as one who bears witness. This "bearing of witness" has two elements. On a modest level, it means the filmmaker is interested in telling us a certain truth—not *the* truth or the eternal message, but rather a very personal statement that says, "This film arises out of my background, feelings, and integrity, and on the basis of what I show and how I show it, you can take it or leave it for what it's worth." On a different level of bearing witness, the filmmaker is one who says: "This is our world. See its joys and be happy. But see its sorrow and learn from it, and don't say that no one ever told you what the world was like." This kind of bearing witness is not something that one does logically. It is something that one does compulsively. It is the fire within that must be stoked.

A friend of mine, the very fine filmmaker Robert Vas, once put it to me this way: "I've brought with me a great many things to talk about. This baggage, this message which nobody asked me to talk about, is absolutely central to me. I can't exist without it. And I must talk about it to audiences that never experienced these things directly."

In this book I have tried to tell you a few things about technique. I can't teach you about passion, but I can tell you this: With technique alone you can become a good filmmaker, but you will not become a great one. For that you need passion: passion for the personal message that no one asked you to talk about; passion for the story that must be told and the facts that must not stay hidden.

Alan Rosenthal was born in England, studied law at Oxford, and has made more than fifty films, mainly in the United States, Canada, and Israel. He helped train Israel Television's film staff and has written three previous books on documentary. He has taught at Stanford University and at the British and Australian National Films Schools and is a senior faculty member of the Institute of Communications at the Hebrew University, Jerusalem. His recent film *Out of the Ashes*, in the WNET Television series "Civilization and the Jews," won a Christopher Award and a Peabody Journalism Award.